LATIN   RHETORICAL   THEORY   IN
THIRTEENTH   AND   FOURTEENTH   CENTURY   CASTILE

LATIN RHETORICAL THEORY
IN THIRTEENTH
AND FOURTEENTH CENTURY CASTILE

BY

CHARLES FAULHABER

UNIVERSITY OF CALIFORNIA PRESS

BERKELEY · LOS ANGELES · LONDON

1972

University of California Publications in Modern Philology

Volume 103

Approved for publication April 23, 1971

University of California Press
Berkeley and Los Angeles
California

◇

University of California Press, Ltd.
London, England

ISBN 0-520-09403-4

Library of Congress Catalog Card No.: 71-635563

PREFACE

THE PRESENT STUDY began life as a dissertation at Yale University, "Latin Rhetorical Theory in Medieval Spain." The change in title reflects more accurately my own contributions and the scope of the work. It remains substantially the same, with the exception of minor stylistic revisions and the correction of certain errors of fact. The Appendix is to be published separately in *Ábaco*, under the title "Retóricas clásicas y medievales en bibliotecas castellanas." Specialists in medieval rhetoric will encounter little that is new in Chapters I and II, but I felt it incumbent upon me at least to sketch rapidly the development of medieval rhetoric for the benefit of those Hispanists unfamiliar with that development.

I have attempted to acknowledge as fully as possible my debt to previous scholars in the notes and bibliography of this study, but there are more personal and immediate debts that deserve special mention.

I must thank Professor Gustavo Correa of Yale for his time and patience in directing this study from its inception as a term paper in his course on medieval Spanish literature in 1963-1964; the Hispanic Society of America, for the grant of a Huntington predoctoral fellowship in the summer of 1968, and especially its director, Dr. Theodore S. Beardsley, the late Clara Louisa Penney, and Mrs. Martha de Narváez; the Fulbright-Hays program for a grant allowing me to spend the academic year 1967-1968 in Spain, and particularly Miss Matilde Medina, assistant director of the Fulbright Commission in Spain; and Professor J. Homer Herriott, now of the University of Wisconsin-Milwaukee, for general counsel and moral support.

Thanks to the good offices of the following directors of libraries and archives I was able to study and make microfilms of many otherwise inaccessible manuscripts: D. Ramón Paz Remolar of the Biblioteca Nacional, Madrid; D. César Real de la Riba of the Biblioteca Universitaria of Salamanca; M. C. Simonnet of the Bibliothèque Municipale of Rouen; P. Ramón Gonzálvez, assistant *canónigo archive-*

ro of the Chapter Library of Toledo; PP. Salvador Pizarro and Rodrigo Madrid, *canónigos archiveros* of the Chapter Library of Cordova; and P. Francisco Álvarez Seisdedos, *canónigo lectoral* of the Biblioteca Colombina y Capitular of Seville. For advice on specific problems I should like to thank PP. Justo Pérez de Urbel and José López de Toro of Madrid, P. José Goñi Gaztambide, *canónigo archivero* of the Chapter Library of Pamplona, Miss Cora E. Lutz of Wilson College, Professor Christopher Cheney of Cambridge, and Professor Harry Caplan of Cornell.

I owe a special debt of gratitude to the friends and colleagues at Yale and the University of California, Berkeley and Davis, who have read all or part of the manuscript: Mr. Michael Nimitz, Mr. Ottavio di Camillo, Professor Edmund T. Silk, Professor Luis Jenaro-MacLennan, Professor Yakov Malkiel, Professor Stephan Kuttner, Professor J. J. Murphy, Professor Jerry R. Craddock, and Professor James Munroe. I cannot adequately thank Miss Lucille Kerr, who has read the manuscript in its entirety with a critical eye and then read proof on the entire manuscript again.

That the imperfections of this study are not more numerous is due in no small measure to the knowledge and advice of all these masters, scholars, and friends.

CONTENTS

CHAPTER I

INTRODUCTION

ERICH AUERBACH remarks, in *Literary Language and Its Public in Late Latin Antiquity and in the Middle Ages*:

> It was only natural that [rhetorical] technique should have influenced literary production at the same time that the rhetoricians should have looked to literature for striking illustrations of their principles. Despite frequent warnings, despite occasional countermovements, which were effective for a time, the two arts merged almost completely in late antiquity. The traces of this fusion may be found throughout the Middle Ages and beyond, both in literature itself and in the terminology of literary esthetics.[1]

Scholars in a number of medieval literatures have been attempting to establish the exact conditions of this fusion for a long time, but particularly since Edmond Faral published *Les arts poétiques du XIIe et du XIIIe siècle: Recherches et documents sur la technique littéraire du Moyen Âge.*[2] In this work Faral edited and studied the *artes poetriae* of Matthieu de Vendôme, Geoffroi de Vinsauf, and Evrard the German, and analyzed others of lesser importance. There was an immediate impact on Chaucerian criticism, an impact whose repercussions are still felt today.[3] Reactions in other literatures have been

---

[1] Trans. by Ralph Manheim, Bollingen Series, 74 (New York: Pantheon Books, 1965), pp. 192-193.

[2] Bibliothèque de l'École des Hautes Études, 238 (Paris: Librairie Honoré Champion, 1924; repr. 1962).

[3] Cf. John M. Manly, "Chaucer and the Rhetoricians," *Proceedings of the British Academy*, 12 (1926), 95-113; Traugott Naunin, *Der Einfluss der mittelalterlichen Rhetorik auf Chaucers Dichtung* (Bonn, 1929); Marie P. Hamilton, "Notes on Chaucer and the Rhetoricians," *PMLA*, 47 (1932), 403-409; James Jerome Murphy, "Chaucer, Gower, and the English Rhetorical Tradition" (unpubl. diss., Stanford University, 1957). Future citations of these and other works will use a comprehensible short title.

[1]

slower in coming, but in the last ten or fifteen years a number of important studies have begun to examine the whole question of rhetoric and medieval Italian and French literature.[4]

If we turn to medieval Spanish literature, however, we find that work based on Faral—indeed, any work on rhetoric—is exceedingly rare. In the period before Faral, only Marcelino Menéndez y Pelayo makes a serious study of rhetorical and poetic theory in Spain. In his *Historia de las ideas estéticas en España* he devotes much attention to the classical theorists born in Spain (Quintilian, the two Senecas, Martial), to St. Isidore of Seville, and to the Arabic and Jewish estheticians of the Middle Ages; but he mentions the later Latin tradition only to dismiss its importance: "Las nociones técnicas seguían aprendiéndose en las *Etimologías,* y no en Quintiliano, ni menos en Cicerón. ... Parece inútil advertir que la *Retórica* y la *Poética* de Aristóteles fueron completamente ignoradas hasta el siglo XIII en todo el Occidente."[5] He disparages the importance of theoretical treatises written by Spaniards and denies their influence on contemporary works in the vernacular:

... la misma filosofía del arte y los estudios técnicos que de ella se derivan, apenas encuentran cultivadores, y aun éstos se limitan a extractar y resumir en áridos compendios o en algún capítulo de los libros enciclopédicos ... retazos brevísimos de las Instituciones de Quintiliano. ... El arte propio y genuino de la Edad Media se desarrolla, entretanto, espontáneo y poderoso, acaudalándose con los despojos de la antigüedad, pero con absoluta independencia de las teorías, que no suele infringir en cuanto son principios de eterna verdad, pero que las más de las veces ignora o desatiende.[6]

Menéndez y Pelayo goes on to quote a short definition of rhetoric from Alfonso the Learned's *Setenario* and rounds out his discussion of rhetorical and poetic theory in the thirteenth century with a paragraph on the Spanish translation of Brunetto Latini's *Livres dou Tré-*

---

[4] Cf., for medieval French literature, Paul Zumthor, *Langue et techniques poétiques à l'époque romane (XIᵉ-XIIIᵉ siècles),* Bibliothèque Française et Romane (Paris: Klincksieck, 1963); and, for Italian, August Buck, "Gli studi sulla poetica e sulla retorica di Dante e del suo tempo," *Cultura e Scuola,* 4 (1965), 143-166.

[5] Ed. by Enrique Sánchez Reyes in the *edición nacional* of Menéndez y Pelayo's *Obras completas,* 3d ed., Vols. I-V (Madrid: Consejo Superior de Investigaciones Científicas, 1962), I, 339n.

[6] Ibid., I, 443-444.

sor. Then he turns to the arts of *gay saber* written during the four-teenth century in the abortive attempt to revive the Provençal lyric and to their more-or-less direct imitations produced in Castile during the fifteenth century—the lost *Arte de trovar* of Enrique de Villena, the *Gaya ciencia* of Pero Guillén de Segovia, and the *Arte de trovar* of Juan del Encina. In the end he states that "a esto se redujo en la Edad Media el estudio técnico de la poesía," and confesses that "no sabemos que se escribiera ninguna Retórica."[7]

Our knowledge of the state of the rhetorical art in medieval Spain has not progressed noticeably since Menéndez y Pelayo's study. Fa-ral's work has spurred exploration of the influence of the *artes poetriae* in Spain to a very limited extent. The first important reference to it occurs in Francisco López Estrada's "La retórica en las 'Gene-raciones y semblanzas' de Fernán Pérez de Guzmán." The author sounds a note which recurs constantly in later studies: "Ignoro cuál podía ser el *Ars poética* que conociese Pérez de Guzmán, pero el fon-do retórico medieval es común en la romanidad y en la zona de su influencia. . . . Aun teniendo en cuenta que el estudio de estas *Ar-tes* en España está aún por realizar, no creo que difiriesen mucho los hispánicos de los recogidos por Faral."[8] Pérez de Guzmán is a fifteenth-

---

[7] Ibid., I, 469, 469n. In the same footnote he mentions that Alfonso de Cartagena translated Cicero's *De Inventione*—edited by Rosalba Mascagna: *La Rethorica de M. Tullio Cicerón*, Romanica Neapolitana, 2 (Naples: Liguori, 1969)—and that Villena, in the introduction to his translation of the *Aeneid*, states that he had previously translated the *Rhetorica ad C. Herennium*; but, like his *Arte de trovar*, this too has been lost.

[8] *RFE*, 30 (1946), 311. López Estrada repeats substantially the same state-ments in his *Introducción a la literatura medieval española*, 3d ed., Biblioteca Románica Hispánica, III, Manuales (Madrid: Editorial Gredos, 1966), p. 101. We find passing references to rhetoric and to the work of Faral in various earlier cri-tics, but no systematic study. Félix Lecoy, for example, refers fleetingly to the *artes poetriae* in his *Recherches sur le "Libro de Buen Amor"* (Paris: Librairie E. Droz, 1938; cf. pp. 210-211). In the same year Ernst Robert Curtius, in a mas-sive review article of H. H. Glunz, *Die Literarästhetik des europäischen Mittel-alters: Wolfram, Rosenroman, Chaucer, Dante*, entitled "Zur Literarästhetik des Mittelalters," *ZRPh*, 58 (1938), 1-50, 129-232, 433-479, applied the theory of rhetorical *topoi* to the *Cid* and the *Carmen Campidoctoris*, seeing in the latter "eine kunstvolle rhetorische Schuldichtung, in der alles auf die Stilkonventionen der mlat. Poesie, nichts auf Volksdichtung hinweist" (p. 168). Ramón Menéndez

century writer who has been exposed, as López Estrada states, to humanistic influences. Thus it seems legitimate to wonder how well he represents the earlier rhetorical tradition in medieval Spain.

The only monograph confined to the study of rhetoric in one author is Carmelo Samonà's *Aspetti del retoricismo nella "Celestina."*[9] Here

---

Pidal objected vigorously to this in "La épica española y la 'Literarästhetik des Mittelalters' de E. R. Curtius," *ZRPh*, 59 (1939), 1-9, stressing the essential historicity of both the *Cid* and the *Carmen Campidoctoris*.

María Rosa Lida also took exception to Curtius' formulations in her review of his article, denying the "extensión de la retórica en la Edad Media": *RFH*, 1 (1939), 185. Her attitude was not completely negative, however, and of all the great critics of medieval Spanish literature she alone was constantly aware of the importance of rhetoric, although nowhere did she make an exhaustive study of it. Thus, in her "Notas para la interpretación, influencia, fuentes y texto del *Libro de buen amor*," she refers to the *artes poetriae* and Faral in the section on "Los retratos del *Buen amor*," *RFH*, 2 (1940), 122-125, foreshadowing the thesis of Zahareas some twenty-five years later (see below, p. 4). In the introduction to her edition of the *Libro de buen amor: Selección*, Colección de Textos Literarios (Buenos Aires: Editorial Losada, S. A., 1941), she states that "la obediencia a las normas de la retórica, elemento común de la enseñanza medieval, estrecha la vinculación de Juan Ruiz con toda la clerecía europea, y explica la presencia de unas mismas características en toda la literatura de la época" (p. 22). She then enumerates the rhetorical techniques used by Juan Ruiz, although without attempting to relate them to any theoretical work. A long excursus in "Las sectas judías y los 'procuradores' romanos: En torno a Josefo y su influjo sobre la literatura española," written ca. 1942-43 as part of a study on Josephus and recently published in *HR*, 39 (1971), 183-213, foreshadows her own later article on Antonio de Guevara (see below, p. 10), tracing his style back to "la prosa italiana latinizante o de las obras latinas del Prerrenacimiento, como las de Boccaccio, cuya primera manifestación en castellano es el estilo del *Corbacho* . . . " (p. 203). She was as yet unaware of its filiation with the *Synonyma* of St. Isidore and the *De Virginitate Sanctae Mariae* of St. Ildefonsus. She returned to the theme in a lengthy review article, "Perduración de la literatura antigua en Occidente (A propósito by [sic] Ernst Robert Curtius, *Europäische Literatur und lateinisches Mittelalter*)," *RPh*, 5 (1951-1952), 99-131. In a later review, of Leonid Arbusow's *Colores Rhetorici* in *RPh*, 7 (1953-1954), 223-225, she states flatly: "Es tan decisiva en la literatura medieval la formación retórica, que toda reseña de su teoría, toda muestra de su material son bienvenidas." Her untimely death undoubtedly prevented her from treating this problem in detail, a task which she was uniquely qualified to do. I am indebted to Professor Yakov Malkiel for most of the references above.

[9] Studi di Letteratura Spagnola, Quaderno II, Facoltà di Magistero dell'Università di Roma (Rome, 1953).

again the problem is whether the work can be considered medie-val at all. Samonà is concerned almost exclusively with the prac-tice of rhetoric in the *Celestina*; he makes little attempt to relate it to anything except contemporary usage and to the immediate rhe-torical tradition from which it sprang. What he has to say about the period before the fifteenth century seems to be taken from López Estrada's article and from a study by María Rosa Lida.

There have been no studies exclusively on rhetoric or rhetorical influence in the earlier period (to the end of the fourteenth century). However, since 1960 a number of monographs on medieval Spanish literature have paid varying amounts of attention to rhetorical in-fluences on individual writers. In every case we find that the auth-ors make a number of assumptions about rhetoric in Spain, either implicit or explicit, which are open to question.

Anthony Zahareas, in *The Art of Juan Ruiz, Archpriest of Hita*, devotes twenty pages to rhetoric in the *Libro de buen amor* and ano-ther thirty to the *Libro's* rhetorical portraits. Although he nowhere specifically discusses the problem of Spanish knowledge of medieval rhetoric, it is apparent, from the critics he cites (Faral, Ernst Robert Curtius, Richard McKeon), that he considers the peninsula to lie completely within the European Latin tradition. The closest he comes to an open acknowledgment of this occurs in the following state-ment: "Because of the intimate symbiosis of Latin and vernacular literatures in the thirteenth and fourteenth centuries, these learned treatises [the *artes poetriae*] are very important for Romance litera-rature."[10]

Carmelo Gariano recognizes the problem more explicitly and at-tempts to counter possible objections to the practice of comparing the theories advanced by the *artes* with Spanish poetic usage:

> ... hubo en la Europa del siglo XII un florecimiento de artes poéticas que se acentuó en el siglo XIII, es decir, en tiempos de nuestro poeta. ... Debido al nue-vo clima cultural que iba difundiéndose por toda Europa, España inclusive, la producción y difusión de aquellas obras fue notable. Es probable, pues, la afir-mación de López Estrada sobre ese punto: es decir, que su alcance entre la gente culta de España corría parejo con el de otros países europeos.

---

[10] (Madrid: Estudios de Literatura Española, 1965), p. 123n.

En cuanto a Berceo, no hay evidencia directa de que él conociera las artes poéticas corrientes; tampoco es conclusive el argumento de que se dan, dentro de su
obra, varios de los recursos estilísticos a la sazón recomendados por los mejores
tratadistas. . . . Por otro lado, no se puede negar que aquellas artes poéticas go-
zaban de mucha popularidad porque, junto con los *auctores*, formaban el núcleo
de la educación liberal medieval. *Auctores* y *artes* fueron materia de estudio en
los ateneos universitarios entonces existentes, y, bajo ese concepto, España no
estaba a la zaga de nadie. Lo cual está corroborado por la estima que la escuela
de Toledo merecía a uno de aquellos antiguos tratadistas medievales, quien la com-
para en prestigio con las de París, Salerno y Bolonia.[11]

I have quoted Gariano at some length in order to present his defense of Spanish knowledge of the *artes* as fully as possible. Aside
from his general references to medieval rhetorical tradition, his specific statements concerning Spain rest on two sources: López Estrada's unsupported affirmation that the situation in Spain "probably"
was similar to that in other parts of Europe, and a reference to the
"school of Toledo" in Geoffroi de Vinsauf's *Documentum de Modo et
Arte Dictandi et Versificandi.* The latter is adduced to buttress the
assertion that Spanish university centers were as up-to-date in their
curriculum as those of the rest of Europe. But Geoffroi is not talking about universities. In this passage he is discussing the amplification of general statements through concrete examples; he cites
Paris, Salerno, Bologna, and Toledo as examples of the general expression "peritos." He assigns a specific, and traditional, specialty
to each of these schools: the trivium to Paris, medicine to Salerno,
law to Bologna—and the quadrivium to Toledo.[12] Since the quadri-

---

[11] *Análisis estilístico de los "Milagros de Nuestra Señora" de Berceo*, Biblioteca Románica Hispánica, II, Estudios y Ensayos (Madrid: Editorial Gredos, 1965),
pp. 18-19.

[12] ". . . re vera 'inter peritos,' cum inter Parisienses, ubi floret scientia trivii,
inter Tholetanos, ubi scientia quadrivii, inter Salernitanos, ubi scientia medicorum, inter Bononienses, ubi scientia legis et decretorum." Faral, *Les arts poétiques*,
p. 283. Toledo also had a reputation as a center for the occult: "Caesar of Heis-
terbach (1222) in his *Dialogus Miraculorum* says that young people in order to
learn *Nigromantia* usually go to Toledo. Günther, *Geschichte des mathematischen
Unterrichts*, 203, n. 2." "'Ecce quaerunt clerici Parisiis artes liberales, Aurelia-
nis auctores, Bononiae codices, Salerni pyxides, Toleti daemones et nusquam mo-
res.' Helinand, in a sermon before the students of the University of Toulouse in
1229." Louis John Paetow, *The Arts Course at Medieval Universities with Special*

vium was the medieval *scientific* curriculum, the statement cited by Gariano tells us nothing about the state of literary theory in Spain; it does not even tell us much about Spanish universities and their curricula, since Toledo technically never had a university.

Another study of Berceo, Joaquín Artiles' *Los recursos literarios de Berceo*, in spite of its ambitious title, makes even less of an attempt to relate Berceo's "literary devices" to contemporary poetic theory. Artiles merely cites the theoreticians' definitions of certain rhetorical devices, as published in Faral, in his discussion of these same devices in the *Milagros*.[13] Gaudioso Giménez Resano notes in his review of the book that the author mentions a limited number of rhetorical figures, such as alliteration, anaphora, and paronomasia, "sin detenerse en otros interesantísimos aspectos que nos ofrece el estudio de la retórica en Berceo."[14]

Finally, we might mention André Michalski's excellent study, "Description in Mediaeval Spanish Poetry." Like Gariano, Michalski goes into the theoretical underpinning of his work in some detail. On the question that interests us he states his position as follows:

This investigation was undertaken under the presumption that medieval Spain was very much a part of Latin Europe, and that its literary expression, whatever might have been its "Spanish particularity" and its indebtedness to Islamic and Hebraic culture, constituted an integral part of "Western-European literature."[15] . . . although none of the important authors of the treatises on rhetoric was Spanish, we know that, given the uniformity of Latin literary culture in the Middle Ages and the speed with which literary themes and manuscripts travelled in both directions across the Pyrenees, the rhetoric taught in Spanish schools and the texts used were substantially the same as elsewhere in Latin Europe.[16]

Reference to Grammar and Rhetoric, University of Illinois, The University Studies, III, 7 (Urbana-Champaign: University Press, 1910), pp. 26n, 14n. See also Samuel M. Waxman, "Chapters on Magic in Spanish Literature," *RHi*, 38 (1916), 325-463. At the time, of course, the line between science and magic was a thin one. But these citations lead us to question even more the statement that literary studies were one of the strengths of the Spanish schools.

[13] Biblioteca Románica Hispánica, II, Estudios y Ensayos (Madrid: Editorial Gredos, 1964); cf. pp. 56, 137, 174-175.

[14] *AEM*, 2 (1965), 683.

[15] (Unpubl. diss., Princeton University, 1964), p. 2.

[16] Ibid., p. 23.

Michalski assumes that there was no "important" Spanish work on rhetoric—the same position Menéndez y Pelayo had adopted seventy-five years previously. He also assumes that rhetorical theories were imported from beyond the Pyrenees and that these theories were not significantly changed on being received in Spain. These assumptions are basic to Michalski's study, but they remain assumptions. Methodologically it makes more sense to determine the actual state of rhetorical theory in medieval Spain by empirical investigation before seeking to determine the effect of that theory on contemporary poetic practice.

Neither Michalski nor anyone else has attempted to do this. Manuel C. Díaz y Díaz pointed out precisely this problem in his discussion of our knowledge of medieval Hispanic Latin before the first Spanish Congress of Classical Studies in 1958:

> . . . nos faltan ensayos sobre el concepto que tenían de la lengua y el estilo los autores mediolatinos, no sabemos casi nada por investigación indiscutible sobre los autores por ellos leídos, porque entre otras faltas de nuestros estudios ignoramos cuáles eran y en qué proporción los autores cuyas obras se conservaban en las Bibliotecas, así como el porqué de la abundancia de copias de cieitos autores en perjuicio de otros.[17]

The situation has not changed appreciably since then.[18]

The basic thrust of the previous review should be clear: There is a tendency, based on inadequate documentation, to equate rhetoric in Spain with rhetoric in the rest of Europe. In the present study I present the documentation upon which such an affirmation must rest. Specifically, I have examined the extant rhetorical treatises written by Spaniards during the Middle Ages and their relationship to contemporary European theory as set forth in *artes poetriae*, *artes praedicandi*, and *artes dictandi*, and I have provided informa-

---

[17] "El latín medieval español," in *Actas del Primer Congreso Español de Estudios Clásicos*, Publicaciones de la Sociedad Española de Estudios Clásicos, 2 (Madrid: Cándido Bermejo, 1958), pp. 565-566.

[18] Francisco López Estrada promises an edition of tbe translation of Brunetto Latini's *Livres* in "Sobre la difusión del *Tesoro* de Brunetto Latini en España (El manuscrito de la Real Academia Sevillana de Buenas Letras)," *Gesammelte Aufsätze zur Kulturgeschichte Spaniens*, Spanische Forschungen der Görresgesellschaft, 1. Reihe, 16 (1960), 137-152.

tion on certain related matters: rhetorical treatises found in medieval Spanish libraries; rhetorical texts, if any, used in medieval Spanish schools; the first references to rhetoric in both Spanish Latin and Spanish vernacular literature; the first discussions of rhetoric in the vernacular; rhetorical treatises still extant in Spanish libraries, their authorship, and the provenience of the extant manuscripts; the conditions under which the non-Spanish manuscripts entered Spain; and the degree to which modern holdings reflect medieval conditions. Some of these matters can be documented in detail, others only partially, and some not at all.

My investigation is both broader and narrower than previous studies on medieval rhetoric. It is broader than Faral's or Thomas M. Charland's *Artes Praedicandi: Contribution à l'histoire de la rhétorique au moyen âge*, which concentrate on one aspect of rhetoric.[19] I examine all facets of rhetorical theory important in Castile during the thirteenth and fourteenth centuries. At the same time it is narrower in the sense that it concentrates on a particular geographical region and a limited historical period. Geographically I restrict my investigation to Castile and León, with occasional references to the adjacent kingdoms of Galicia and Navarre. I do not treat rhetoric in Catalonia and Aragon. The cultural tradition of the eastern part of the peninsula, because of its closer ties with France and Italy, varies considerably from that of the center and the northwest. Conclusions valid for one region may not be valid for the other. Chronologically I concentrate upon the thirteenth and fourteenth centuries, although I treat the earlier period with as much detail as possible. I have chosen the year 1400 as a convenient cut-off point; increasingly after that date the nature and quantity of rhetorical theory begin to change under the influence of early Italian humanism.

There are several problems which I shall not treat but which should be mentioned, if only to point out their significance for the history of rhetorical influence in medieval Spanish literature. There is, for example, the continuing stylistic imitation throughout the Middle Ages of St. Ildefonsus' *De Virginitate Sanctae Mariae contra Tres In-*

---

[19] Publications de l'Institut d'Études Médiévales d'Ottawa, 7 (Ottawa: Institut d'Études Médiévales, 1936).

fideles. In "Fray Antonio de Guevara: Edad Media y Siglo de Oro español," María Rosa Lida traces briefly the trajectory of this style, characterized by its short periods, rhymed prose, contrasts, and heavy use of synonyms, in the vernacular literature.[20] José Amador de los Ríos shows the use of the same style in Spanish Latin prose, particularly in the chronicles of the high Middle Ages.[21] But the comments of these two critics serve merely as an introduction to the problem, which merits a thorough study.

I am not concerned with the development of the *cursus*, the use of rhythmic cadences at the end of periods, in the vernacular literatures, in imitation of the style employed in the papal Curia starting in the twelfth century and later in the royal chancelleries. The study of this phenomenon belongs to the realm of rhetorical practice rather than to that of theory.

Nor do I attempt to list and discuss every rhetorical figure mentioned in the various treatises examined. Such figures were readily available to the medieval author in the classical rhetorics, in all of the varieties of medieval rhetoric, and even in grammar books. What is more, these lists of rhetorical figures are basically the same and are derived from that given in Book IV of the *Rhetorica ad C. Herennium.*[22] Thus the mere fact that an author lists rhetorical devices indicates nothing about the particular rhetorical tradition he may be following. For that reason I am concerned with the broader rhetorical patterns and literary ideas which more accurately characterize each tradition.

---

[20] *RFH*, 7 (1945), 346-388. John of Garland, in his *De Arte Prosayca Metrica et Rithmica*, calls this the "stilo ysidoriano," probably because it is first found in St. Isidore's *Synonyma de Lamentatione Animae Peccatricis.* But his definition of it is so brief that no medieval writer could have used it as a guide. Cf. the ed. of Giovanni Mari in *RF*, 13 (1902), 929; cited by Gariano, p. 198.

[21] *Historia crítica de la literatura española*, 7 vols. (I-III, Madrid: Imp. José Rodríguez, 1861-1863; IV-VI, Madrid : Imp. José Fernández Cancela, 1863-1865; VII, Madrid: Imp. Joaquín Muñoz, 1865). Cf. esp. I, 416-417; II, 48-49, 58, 65, 101-102, 142-143, 150, 155-156, 182, 316-318; VI, 246. See also Francisco Rico, "Las letras latinas del siglo xii en Galicia, León y Castilla," *Ábaco*, 2 (1969), 53, 67.

[22] Faral, *Les arts poétiques*, pp. 52-54.

Finally, I do not enter into the thorny problem of the relationships between western and Arabic literary theory, both basically offspring of Greek rhetoric. So much research remains to be done by Latinists and Arabists that it would be futile to discuss those relationships here. At this stage it is more important for both groups of scholars to publish the basic texts and define as accurately as possible the internal development of each tradition on the basis of those texts before going into their possible cross-connections. Such basic research is all the more important in view of the fact that the interrelationship of Christian, Moslem, and Jewish elements has been a crux of medieval Hispanic scholarship, literary and historical, since the publication of Américo Castro's seminal *España en su historia* in 1948.

This cannot be the definitive study of rhetoric in medieval Spain; at most it is but a start. Too much unpublished material remains to be examined. But incomplete as it is, this investigation will, I hope, establish the broad outlines of the Spanish rhetorical tradition and focus attention on the most influential rhetorical genres and works. In so doing it will also point out the scholarly and critical tasks that must be undertaken if we are ever to attain a more precise and profound understanding of that rhetorical tradition and its contribution to the evolution of medieval Spanish literature.

In the organization of this study, Chapter II serves as a general introduction to the history of Latin rhetoric in the Middle Ages, and attempts to determine which of its elements were present in Spain on the basis of contemporary sources— what little is known of medieval schools, the records of medieval libraries, and the reflection of medieval conditions in modern Spanish library holdings. Chapter III deals with the same problem through an examination of references to rhetoric and the other arts of the trivium in Spanish Latin and vernacular literature. Chapter IV presents a cursory study of two non-Spanish rhetoricians in Spain, Ponce of Provence and Geoffrey of Everseley, and a detailed study of two rhetorical treatises written in Latin by Spaniards during the thirteenth and fourteenth centuries, the *Dictaminis Epithalamium* of Juan Gil de Zamora, collaborator of Alfonso X and tutor of his son Sancho IV, and the *Breve Compendium Artis Rethorice* of Martín de Córdoba.

CHAPTER II

LATIN RHETORIC IN MEDIEVAL SPAIN:
EVIDENCE OF CONTEMPORARY SOURCES

LATIN RHETORIC DURING THE MIDDLE AGES

RATHER than trace the development of rhetoric from its beginnings in Greek Sicily or even from its establishment in Rome, it is sufficient for our purposes to start with the Latin rhetorical tradition as it is given during the period of transition from Antiquity to the Middle Ages, from 400 to 600 approximately. At the beginning of this period refinements are still being introduced into the Latin rhetorical tradition; at the end, that tradition has hardened into doctrine in the summaries of the encyclopedists Cassiodorus Senator, Martianus Capella, and Seville's St. Isidore.[1]

Treatises on rhetoric known during this period can be divided roughly into two groups: those which present a comprehensive and coherent philosophy of rhetoric and its functions, and those which are more narrowly concerned with the technical problems of rhetoric. The first group is represented by the Ciceronian treatises, Quintilian's *Institutio Oratoria*, and, to a lesser extent, the pseudo-Ciceronian *Rhetorica ad C. Herennium*. The second group, composed generally of la-

---

[1] The material for the following outline is drawn chiefly from Charles S. Baldwin, *Medieval Rhetoric and Poetic (to 1400), Interpreted from Representative Works* (New York: The Macmillan Company, 1928; repr. Gloucester [Mass.]: Peter Smith, 1959); Richard McKeon, "Rhetoric in the Middle Ages," *Speculum*, 17 (1942), 1-32; and James Jerome Murphy, "Chaucer, Gower, and the English Rhetorical Tradition" (unpubl. diss., Stanford University, 1957). See also the latter's admirably clear and succinct summary at the beginning of his "Rhetoric in Fourteenth-Century Oxford," *Medium Aevum*, 34 (1965), 1-20. I have reorganized it for my own purposes. I shall be concerned primarily with enumerating the various treatises and grouping them into broad categories.

ter works based on the aforementioned, includes the *Ars Rhetorica* of Julius Victor, the *Institutiones Oratoriae* of Sulpitius Victor, the *Artis Rhetoricae Libri* of C. Chirius Fortunatianus, and the even more restricted treatises of Aquila Romanus, Rutilius Lupus, Julius Rufinianus, and others.[2]

What will become a dominant characteristic of the development of medieval rhetorical theory is already manifest in the late classical period. The comprehensive treatises, which discuss rhetoric in its relationship with man's whole life and as a necessary adjunct to the conduct of human affairs, are gradually superseded by treatises which take the philosophy behind rhetoric for granted; concerned with solving particular problems, they draw upon the techniques presented in the earlier treatises and elaborate these techniques as new problems arise. The most extreme examples of this tendency toward pragmatism occur in the treatises grouped under the name of the Second Sophistic. Of these works Hermogenes' *Progymnasmata*, translated into Latin by Priscian as *De Praexercitamina Rhetoricis*, is probably the best known.[3] According to Murphy, "emphasis is upon rules and methods, to the extent that the ancient concept of *topos* or *locus* is replaced by long lists of specific directions about things to be done. A writer or speaker wishing to describe a person, for instance, can rely on specific, detailed directions rather than upon his own inventive ability."[4]

The manuscript tradition of the comprehensive treatises reflects the influence of this tendency toward pragmatism. Three of Cicero's six treatises on rhetoric, *De Oratore*, *Brutus*, and *Orator*, were virtually unknown in the Middle Ages; and it is precisely these treatises which present the most mature development of Ciceronian rhetorical theory. *De Inventione*, an incomplete and schematic text, strong on specific instructions, is far and away the most popular of the Ciceronian

---

[2] These later treatises are gathered together in *Rhetores Latini Minores*, ed. by Carolus Halm (Leipzig: In aedibus B. G. Teubneri, 1863; repr. Frankfurt am Main: Minerva GMBH, 1964).

[3] In Halm, pp. 551-560.

[4] "Chaucer, Gower," pp. 26-27.

treatises during the Middle Ages.⁵ Its popularity was equaled in the low Middle Ages by that of the anonymous *Rhetorica ad C. Herennium*, just as schematic and very similar in treatment, so similar in fact that after the twelfth century the two works were frequently found together and were both attributed to Cicero. The *Ad Herennium* was particularly useful for its long list of figures of thought and speech in Book IV.

During the greater part of the Middle Ages, Quintilian's *Institutio Oratoria* was available only in a badly mutilated version. Books V-VIII, IX, X, and XII were missing completely or in part.⁶ Thomas E. Marston states that "on the basis of this version most medieval scholars considered the *Institutio* as a moral writing rather than a work on education."⁷ The strictly rhetorical portions were among those missing; the *Institutio* exerted a negligible influence on the development of medieval rhetoric.

It is impossible to state how far the trend toward pragmatism had gone by the beginning of the Middle Ages. Nevertheless, it is interesting to note that the encyclopedists, who compiled what they considered to be the most important elements of classical knowledge in organized syntheses, drew heavily upon abstracts of or commentaries on the earlier texts, not upon those texts themselves. Thus in Book V of his *De Nuptiis Philologiae et Mercurii et de Septem Artibus Liberalibus*, the fifth-century compiler Martianus Capella follows Fortunatianus for the organization of his comments on rhetoric and follows Aquila Romanus almost word for word in his discussion of the rhetorical figures.⁸ Cassiodorus Senator, the first of the great Christian encyclopedists (ca. 490-ca. 583), also bases the discussion of rhetoric in his *Institutiones* on Fortunatianus.⁹ St. Isidore, in turn,

---

⁵ Hilda Buttenweiser, "The Distribution of the Manuscripts of the Latin Classical Authors in the Middle Ages" (unpubl. diss., University of Chicago, 1930), p. 24.

⁶ Priscilla S. Boskoff, "Quintilian in the Late Middle Ages," *Speculum*, 27 (1952), 71-72.

⁷ "Quintillian's *Institutiones Orationae*," *YULG*, 32 (1957), 6-7.

⁸ Murphy, "Chaucer, Gower," p. 31; and María Ángeles Galino, *Historia de la educación*, Vol. I: *Edades antigua y media*, Biblioteca Hispánica de Filosofía (Madrid : Editorial Gredos, 1960), pp. 478-479.

⁹ Murphy, "Chaucer, Gower," p. 37; Galino, *Historia de la educación*, I, 481.

grounds his treatment of rhetoric in Book II of the *Etymologiae* on Cassiodorus.

The pragmatic approach to rhetoric also accounts for its increasing disintegration in the later Middle Ages. Richard McKeon has traced in broad outline the history of this phenomenon and concludes, paradoxically, that rhetoric as such has no history during this period. It must always be discussed in terms of something else. On the one hand, starting with Boethius it becomes methodologically involved with dialectic; on the other hand, its subject matter, the "substantive consideration of law," was transferred to the domain of theology.[10] Yet there is a third aspect to rhetoric, one to which McKeon rather slightingly refers as "a simple art of words."[11]

It is precisely this "simple art of words" which had the most extraordinary development in the later Middle Ages, beginning in about the eleventh century. But to trace this development we must break McKeon's "simple art" into its component parts: *ars dictaminis, ars praedicandi*, and *ars poetriae*. In spite of the early exposition of the art of preaching by St. Augustine in Book IV of his *De Doctrina Christiana*, showing how pagan rhetoric can aid the Christian preacher,[12] it was the art of letter-writing which first established itself as an independent discipline within the general study of rhetoric. Simplifying a very complex process for the sake of brevity, we may say that *dictamen* had its origins in the need for fixed rules for the composition of official documents and letters. Its first important author was Alberic of Monte Cassino, who wrote a *Breviarium Dictaminis* and a *Flores Dictaminum* in the latter part of the eleventh century.[13] In the twelfth century the art continued to develop in Italy and also in France, more or less independently. Orléans was the center of a vigorous school of *dictamen* in the second half of the twelfth century, a school which emphasized, so far as was possible, a return to classical Latinity.

---

[10] McKeon, "Rhetoric in the Middle Ages," p. 27.

[11] Ibid., p. 15.

[12] Robert O. Payne, *The Key of Remembrance: A Study of Chaucer's Poetics* (New Haven: Yale University Press for the University of Cincinnati, 1963), pp. 41-42.

[13] Luis Vázquez de Parga, "Literatura latina medieval," *RUO*, 10 (1948), 22.

The *ars dictaminis* was virtually revolutionized in the thirteenth century by scholars associated with the schools of Bologna, who turned it into an adjunct of the disciplines of law. The founder of this later Italian school of *dictamen*, which held sway throughout the low Middle Ages, was Buoncompagno of Bologna (fl. XIII inc.), who claimed that his *Rhetorica Novissima* owed nothing to Cicero (probably a cut aimed at the school of Orléans), but was based on the usage of the Roman Curia.[14] The most famous exponent of this school was Guido Faba (see below, p. 47).

From the very beginning *dictamen* had followed two divergent but complementary tendencies. The first considered it from a theoretical point of view, giving general rules for the composition of all letters. The second was more pragmatically oriented. It merely offered a series of form letters to be imitated by chancery notaries. Buoncompagno and Guido wrote both theoretical and practical works; by the beginning of the fourteenth century, however, theory was virtually eliminated while form books became more voluminous. *Dictamen* by that time was almost wholly oriented toward law; and treatises such as Rolandinus Rodulphus Passagerius' *Summa Artis Notariae* present only those forms necessary for the drawing up of legal documents.[15] Late medieval treatises which are more than collections of stock phrases to suit the usual requirements of official epistolary usage are very few.

The *artes poetriae* of the Middle Ages, the second major rhetorical discipline to develop, had little to do with classical treatises. The *Poetics* of Aristotle was virtually unknown until well into the thirteenth century,[16] and Horace's *Epistola ad Pisones*, which was known, exerted little influence even on the work of those who cite it. What the Middle Ages knew as *poetria*, starting in the twelfth century, was actually an amalgam of rhetorical and metrical theory designed more for the schoolroom than for the poet's study. The *Laborintus* of Evrard the German is in fact subtitled *De Miseriis Rectorum Schola-*

---

[14] Murphy, "Chaucer, Gower," p. 57. Cf. also Augusto Gaudenzi, "Sulla cronologia delle opere dei dettatori Bolognesi da Boncompagno a Bene di Lucca," *BISI*, 14 (1895), 85-161.

[15] Murphy, "Chaucer, Gower," p. 55.

[16] Menéndez y Pelayo, *Ideas estéticas*, I, 393-394.

rum.[17] As Murphy points out, "the *artes poetriae* were composed by professional teachers of *ars grammatica*. Moreover, they refer to problems of teaching versewriting, and display a constant regard for the larger *ars grammatica* of which they form a part."[18]

Of these *artes* the most important remain those treated by Faral, in particular the *Ars Versificatoria* of Matthieu de Vendôme, the *Poetria Nova* of Geoffroi de Vinsauf, and the *De Arte Prosayca Metrica et Ritmica* of John of Garland. The earliest is Matthieu's *Ars Versificatoria*, written before 1175.[19] The sources used reflect the intellectual atmosphere at Orléans, where Matthieu both studied and taught, during the so-called Renaissance of the twelfth century. Horace is cited extensively, as are *De Inventione* and the *Rhetorica ad C. Herennium*, but all are checked against Book II of St. Isidore's *Etymologiae*.[20]

Geoffroi's *Poetria Nova*, written between 1208 and 1213, is the most popular of the three works if the number of extant manuscripts is any indication. Faral mentions forty-three specifically and adds, "et cette liste, donnée seulement à titre d'indication, est très loin d'être complète."[21] As we shall see at the end of this chapter, three manuscripts in Spanish libraries must be added to it. Like Matthieu de Vendôme, Geoffroi turned to the classical authors but relied especially on the *Rhetorica ad C. Herennium*.[22]

The Englishman John of Garland's treatise is later than the other two (after 1229) and more comprehensive.[23] He tries, without much success, to include both *dictamen* and *poetria* in one work. He also devotes more attention than the other theorists to the purely technical questions of versification. It is a *summa* of contemporary rhetorical theory, probably the last such *summa* written.

---

[17] Hastings Rashdall, *The Universities of Europe in the Middle Ages*, ed. by F. M. Powicke and A. B. Emden, 3 vols. (Oxford: At the Clarendon Press, 1936), I, 448-449.

[18] "Chaucer, Gower," p. 88.

[19] Faral, *Les arts poétiques*, p. 3.

[20] Baldwin, *Medieval Rhetoric*, pp. 185-187; Ellis Gale Shields, "The Gawain-Poet and the Latin Rhetorical Tradition" (unpubl. diss., University of Southern California, 1956), pp. 12-13.

[21] *Les arts poétiques*, p. 28.

[22] Shields, "The Gawain-Poet," p. 14.

[23] Faral, *Les arts poetiques*, p. 41.

Many of the *artes praedicandi* are also called *summae*, although the title usually promises rather more than it delivers. Of the separate arts based on classical rhetoric, this one has the longest history, going back ultimately to St. Augustine. The subject was treated sporadically throughout the Middle Ages, most conspicuously in Hrabanus Maurus' *De Clericorum Institutione* (ninth century) and in Alain de Lille's *Summa de Arte Praedicatoria* (twelfth century), but arts of preaching did not multiply noticeably until the thirteenth century.[24]

Whereas the older treatises had been concerned with generalized counsel on the preacher's duties, the thirteenth-century treatises emphasized the rules of the thematic sermon. This sort of sermon, taking as its theme the scriptural text for the day and developing it according to elaborate techniques, probably came about through the confluence of two powerful currents: the invasion of the nascent universities by dialectic and the rise of the great preaching orders, the Franciscans and the Dominicans.[25] The thematic sermon appears fully developed at the University of Paris by 1230, before the first theoretical arts setting it forth were written.[26] Until its decline in the late fifteenth century, the bulk of the *artes praedicandi*—and nearly 300 are known—were produced by members of the two mendicant orders.[27] Moreover, the most influential of these *artes* were also due to these orders: Charland cites the *De Eruditione Praedicatorum* of Humbert de Romans, fifth general of the Dominicans (1254-1263) and publishes, as one of the two texts which set forth the theory of the thematic sermon in its most complete form, the *De Modo Componendi Sermones cum Documentis* of the Dominican Thomas Waleys (fourteenth century).[28]

Of all the forms of medieval rhetoric, the *ars praedicandi* moved farthest from the techniques of the classical art, retaining only the classical *colores*.[29] Paradoxically, the *ars praedicandi* is closest to clas-

---

24 For Hrabanus Maurus cf. Murphy, "Chaucer, Gower," pp. 46-47.
25 M.-D. Chenu, "Introduction" to Charland, *Artes Praedicandi*, p. 9.
26 Murphy, "Chaucer, Gower," p. 71.
27 Ibid., pp. 66-67.
28 *Artes Praedicandi*, pp. 47, 325-403.
29 Murphy, "Chaucer, Gower," p. 143.

sical rhetoric in spirit, since it is the only one of the medieval arts to deal with the spoken word.[30]

The second half of the thirteenth century saw the first attempts at translating Latin rhetoric into the vernaculars. The Florentine Brunetto Latini translated *De Inventione* into Italian before 1260 and then utilized a free version of this as the third book of his *Livres dou Trésor*, written in French.[31] An Italian paraphrase of the *Rhetorica ad C. Herennium*, variously ascribed to one Guidotto da Bologna or to a Bono Giambono, appeared before 1266; and the Frenchman Jean d'Antioche de Harens combined these two classical rhetorics in 1282 in a work which he called *Rettorique de Marc Tulles Cyceron*.[32] Direct translations into Spanish do not occur until the fifteenth century and are not found in English until the sixteenth.[33]

In the fourteenth century there was not much change in the rhetorical doctrines or the sources from which they were taken; the medieval *artes* continued to play a major role. But by the end of that century the concept of rhetoric was changing rapidly under the impact of humanism. The complete Quintilian was discovered in St. Gall by Poggio in 1416;[34] and the "greater Cicero"—*De oratore, Orator,* and *Brutus*—was rediscovered, the *Brutus* literally so, in 1421.[35] Rhetoric as the classical authors conceived it was reviving; and rhetorical theory was beginning to lose the accumulated accretions and distortions of the medieval period.

CONTEMPORARY EVIDENCE FOR LATIN RHETORIC IN MEDIEVAL SPAIN

The degree to which the Iberian Peninsula participated in the evolution of Latin rhetoric as described above, or even in the use of

---

[30] Baldwin, *Medieval Rhetoric*, p. 230.

[31] Murphy, "Chaucer, Gower," pp. 50-51.

[32] Ibid., pp. 51-52.

[33] Ibid., p. 52.

[34] Buttenweiser, "The Distribution of the Manuscripts," pp. 24-25.

[35] Arthur A. Tilley, "The Early Renaissance," in *Decline of Empire and Papacy*, Vol. VII of the *Cambridge Medieval History*, ed. by J. B. Bury et al. (New York: The Macmillan Company, 1932; Cambridge: At the University Press, 1932), p. 762.

that rhetoric, has heretofore been more a matter for speculation than for detailed research. The reasons for the lack of such research are fairly obvious. As R. R. Bolgar points out, "the historian has to depend not incidentally (as is often the case), but primarily, on the results obtained in a field which ranks among the most difficult that scholars have ever tackled."[36] He is referring to the problems of finding out exactly what books were available to the medieval schoolmen in the libraries of the time, what books were used as texts in the schools, and what medieval teachers and students were looking for in those books.

If these problems are difficult for medieval research in other areas of Europe, the difficulties are compounded in Spain. There has been no general study of medieval libraries since Rudolf Beer's *Handschriftenschätze Spaniens*.[37] Nor has there been a comprehensive history of Spanish education in the Middle Ages since the appearance of Vicente de la Fuente's *Historia de las universidades, colegios y demás establecimientos de enseñanza en España* (1884-1889).[38] Studies on the history of the Spanish universities have all been concerned with the evolution of the university as an institution, with its political and legal aspects rather than with its educational ones. C. M. Ajo's *Historia de las universidades hispánicas*, the latest and most detailed of these studies, concentrates, like the others, on the origins and constitutional history of the universities.[39] Finally, catalogues of modern Spanish libraries have until very recently been almost nonexistent, and even the best have suffered from serious deficiencies. The *Inventario general de manuscritos de la Biblioteca Nacional* of Madrid is a notable and welcome exception, but its nine volumes (to date) include less than 3,000 of the library's 30,000 manuscripts.[40]

---

[36] *The Classical Heritage and Its Beneficiaries: From the Carolingian Age to the End of the Renaissance*, Harper Torchbooks, The Academy Library (New York: Harper and Row, 1964), p. 6.

[37] Vienna: In Commission bei F. Tempsky, 1894.

[38] 4 vols. (Madrid: Imprenta Viuda de Fuentenebro, 1884-1889).

[39] 6 vols. (Madrid: Imprenta La Normal, 1957-1966); in progress.

[40] Dirección General de Archivos y Bibliotecas, Catálogos de Archivos y Bibliotecas, 18 (Madrid: Ministerio de Educación Nacional, Dirección General de Archivos y Bibliotecas, Servicio de Publicaciones, 1953-1970); in progress.

Because of the lack of comprehensive studies and detailed catalogues, the historian interested in the intellectual development of Spain during the Middle Ages must have recourse to other sources, both published and unpublished: collections of documents, cartularies of medieval monasteries, and chapter records of medieval cathedrals. Not infrequently such documents contain references to libraries, to books lent under pledge to different individuals, to the schoolmasters employed (*magister scholae, capiscol*); less frequently they contain complete or partial library catalogues. Supplementing the documents are secondary sources of varying value. Of minor importance are the municipal and ecclesiastical histories of the sixteenth and seventeenth centuries; certain notable exceptions are those based more strictly on documentary evidence, much of which has disappeared in the intervening centuries.[41] The eighteenth century saw the first systematic attempts at organizing and cataloguing the medieval documents in the work of P. Enrique Flórez, the first editor of *España sagrada*, and in that of P. Andrés Burriel. Most of the latter's studies and transcriptions lie unpublished in Madrid's Biblioteca Nacional. Such efforts were continued in the nineteenth century, most notably in Jaime Villanueva's *Viaje literario a las iglesias de España*.[42] Unfortunately this work is of virtually no use to us since it is confined to the kingdom of Aragon. No comparable collections of documents for other regions of Spain appeared in the latter part of the nineteenth century or in the twentieth.

Many less ambitious modern studies are of highest importance for the information they yield about education or libraries in specific places at specific times, but the results are fragmentary. Of the area in which we are particularly interested, the center and northwest of the peninsula, Galicia and León have received the most attention. We have a reasonably good idea of the intellectual conditions in these regions through the eleventh century. Our knowledge of other areas

---

[41] Prudencio de Sandoval, *Primera parte de las fvndaciones de los monasterios del glorioso padre San Benito* . . . (Madrid: Luis Sánchez, 1601); Ambrosio de Morales, *Viage* . . . *a los reynos de León, y Galicia, y principado de Asturias* . . . , ed. by Henrique Flórez (Madrid: por A. Marín, 1765).

[42] 22 vols. (Madrid: Imprenta Real et al., 1803-1852).

is scanty for the early period. The low Middle Ages, especially the thirteenth and fourteenth centuries, have been neglected everywhere.

I do not pretend to have made an exhaustive survey of all the available sources. A good share of them still slumber untouched and unknown in Spanish archives and libraries. I have been able to examine *in situ* a small number of these unpublished documents and a reasonable number of the older histories. But by far the greater part of the information upon which the following remarks are based has been gleaned from modern studies and editions.

MEDIEVAL EDUCATION IN SPAIN

The schools of Visigothic Spain, which reached their apogee under St. Isidore early in the seventh century, seem to have collapsed as completely as did other Visigothic institutions under the onslaught of the Moslems. Information about the Christian schools of the north (presumably monastic as in other parts of contemporary Europe) is remarkably scarce. The documents that remain tell us nothing and the narrative sources are hardly more enlightening. The only references in the latter occur when the education of princes comes under discussion. The *Historia Silense* states that Bermudo the Deacon (reigned 789-791) was given over to "literarum studiis" from his youth by order of his father.[43] The only problem is that the anonymous monk of Silos was writing in the twelfth century.[44] Even if the reference is exact, we can only conjecture what the content of the "literary studies" was. The Silense's other reference to royal studies is also inconclusive. He states with regard to the children of Fernando the Great (reigned 1035-1065): "Rex vero Fernandus filios suos et filias ita censuit instruere, vt primo liberalibus disciplinis, quibus

---

[43] Ed. by Justo Pérez de Urbel and Atilano González Ruiz-Zorrilla, Escuela de Estudios Medievales, Textos, 30 (Madrid: Consejo Superior de Investigaciones Científicas, 1959), p. 142; cited by José Amador de los Ríos, "Estudios sobre la educación de las clases privilegiadas de España durante la Edad Media," *RE*, 10 (10 Oct. 1869), 405.

[44] His probable source, the *Chronica Adefonsi Regis*, written in the late ninth century, is silent upon this point. Cf. ed. of Antonio Ubieto Arteta, Textos medievales, 3 (Valencia: Gráficas Bautista, 1961), pp. 46-47.

et ipse studium dederat, erudirentur. . . ."[45] The phrase is quoted almost verbatim from Einhard's *Vita Caroli*,[46] the biography of Charlemagne. While it may indicate something about trans-Pyrennaic influence in Spain (and we do know that the Cluniac reform penetrated into Spain during the reign of Fernando I), it cannot be said to offer conclusive evidence of Spanish educational practice.

The documents provide only indirect testimony about the schools of the time. Histories, deeds, wills, donations continue to be written; presumably their authors studied in monastic or episcopal schools. Such presumptions are confirmed by documents like the testament of St. Rudesindus (fl. 900), which honors the memory of his master, Sabaric II, bishop of Mondoñedo.[47] (This assumes, of course, that the title *magister* indicates a teacher-student relationship.) In the twelfth century the saint's hagiographer, Ordoño of Celanova, gives additional evidence: "Cum in primo tenere etatis flore litterarum studiis traderer, per tanti studii sudores . . . ."[48] As with Bermudo the Deacon, however, this quotation tells us more about the twelfth century than it does about the ninth.

Not until the eleventh century do we come upon concrete evidence of organized schools. Ironically, the earliest reference is to the destruction of a school, that of San Pedro de Rocas, in Galicia, through the negligence of the students: "Per negligentiam puerorum, qui in schola adhuc litteras legebant, domus ipsa . . . ab igne de nocte est succensa."[49] We note again that the students studied "letters" but are still not told what those letters consisted of. A school existed

---

[45] Ed. cited, p. 184; cited by Amador de los Ríos, "Estudios," p. 405.

[46] "Liberos suos ita censuit instituendos, ut tam filii quam filiae primo liberalibus studiis, quibus et ipse operam dabat, erudirentur . . . . "; cited by Pérez de Urbel and González Ruiz-Zorrilla in their ed. of the *Historia Silense*, p. 184.

[47] In *ES*, XVIII, 69; cited by Jules Tailhan, "Appendix sur les bibliothèques espagnoles du haut moyen âge," in *Bibliothèques*, Vol. III of *Nouveaux mélanges d'archéologie, d'histoire et de littérature sur le moyen âge*, ed. by Ch. Cahier (Paris: Firmin Didot Frères, Fils et Cie, 1877), p. 282.

[48] *S. Rudesindi Miraculo*, II, n. 15; cited in Tailhan, p. 286.

[49] Privilege of Alfonso V; cited by José Amador de los Ríos, "Del estado y educación de las clases sociales en España durante la Edad-Media: Medios científicos que labran la educación de la clerecía española," *RUM* (2ª época), 3 (1874), 488.

also at Santiago de Compostela in the eleventh century. In 1073 the bishop of León, Pelayo, writes that he was reared and instructed in ecclesiastical doctrine in Santiago.[50] Toward the end of the century Diego Gelmírez, first archbishop of Santiago, also went through that same school,[51] which he later reformed: "Clericos . . . a diversis partibus colligens, locato de doctrina eloquentiae magistro et de ea quae discernendi facultatem plenius administrat, ut nos ab infantiae subtraheret rudimentis, suo nos commendavit imperio."[52]

The *Versus ad Pueros* from the monastery of San Millán de la Cogolla, dated 1122, offers the first indications of the content of literary studies in Spain. This poem, perhaps intended to encourage the students of the monastic schools in their studies, mentions briefly Virgil and Cato, whose moralizing *Disticha* served as an elementary primer throughout the Middle Ages.[53]

It is possible that the recommendations of the councils of Coyanza and Compostela in 1055 and 1056, respectively, stimulated the growth of Spanish schools. The earlier council ordered clerics to teach all children the Credo and Pater Noster so that they knew them by heart.[54] The council of Compostela was even more explicit, ordering

---

[50] *ES*, XXXVI, escr. 28; cited by Tailhan, "Appendix," p. 282.

[51] *Historia Compostellana*, Bk. II, ch. 2; cited by H. Sancho, "La enseñanza en el siglo xii," *CT*, 9 (1914), 55.

[52] *Historia Compostellana*, Bk. I, ch. 20; cited by Amador de los Ríos, "Del estado y educación," p. 493.

[53] "Pervigil oro legas cecinit / quod musa maronis," "neglige ne iubenis relegens / pia facta Catonis" (Madrid, Biblioteca de la Real Academia de la Historia, cód. 46, ff. 170v-171r). Ed. by Amador de los Ríos in his *Historia crítica*, II, 339-340; in places he has overcorrected the text. Justo Pérez de Urbel gives a free translation in his *Semblanzas benedictinas*, 2 vols. (Madrid: Editorial Voluntad, 1926), II, 199-200. I am indebted to P. Pérez de Urbel for bringing this text to my attention. A reference to the nymph Camena in the first lines ("Fistula pange melos puero / meditante Camena") brings to mind Martianus' *De Nuptiis*, ed. by Adolf Dick (Leipzig: In aedibus B. G. Teubneri, 1925), pp. 50.20, 80.14. It seems likely that either the *De Nuptiis* or a commentary on that work was a source of the poem.

[54] "Doceant autem clerici filios Ecclesias et Infantes ut simbolum et orationem Dominicam memori ter teneant"; cited by Vicente de la Fuente, "Estudios y enseñanza en España: Escuelas regias y clericales en los siglos x y xi," *RUM* (2ª época), 4 (1874), 26.

schools established so that all priests might know perfectly the principal parts of the Mass.[55] These Spanish injunctions were reinforced by the general councils of the whole church, Lateran III and IV, in 1179 and 1215. In the former, Pope Alexander III ordered each cathedral to establish a benifice for a master to teach the clerics of that church and poor students.[56] In the latter, Innocent III, observing that "in multis ecclesiis id minime observatur" (referring to the previous decree), ordered that "non solum in qualibet cathedrali ecclesia, sed etiam in aliis quarum sufficere poterunt facultates constituatur magister idoneus . . . qui clericos ecclesiarum ipsarum et aliarum gratis in gramaticae facultates ac aliis instruat justa posse."[57]

It is difficult to ascertain to what extent these decrees were carried out,[58] but apparently the earlier ones had some effect in Spain. Coupled with the influence of the Cluniac reform in the eleventh century and that of the Cistercian reform in the twelfth, the ever-growing necessity for educated men to conduct the ecclesiastical and political business of a reviving Europe, and the necessity for staffing increasing numbers of churches as the Reconquest moved south, these decrees led to the establishment of numerous cathedral schools. In the second quarter of the twelfth century we find schoolmasters (*magistri scholae*) signing many documents as witnesses: so schools of some sort must have existed. In Salamanca there is a *magister scholae* in 1131, in Astorga in 1154, in Toledo in 1172, in Cuenca in 1183, in León and Segovia in 1190, and in Tuy in 1203.[59] In the thirteenth

---

[55] "Hi autem Abbates per propias Ecclesias canonicas faciant scholam . . . ." In José Saenz de Aguirre, *Collectio Maxima Conciliorum Omnium Hispaniae et Novi Orbis*, ed. by José Catalani, 6 vols. (Rome: Antonius Fulgonius, 1753-1755), IV, 413.

[56] Vicente Beltrán de Heredia, "La formación intelectual del clero según nuestra antigua legislación canónica (siglos xi-xv)," *Escorial*, 3 (1941), 290-291.

[57] Cited by Sancho, "La enseñanza en el siglo xii," p. 61.

[58] "Dos célebres canonistas, Bernardo de Parma (m. 1266) y el Ostiense (m. 1271), atestiguan que en su tiempo el decreto lateranense continuaba incumplido," Beltrán de Heredia, "La formación intelectual del clero," p. 292.

[59] For Salamanca, Toledo, and León, cf. Sancho, "La enseñanza en el siglo xii," pp. 55-56; for Astorga and Segovia, cf. Fuente, "Estudios y enseñanza en España," pp. 30-31; for Cuenca, cf. Vicente de la Fuente, *Historia eclesiástica de España*, 2a ed. corr. y aum., 6 vols. (Madrid: Impresores y Libreros del Reino, 1873), IV,

century such subscriptions are so common that we are led to believe
that every cathedral maintained a school of some sort.

Some light on common Spanish practice and curriculum at the
time is thrown by Berceo's references to his heroes' education in the
Vida de Santo Domingo de Silos and in the *Vida de San Millán.*
Lives of saints are suspect, and rightly so, for their uncritical repetitions of commonplaces. But if such commonplaces tell us nothing
about the saint in question, they do give some indication of conditions at the time the life itself was written. Berceo's descriptions of
the education of Santo Domingo of Silos and of San Millán are remarkably similar, in spite of the fact that the two saints lived some six
centuries apart (San Millán in the fifth century and Santo Domingo
in the eleventh). Of San Millán Berceo says (stanzas 21-22):

> demostróli los psalmos   por fer su oración;
> con la firme femencia   dióli tal nudrición,
> qe entendió la forma   de la perfectïón.
>
> Fue en poco de tiempo   el pastor psalteriado,
> de imnos e de cánticos   sobra bien decorado,
> en toda la doctrina   maestro profundado,
> faziése el maestro   mismo maravellado.[60]

He expands this description slightly in the *Vida de Santo Domingo
de Silos,* but it remains essentially the same (stanzas 37-39):

> Uinie a su escuela el infant grand mannana;
> Non auie a deçirgelo nin madre nin ermana,
> Non façie entre dia luenga meridiana,
> Ouo algo apreso la primera semana.
>
> Fue en poco de tiempo al infant salteriado,
> De ymnos, & de canticos, bien gent decorado,
> Euangelios, epistolas aprisolas priuado.
> Algun mayor leuaua el tiempo mas baldado.

229n; for Tuy, cf. Prudencio de Sandoval, *Antigveded dela civdad, y iglesia cathedral
de Tvy, y delos obispos qve se save aya auido en ella* (Braga: Fructuoso Lourenço
de Basto, 1610), f. 140r-v.

[60] *La "Vida de San Millán de la Cogolla" de Gonzalo de Berceo,* ed. by Brian Dutton, Colección Támesis, Serie A, Monografías, IV (London: Támesis Books Limited
[1967]), p. 88.

Bien leye, & cantaua sin ninguna pereza,
Mas tenie en el seso toda su agudeza.[61]

The schools described here are little more than grammar schools for the parish clergy.

Thus in the period to the end of the twelfth century evidence regarding even the existence of Spanish schools is exceedingly scarce, and evidence on the curriculum followed in those schools is all but absent. There are no intellectual centers in León or Castile comparable to those existing in the high Middle Ages in monasteries like Jarrow in England, Bobbio in Italy, St. Gall or Fulda in Germany, Fleury or Corbie in France, or even Ripoll in Catalonia. In the latter period episcopal schools do not develop into centers for higher studies as they did in Chartres, Paris, and Bologna. If Berceo's descriptions are correct—and the available evidence indicates that they are—the generality of Spanish schools of this period are merely grammar or singing schools intent upon turning out clerics provided with the basic knowledge for caring for the religious necessities of their flocks. The Latin literary productions of this period, chiefly chronicles such as that of Alfonso III in its various recensions, the *Albeldense*, and the *Silense*, show very little stylistically that would lead us to qualify this statement.[62]

By the beginning of the thirteenth century, however, the situation was beginning to change. Using the cathedral schools of Palencia and Salamanca as nuclei, universities, "estudios generales," were established in those cities. That of Palencia was established by Alfonso VIII of Castile at the urging of the bishop of the city, Tello Téllez de Me-

---

[61] I follow the paleographic edition of Fr. Alfonso Andrés, *Vida de Santo Domingo de Silos: Edición crítico-paleográfica dèl códice del siglo XIII* (Madrid: Padres Benedictinos, 1958), p. 5.

[62] The famous school of translators of Toledo was also in existence from about the middle of the twelfth century under D. Raimundo of Salvetat; but it worked almost exclusively with scientific and logical works. As we shall see in Chapter III, Dominicus Gundisalvus is the exception to this. Francisco Rico, however, finds a certain amount of familiarity with literary and rhetorical technique in works such as the *Garcineida*, *Historia Compostellana*, *De Consolatione Rationis* of Petrus Compostellanus, etc.; but in the end he states that the achievement of Latin letters in twelfth-century Spain was modest at best: "Las letras latínas," p. 89.

neses, around the year 1212.⁶³ In spite of the concession by Honorius III of church rents for the support of the university in 1220 and
1225, it apparently lost ground rapidly to Salamanca.⁶⁴ Soon there-
after it ceased to exist, but was functioning again in 1243 when Rodrigo Jiménez de Rada mentions it in his *De Rebus Hispaniae Ges-
tis* (Book VII, ch. 34), and probably lapsed to the status of an "estudio particular" sometime after the middle of the thirteenth century. With regard to what was taught at Palencia, don Rodrigo
states that Alfonso VIII called together learned men from Gaul and
Italy of "all faculties."⁶⁵ Lucas de Tuy elaborates on this somewhat:
"Adefonsus evocavit magistros theologicos et aliarum artium libera-
lium, et Palentiae scholas constituit."⁶⁶ Honorius III's bull of 1220
states that salaries are to be provided for masters in theology, canon
law, logic, and "auctores," the latter presumably referring to gram-
mar.⁶⁷

Alfonso IX of León officially established the "studium generale"
of Salamanca, probably about the year 1218.⁶⁸ The oldest extant
document concerned with the university, however, a privilege of Fernando III, *el Santo*, dates only from the year 1243. It guarantees
the safety and freedom of students and masters and confirms "aquellas costumbres e aquellos fueros que hobieron los escolares en Salamanca en tiempo de mio padre," but tells us nothing about those cus-
toms or the disciplines taught there.⁶⁹

---

⁶³ Vincente de la Fuente, "Historia de los establecimientos de enseñanza en España: Universidad de Palencia," *RUM* (2ª época), 4 (1874), 518.

⁶⁴ Jesús San Martín, *La antigua universidad de Palencia* (Madrid: Afrodisio
Aguado, 1942), pp. 77-78.

⁶⁵ Amador de los Ríos, "Del estado y educación," p. 496n.

⁶⁶ *Chronicon Mundi*, ed. by Andreas Schottus in his *Hispaniae Illvstratae sev
Rervm Vrbivmq. Hispaniae, Lvsitaniae, Aethiopiae et Indiae Scriptores Varii*,
4 vols. (Frankfurt: Apud Claudium Marnium, et Haeredes Iohannis Aubrij, 1603-
1608), IV, 109; cited by Vicente Beltrán de Heredia, *Los orígenes de la Universidad de Salamanca*, Acta Salmanticensia, Historia de la Universidad, I, 1 (Salamanca: Universidad de Salamanca, 1953), p. 9.

⁶⁷ San Martín, *La antigua universidad de Palencia*, pp. 77-78.

⁶⁸ Beltrán de Heredia, *Los orígenes*, p. 17.

⁶⁹ Enrique Esperabé y Arteaga, *Historia pragmática e interna de la Universidad de
Salamanca*, 2 vols. (Salamanca: Imp. Francisco Núñez Izquierdo, 1914-1917), I, 19.

The first document that gives us information about Spanish university studies in the thirteenth century is the privilege of Alfonso the Learned establishing eleven chairs at Salamanca in 1254, only two years after his accession to the throne. There were to be three masters of canon law, one of civil law with a "bachiller" under him, two of logic, two of grammar, two of medicine, and one of organ.[70] Beltrán de Heredia points out the preponderance of the study of law and explains it as a result of the king's own interest in that discipline.[71] He briefly traces the history of law at Salamanca and concludes that the University of Salamanca "fue desde el principio eminentemente jurídica, como la de París fue teológica."[72] This interest in law is important for what it indicates about the study of the *ars dictandi*, which was closely linked to the study of law in the thirteenth century.

Of the other chairs, the only ones of interest to us are those of grammar. Beltrán de Heredia explains why there are two each for grammar and logic: each of these disciplines was subdivided, grammar into grammar and rhetoric, and logic into dialectic and the *Summulas*.[73] There is, however, no evidence to indicate that such a division did in fact exist. Title 31, law 3 of the second *partida* states that "cuantas son las esciencias tantos deben ser los maestros que las muestren, así que cada una de ellas haya un maestro a lo menos."[74] In other words, it is possible to have more than one master for each "science," and that would probably apply to logic and grammar. These were basic courses which all students had to take in order to advance to the higher faculties of law, medicine, and—in the fifteenth century— theology. It seems reasonable to assume that they would need more than one master.

---

[70] Ed. by Ajo, in his *Historia de las universidades hispánicas*, I, 438-440; cited by Beltrán de Heredia, *Los orígenes*, p. 31.

[71] Beltrán de Heredia, *Los orígenes*, p. 40.

[72] Ibid., p. 44.

[73] Ibid., p. 46.

[74] *Las siete partidas del rey don Alfonso el Sabio*, ed. by La Real Academia de la Historia, 3 vols. (Madrid: Imprenta Real, 1807), II, 341; cited by Beltrán de Heredia, *Los orígenes*, p. 39.

Title 31 of the second *partida* also sets forth the courses to be given at an "estudio general," and these citations do tend to bear out Beltrán de Heredia's contention that rhetoric was taught in the thirteenth century in Spain. The first law of this title states that an "estudio general" has "maestros de las artes, así como de gramática, et de lógica, et de retórica, et de arismética, et de geometría, et de música et de astronomía, et otrosí . . . maestros de decretos et señores de leyes."[75] And in the third law it is recognized that it may not be possible to maintain a complete faculty: "Pero si de todas las ciencias non pudiesen haber maestros, abonda que haya de gramática, et de lógica, et de retórica, et de leyes et de decretos."[76] Thus the bare minimum for a university consists of the arts faculty and the faculty of law.

However, there are obvious discrepancies between Alfonso's juridical formulations and his actual practice. He mentions medicine nowhere, yet establishes two chairs for it at Salamanca; he does mention the sciences of the quadrivium, yet does not establish chairs for them. The most one can say with regard to rhetoric is that the situation is ambiguous. Even granting Beltrán de Heredia's assumption that rhetoric was taught at Salamanca, nothing can be known about the books used in teaching it.

The later history of the University of Salamanca in the thirteenth and fourteenth centuries has yet to be written. Information about the curriculum is available only for widely separated points during this period. In 1313 the same chairs established by Alfonso X are mentioned in a bull of Clement V: canon and civil law, medicine, logic, and grammar.[77] The university would seem to have remained about the same size during this whole period, if the *rotuli* published by Beltrán de Heredia can be believed. He cites in particular two at the end of this period, from the years 1381 and 1393. In the former 342 persons are listed, "aproximadamente del 80 al 90 por cien-

---

[75] *Siete partidas*, II, 340; cited by Beltrán de Heredia, *Los orígenes*, p. 39.

[76] *Siete partidas*, II, 341; cited by Beltrán de Heredia, *Los orígenes*, p. 39.

[77] Vicente Beltrán de Heredia, *Bulario de la Universidad de Salamanca* (*1219-1549*), Acta Salmanticensia, Historia de la Universidad, XII, Vol. I (Salamanca: Universidad de Salamanca, 1966), p. 336.

to del personal docente y discente."[78] Of these, nine are listed as professors: three of canon law, two of civil law, two of grammar, one of theology, and one of music.[79] In the 1393 *rotulus* there are ten professors out of a total of 122 individuals, six in canon law, two in civil law, and two in grammar.[80] So, although the composition of the teaching faculty varies, the number is about the same as that established by Alfonso the Learned in 1254.

Not until the beginning of the fifteenth century does a professor of rhetoric appear at the University of Salamanca. In a request for a benefice addressed to Benedict XIII on October 14, 1403, one Bartholomaeus Sancius de Firmo is identified as "magistro rhetoricae in studio Salamantin."[81] It is significant that this master should be of Italian origin. Beltrán de Heredia states that "los humanistas italianos, de origen o de adopción, comenzaban ya a orientarse hacia la Academia salmantina."[82] Did they bring with them the disciplines then in vogue in Italy?

Aside from the material just cited, the early period of the University is lacking in documents about its academic history. We know nothing of the exact curriculum studied in any of the faculties and have no lists of the texts studied at Salamanca at any time through the end of the fourteenth century.

The situation is substantially the same for the other Spanish schools and universities founded in the thirteenth and fourteenth centuries.

---

[78] Ibid., I, 57; the *rotuli* were lists of clerics for whom benifices were requested, not registers of matriculated students. But since all students were clerics the lists are probably reasonably complete.

[79] Ibid., I, 58.

[80] Ibid., I, 62.

[81] Ibid., I, 556. The account books of the university from the years 1406-1408 (the only ones left from the period before 1500) confirm the fact that the chair of rhetoric was a recent innovation. In the accounts of the year 1406, the sum of 2000 *maravedís viejos* was expended on the four "cátedras extraordinarias nuevas de filosofía, gramática, vibria [Biblia] e retórica . . . ." The same amount is noted in the accounts of the next two years: Vicente Beltrán de Heredia, *Cartulario de la Universidad de Salamanca (1218-1600)*, Acta Salmanticensia, Historia de la Universidad, XVII, Vol. I (Salamanca: Universidad de Salamanca, 1970), pp. 659-661.

[82] *Bulario*, I, 67.

In the thirteenth century two major schools—technically not universities—were founded, one in Seville by Alfonso the Learned in 1254
for the study of "latin e de arabigo," and one in Alcalá de Henares
by his son Sancho IV in 1293.[83] Occasional documents confirm the
existence of the school of Seville in the thirteenth and fourteenth centuries,[84] but nothing confirms that of Alcalá until 1421.[85] The foundation privilege of the school of Alcalá has traditionally been cited
as evidence that a university existed at that time in Valladolid, since
Sancho IV granted the former "todas aquellas franquezas que ha
el estudio de Valladolid."[86] Beltrán de Heredia cogently argues that
at this time Valladolid was an "estudio particular, fundado por el
municipio," not a *studium generale.*[87] In fact, Valladolid was not el-
evated to the status of university until 1346, when Clement VI granted a petition of Alfonso XI to that effect.[88]

Canonical legislation concerning the establishment of grammar schools
in every cathedral seems to have borne fruit in Spain. A few examples of churches with *maestrescuelas* or grammar masters in the thirteenth and fourteenth centuries confirm this statement, although the
mention of a *maestrescuela* may be less than conclusive evidence for
the existence of a school. In 1293 the "maestrescuela" of Palencia
could not write his own name.[89] In contrast, no less a scholar than
Lucas of Tuy was *maestrescuela* and bishop-elect of Tuy in 1239.[90]
Calahorra had a school in 1240, and in 1260 the synod of that diocese,
meeting in Logroño, ordered each of the archdeaconries to provide for
two masters of grammar "e ansí non podrán haber excusas que non
saben fablar latín e pronunciar."[91] León had one *maestrescuela* in

---

[83] Ajo, *Historia de las universidades hispánicas*, I, 440, 451-452.

[84] Alonso Morgado, *Historia de Sevilla . . . hasta nuestros tiempos* (Seville: Andrea Pescioni y Iuan de León, 1587), ff. 101v-102r; Beltrán de Heredia, *Bulario*,
I, 197, 198.

[85] Beltrán de Heredia, *Bulario*, I, 198.

[86] Ed. by Ajo, in his *Historia de las universidades hispánicas*, I, 451.

[87] Beltrán de Heredia, *Bulario*, I, 201.

[88] Ibid., I, 200-201.

[89] Vicente Beltrán de Heredia, "La formación intelectual del clero de España
durante los siglos XII, XIII y XIV," *RET*, 6 (1946), 337n.

[90] Sandoval, *Antigvedad dela civdad . . . de Tvy*, ff. 148r-149r.

[91] Beltrán de Heredia, *Bulario*, I, 206.

1224 and two in 1241.[92] In 1363 and 1366 we find documents referring to masters of grammar in the same city.[93] Calatayud had a *maestrescuela* in 1242.[94] The cathedral archive of Oviedo contains documents signed by the *maestrescuela* in 1254, 1296, and 1300.[95] Toledo had a *maestrescuela* in 1265 and 1359.[96] The constitutions of the diocese of Toledo written in the fourteenth century require the cathedral to maintain "sufficientem et idoneum magistrum, qui apud civitatem toletanam in grammatica, et dialectica scholas publice legat."[97] Lope de Haro established a chair of grammar in Sigüenza in 1269, and in 1343 the cathedral had a master "in grammaticalibus et logicalibus."[98] Lugo had its *maestrescuela* in 1271,[99] and that of Cordova subscribed a petition to the pope in 1277.[100] Cuenca had a *maestrescuela* in 1289,[101] and in 1380 it had a master of grammar.[102] The schools of Palencia continued to exist in the fourteenth century on a reduced scale.[103] In 1338 a benefice was requested for a master who had taught grammar in Segovia for seven years.[104] Santiago had a grammar school at the end of the fourteenth century.[105]

---

[92] Fuente, "Estudios y enseñanza," p. 29.

[93] Beltrán de Heredia, *Bulario*, I, 206.

[94] Fuente, "Estudios y enseñanza," p. 31.

[95] Santos García Larragueta, ed., *Catálogo de los pergaminos de la Catedral de Oviedo* (Oviedo: Diputación de Asturias, Instituto de Estudios Asturianos, 1957), pp. 129, 185, 194-195.

[96] Gil González Dávila, *Teatro eclesiástico de las iglesias metropolitanas, y catedrales de los reynos de las dos Castillas. Vidas de sus arzobispos, y obispos, y cosas memorables de sus sedes*, 3 vols. (I, Madrid: Francisco Martínez, 1645; II, Madrid: Pedro de Horna y Villanveva, 1647; III, Madrid: Diego Díaz de la Carrera, 1650), I, 545, 551.

[97] Amador de los Ríos, *Historia crítica*, III, 223n-224n.

[98] Beltrán de Heredia, *Bulario*, I, 207.

[99] García Larragueta, *Catálogo*, p. 150.

[100] Antonio Ballesteros-Beretta, *Alfonso X el Sabio*, Consejo Superior de Investigaciones Científicas, Academia "Alfonso el Sabio" (Murcia) (Barcelona-Madrid: Salvat Editores, S.A., 1963), pp. 836-837.

[101] Juan Pablo Martyr Riço, *Historia de la muy noble y leal ciudad de Cuenca* (Madrid: Herederos de la Viuda de Pº. de Madrigal, 1629), pp. 156-160.

[102] Beltrán de Heredia, *Bulario*, I, 208.

[103] Ibid., I, 200, 419.

[104] Ibid., I, 209.

[105] Ibid., I, 205.

Ecclesiastical measures were renewed in 1322 when the provincial council of Valladolid ordered each diocese as well as all monasteries with sufficient means to establish two or three grammar schools and to support masters of logic in the larger cities. One of every ten beneficed clerics must be sent to a university to study theology, canon law, or liberal arts. From evidence concerning grammar schools it would seem likely that the former provision at least was carried out. The higher studies may have been neglected: in 1339 the archbishop of Toledo, Gil de Albornoz, gave each church six months to send one out of every ten of its clerics away for higher studies, which would indicate that some of the churches were dilatory.[106] Such students were sent not only to Salamanca and Lérida (after 1300), the two major Spanish universities, but also to Paris, chiefly for theology, and to Bologna, chiefly for law. In 1364 Cardinal Gil de Albornoz founded the "colegio hispánico" of Bologna for Spanish students studying in that city. Peninsular students also attended the universities of Montpellier, Toulouse, and Avignon because of their proximity to Spain.[107] However, it is impossible to estimate the proportion of students attending foreign universities to those attending peninsular ones.

To sum up our survey of education in Castile and León during the thirteenth and fourteenth centuries, it would seem that schools multiplied to such an extent that probably no diocese was without at least one. The majority of these schools, however, taught little more than grammar, since the average cleric was required to know only the bare minimum necessary for celebrating divine office, "lectura, canto y construcción latina."[108]

Higher studies were available at least at Salamanca and (after 1346) at Valladolid; possibly some of the larger "estudios particulares" had one or more of the higher faculties. There is no indication that rhetoric was taught anywhere before the beginning of the fifteenth century. Law was always important at Salamanca, and it is within the

---

[106] Beltrán de Heredia, "La formación intelectual del clero según nuestra antigua legislación," p. 294.

[107] Cf. Beltrán de Heredia, "La formación intelectual del clero de España," pp. 338, 339, 340n-341n, 344n-345n; idem, *Bulario*, I, 28, 29, 50, 51, 52, 54, 59, etc.

[108] Beltrán de Heredia, *Bulario*, I, 37.

bounds of possibility that *ars dictaminis* was taught there as part of the law curriculum. If it was, it never reached the point of being considered a separate discipline as at Bologna.[109] Even conceding this point, there is no evidence to show what texts might have been used to teach *dictamen* or any other form of rhetoric.

MEDIEVAL SPANISH LIBRARIES

For specific indications about the availability of rhetorical texts in Spain during the Middle Ages, we must turn to the extant records of medieval libraries. Again, these are not nearly so abundant as we might wish. The information at hand concerns primarily monastic libraries in the high Middle Ages and cathedral libraries in the low Middle Ages, reflecting rather faithfully the decline of the monastic school and the growth of the cathedral school during this period.

In the high Middle Ages, as Menéndez y Pelayo states and Sánchez Albornoz reiterates, manuscripts of the pagan classics were exceedingly rare.[110] St. Eulogius of Cordova made a journey to the monasteries of Aragon and Navarre in the year 849 in search of books. He says that he visited the schools of Leire, Cillas, Urdax, and Igal and was given copies of the *Aeneid*, the *Satires* of Horace and Juvenal, the works of Porfirius, the fables of Avianus, St. Augustine's *City of God*, the *Sacred Epigrams* of Aldhelm, and a collection of hymns.[111] Almost the same classical and early medieval works are found in the earliest Spanish library catalogue still extant, from the year 882: the *Aeneid*, five satires of Juvenal, the *De Consolatione Philosophiae* of Boethius, and the *Disticha Catonis* as well as the works of the Christian Latin poets—Prudentius, Sedulius, St. Avitus, and Dracontius.[112] This catalogue has traditionally been thought to list the library of

[109] Rashdall, *The Universities of Europe*, I, 110n-111n.

[110] Menéndez y Pelayo, *Ideas estéticas*, I, 338n ; Claudio Sánchez Albornoz, "Notas sobre los libros leídos en el reino de León hace mil años," *CHE*, 1-2 (1944), 226.

[111] Amador de los Ríos, "Del estado y educación," p. 486n.

[112] Ed. by Gustavus Becker, in his *Catalogi Bibliothecarum Antiqui* (Bonn: Apud Max. Cohen et filium [Fr. Cohen], 1885), pp. 59-60.

the cathedral of Oviedo, but Díaz y Díaz has recently suggested that it may come from a monastery in Cordova or Toledo—in other words, that it may represent the Mozarabic tradition.[113]

The rather curious agreement between this inventory and the list of books donated by the abbot Cixila to the monastery of St. Cosme and Damian of Abellar (near León) in 927 tends to reinforce this idea. Again we find Cato, the Christian poets, Juvenal, and the *Aeneid*. As Juan Eloy Díaz Jiménez points out, the monastery was probably founded by Mozarabic monks seeking refuge from the religious persecutions of the Moslems; the books listed probably accompanied them from the south.[114]

Much more typical of tenth-century monastic libraries in the north are the books donated by Tehoda and Argonta to the monastery of St. Julian and St. Basilisa in 930: "Libros tamen etiam ecclesiasticos pasionum I, antifonarios II, orationum I, ordinum I, commicum I, racionale I, precum I, libellum de virginitate Sancte Marie I, Bibliotecam ibidem pater meus domnus Aldroitus dedit, ego tamen confirmo."[115] These are the Bible, the basic liturgical works, and, more often than not, St. Ildefonsus' *De Perpetua Virginitate Sanctae Mariae*. More important, however, is the fact that St. Isidore's *Etymologiae* is frequently found in these primitive libraries. The work is mentioned in the donation of St. Gennadius to the church of San Pedro de Montes in Galicia in 915,[116] and it occurs at least ten more times in inventories from the tenth century in Galicia, León, and Castile.[117] It is the only work containing information on rhetoric found during this period.

---

[113] Manuel C. Díaz y Díaz, *Index Scriptorum Latinorum Medii Aevi Hispanorum*, Acta Salmanticensia, Filosofía y Letras, XIII (Salamanca: Universidad de Salamanca, 1958-1959), p. 131.

[114] "Inmigración mozárabe en el reino de León: El monasterio de Abellar o de los santos mártires Cosme y Damián," *BRAH*, 20 (1892), 128-129.

[115] Romualdo Escalona, *Historia del real monasterio de Sahagún* . . . , ed. by Joseph Pérez (Madrid: J. Ibarra, 1782), p. 387; cited by Beer, *Handschriftenschätze Spaniens*, pp. 400-401.

[116] Sandoval, *Fvndaciones*, 3d foliation, f. 28r.

[117] Manuel C. Díaz y Díaz, "Isidoro en la edad media hispana," in *Isidoriana* (*Colección de estudios sobre Isidoro de Sevilla*), ed. by Manuel C. Díaz y Díaz (León: Centro de Estudios "San Isidoro," 1961), pp. 369-370.

Developments during the next two centuries are exceedingly difficult to trace. The relative abundance of library inventories and records of book donations falls off sharply in the eleventh century and virtually disappears in the twelfth. There is only one reference to the *Etymologiae* during this time, in a donation of books by Urraca, daughter of Fernando I and sister of Alfonso VI, to the monastery of San Pedro de Eslonza in 1099.[118] It is difficult to account for this lack of information on medieval libraries when an extensive cultural revolution (the Cistercian reform and the concomitant introduction of the Roman liturgy and Carolingian script) was occurring in Castile and León. Perhaps it is related to the loss of enthusiasm for copying manuscripts in general, which seems to have been a consequence of the switch from Visigothic to Carolingian script.[119] The lack of information may be only apparent, in the sense that scholars have dedicated their efforts to the earlier period and neglected documents from the latter. If the falling-off in the number of documents is real, it may reflect a situation in which books were relatively abundant and thus ceased to be specifically mentioned in wills and donations. The bulk of our information from the earlier period comes not from inventories per se but rather from such donations. Then, a book was a rare and valuable possession; in the latter period it was presumably less rare and perhaps less valuable.

For whatever reason, there is a hiatus of about a century in references to Spanish libraries.[120] When such references begin to reappear, they more often occur as inventories of books owned by cathedrals or by individuals rather than as donations. In the thirteenth century

---

[118] Sandoval, *Fvndaciones*, 2d foliation, ff. 37v-38r; cited by Beer, *Handschriftenschätze Spaniens*, p. 224.

[119] Rico, "Las letras latinas," p. 15n.

[120] The library of the Escurial does contain a twelfth-century manuscript (z. II. 10) which lists a number of books given by Pope Celestinus to the church of St. Floridus, including a "rhetoricam." *Bibliotheca Patrum Latinorum Hispaniensis*, ed. by Gustav Loewe and Wilhelm von Hartel (Vienna: Carl Gerold's Sohn, 1887), I, 26-27. Dorothy Grosser, following Max Manitius, states that the library referred to is Spanish and that the rhetoric is *De Inventione*, but neither she nor Manitius supports these assertions with concrete evidence. "Studies in the Influence of the *Rhetorica ad Herennium* and Cicero's *De Inventione*" (unpubl. diss., Cornell University, 1953), p. 194.

reference is made to cathedral libraries in Santiago de Compostela (1226), Toledo (ca. 1260), Salamanca (1267), Cordova (1274), and Burgo de Osma (XIII ex.). The majority of these libraries seem to have been founded with books donated by various bishops. That of Compostela was originally the library of Bishop Bernard II.[121] The chapter library of Salamanca appears to have come into existence in 1267 with a gift from Bishop Domingo Martínez.[122]

The oldest cathedral library to which we find reference, that of Compostela, contains the first Spanish mention of works of rhetoric as independent entities. In the 1226 catalogue, along with an entry for a "Prescianus major," is the following: "Item due Retorice, in hoc volumine."[123] In her study of the influence of the *Rhetorica ad C. Herennium* and Cicero's *De Inventione*, Dorothy Grosser has shown that after the appearance of a joint edition of the two works in the twelfth century, manuscripts containing both works multiply extraordinarily.[124] It is, then, not unreasonable to assume that a single manuscript containing two rhetorics and appearing in Spain in 1226 will contain precisely these two treatises. If this assumption is correct, we can move the first documented appearance of these texts in Spain forward by almost half a century.[125]

The library of the cathedral of Sigüenza is of importance because it is one of the few whose growth can be traced over a lengthy period in the thirteenth and fourteenth centuries. Founded by a Bishop Rodrigo early in the thirteenth century, the library's first inventory records seventeen books, none of which concerns rhetoric. The 1242 inventory lists twenty books, but again no rhetorical treatises.[126] At the beginning of the fourteenth century 144 books are found, of which two are rhetorical treatises: Alain de Lille's *Summa de Arte*

---

[121] H[enri] Omont, "Catalogue de la bibliothèque de Bernard II, archevêque de Saint-Jacques-de-Compostelle (1226)," *BEC*, 54 (1893), 327.

[122] Florencio Marcos Rodríguez, "La antigua biblioteca de la catedral de Salamanca," *HS*, 14 (1961), 284.

[123] Omont, "Catalogue," pp. 331-332.

[124] "Studies in the Influence," p. 200.

[125] See below, p. 40.

[126] J[osé] Rius Serra, "Inventario de los manuscritos de la Catedral de Sigüenza," *HS*, 3 (1950), 432-433.

Praedicatoria and the *Summa Dictaminis* of one Master Bernard.[127] In 1339 the library has virtually doubled in size to 280 books. Besides three copies of Priscian and the Latin vocabulary of Papias, which confirm the existence of a grammar school,[128] there are two copies of Alain de Lille's *Summa*, an *Ars Notandi*, and "otro libro versificación."[129] Whether the latter refers to a treatise on versification or to a work written in verse is debatable; it makes more sense grammatically to assume that it refers to a work on versification. The rhetorical treatises conserved in the medieval library of Sigüenza were obviously there for practical reasons—to aid the preacher in composing his sermons (*ars praedicandi*) and to aid the chapter in conducting its business (*Summa Dictaminis, Ars Notandi*).

Because of the central position of Toledo, both geographically and culturally, the attempt to establish its library resources in the thirteenth and fourteenth centuries is not without interest. It is there presumably that Rodrigo Jiménez de Rada assembled the sources he needed for his historical works and there also that Alfonso the Learned did the same for his own historical, legal, and scientific works.

We have ample information about books in Toledo, but it is scattered. Apparently the cathedral of Toledo formed its library slowly. There is evidence of its existence around 1260 in the form of an inventory made during the archbishopric of D. Sancho, brother of Al-

---

[127] Ibid., pp. 434-435. It is impossible to say which of the various Bernards known to have written *artes dictandi* is indicated by the Sigüenza inventory. One twelfth-century treatise was written in France by a Bernard whom C.-V. Langlois tried to identify with Bernard Silvester: "Questions d'histoire littéraire: Maître Bernard," *BEC*, 54 (1893), 243. Hermann Kalbfuss published the treatise of Bernard of Bologna, also from the twelfth century, in "Eine Bologneser *Ars dictandi* des XII. Jahrhunderts," *OF*, 16 (1914), ii, 1-35. And the *Dictaminis* of Berardus Caraccioli of Naples (apostolic notary from 1261 to 1287) is sometimes found in the MSS attributed to "Bernardus de Neapoli." Harry Bresslau, *Handbuch der Urkundenlehre für Deutschland und Italien*, 4th ed., Vol. II, part i ed. by Harry Bresslau, part ii ed. by Hans-Walter Klewitz (Berlin: Verlag Walter de Gruyter & Co., 1968), pp. 267-268.

[128] In 1343 the cathedral had a master of grammar and logic (see above, p. 33).

[129] Rius Serra, "Inventario," pp. 439-445; the *Ars notandi* begins "Ne contractus"; the "libro versificación," "Semper ego adiutor." I have not been able to identify either text in the standard lists of *initia*.

fonso the Learned (1251-1261);[130] at that time it contained only bib-lical texts and commentaries and a certain number of works on ca-non and civil law. We also know that at least four of the archbishops of Toledo in the thirteenth century owned personal libraries. That of Rodrigo Jiménez de Rada was willed on his death to the monas-tery of S. María de Huerta near Guadalajara. Unfortunately his will does not enumerate his books, nor is there any way of identifying them from among those confiscated from the monastery during the desamortization of 1835.[131] The testament of Archbishop Juan de Medina in 1248 gives a small inventory of his books, and there is an inventory of books that belonged to Archbishop Sancho, son of Jai-me I of Aragon, in 1275. Neither of them had any rhetorical works.[132]

There are two detailed inventories of the books of Gonzalo García de Gudiel, who became royal notary for Castile in 1270.[133] The first was made when he was promoted from the archdeaconry of Toledo to the bishopric of Cuenca in 1273, the second when he assumed his duties as archbishop of Toledo in 1280.[134] In 1273 don Gonzalo owned "un libro de Notaría" and "unos tratados, retórica de Tullio vieya et nueva en un volumen."[135] This is the first Spanish reference to *De Inventione* and the *Rhetorica ad C. Herennium* by name, although it is reasonably certain that these works are also referred to in the 1226 inventory from Compostela. Dorothy Grosser states that this

[130] In *Liber Secundus Privilegiorum Ecclesiae Toletanae*, Madrid, Archivo His-tórico Nacional; cited by Agustín Millares Carlo, *Nuevos estudios de paleografía española* (México: Casa de España en México, 1941), p. 45. I have used a photo-graph of the eighteenth-century copy in London BM MS. Eg. 1881, ff. 118r-122r: "Inventario de Ropas, Alahajas, Libros, y otras cosas que se hizo por los Años de 1260 . . . ."

[131] José Gómez Pérez, "Manuscritos del Toledano," *RABM*, 63 (1957), 162.

[132] Manuel Alonso Alonso, "Bibliotecas medievales de los arzobispos de Toledo," *RyF*, 123 (1941), 299-300.

[133] E[velyn] S. Procter, "The Castilian Chancery during the Reign of Alfonso X, 1252-84," in *Oxford Essays in Medieval History Presented to Herbert Edward Sal-ter* (Oxford: At the Clarendon Press, 1934), p. 115.

[134] Alonso Alonso, "Bibliotecas medievales," p. 301.

[135] *Ibid.*, pp. 303-304; first ed. by Fernando Martínez Marina in his *Ensayo histórico-crítico sobre la legislación y principales cuerpos legales de los reinos de León y Castilla* (Madrid: Hija de don Joaquín Ibarra, 1808), p. 7, but attributed to Bish-op Gonzalo Palomeque.

is the first occurrence anywhere of the designation of the *De Inventione* as the "old" rhetoric of Cicero and of the *Ad Herennium* as the "new." In other European countries this designation is not found until the fourteenth century.[136] In 1280 an "ars notarie" is again found, but the Ciceronian rhetorics have disappeared. In exchange we find a "rethorica Aristotelis."[137] Given the date and the location of this text, we may justifiably identify it with Hermann the German's translation, finished in Toledo before 1256, of Averroes' commentary on the *Rhetorica*.[138] The translations of Hermann provide additional evidence for the presence of *De Inventione* and the *Rhetorica ad C. Herennium* in Spain as well as for that of Horace's *Ars Poetica*, which is mentioned in no contemporary catalogue. In both the *In Poeticam* and *In Rhetoricam*, Hermann mentions the use of the Latin works in making his translation.[139] That don Gonzalo was interested in the work of the translators of Toledo, and specifically in the translations of Averroes, is indicated by the following quotation from the 1273 inventory: " . . . todos los comentos de Abenrost . . . et es el primer escripto de la mano del trasladador."[140] It is highly likely that the translator in question is Hermannus Alemannus himself.

The first reference to an institutional library in Toledo other than that of the cathedral is an inventory of the conventual library of S. Clemente from the year 1331. The books are strictly religious.[141]

---

[136] "Studies on the Influence," p. 195.

[137] Alonso Alonso, "Bibliotecas medievales," pp. 305-306.

[138] Cf. José María Millás Vallicrosa, *Las traducciones orientales en los manuscritos de la biblioteca catedral de Toledo* (Madrid: Consejo Superior de Investigaciones Científicas, Instituto Arias Montano, 1942), p. 55; *Aristoteles Latinus, Pars Prior*, ed. by Georgius Lacombe et al., Union Académique Internationale, Corpus Philosophorum Medii Aevi (Rome: La Libreria dello Stato, 1939), p. 212. The translation of the *Commentarium Medium* to the *Poetica* of Aristotle is dated 1256; in it Hermann states that he had previously translated the *In Rhetoricam*.

[139] *Aristoteles Latinus, Pars Prior*, pp. 211, 212.

[140] Alonso Alonso, "Bibliotecas medievales," p. 304.

[141] Madrid, Biblioteca Nacional, MS. 13058, f. 2r; ed. by Juan Pérez de Guzmán, "El libro y la biblioteca en España durante los siglos medios," *EM*, 202 (Oct. 1905), 123-124; repr. by Ramón Fernández Pousa (who believed it unedited) in "Catálogo de una biblioteca española del año 1331: El monasterio de San Clemente, de Toledo," *RBN*, I (1941), 48-50.

The second inventory of the cathedral library dates from about the same time. The library, of about 190 books, was apparently kept in the *sagrario* rather than in a room of its own.[142] The only item of interest to us from this inventory is an "ars praedicandi," otherwise unidentified.[143] In 1374 the cardinal archbishop of Toledo, Gil de Albornoz, directed in his will that "restituantur eidem Archiepiscopus [sic] Toletane omnes libri in quibus inveniantur scriptum in postis vel in cartis vel a principio vel in fine quod sunt ecclesie Toletane."[144] His successor as archbishop, don Pedro Tenorio, left all his books to the cathedral chapter in 1383, along with 1,000 florins for the purchase of three books in Paris and the construction of a library. In the meantime the books that he had donated were to be placed "in sacrario seu thesauraria dicte Ecclesie Toletane."[145] It is evident, therefore, that the library of the cathedral of Toledo was of considerable size by the first half of the fourteenth century, that it was originally kept in the sacristy or treasury of the cathedral, and that it did not receive a home of its own until after 1383.

There is no further indication of the size of the library until 1455, when an inventory mentions 400 or 500 separate works. The number must remain vague because the catalogue has never been completely published.[146] Among the items included in the part that was published are the *Rhetorica ad C. Herennium*, *De Inventione*, and a *Tabula de Arte Dictandi* of the thirteenth century Italian notary Ricardo de Pofi.[147] All three copies of these works are still extant, the classical

---

[142] Luis Pérez de Guzmán, Marqués de Morbecq, "Un inventario del siglo xiv de la Catedral de Toledo (La Biblia de San Luis)," *BRAH*, 89 (1926), 374.

[143] Ibid., p. 402.

[144] "Copia del testamento y codicilio de D. Gil de Albornoz, cardenal arzobispo de Toledo," Madrid, Biblioteca Nacional, MS. 13023, f. 164v.

[145] "Donación que hizo de su librería el Arzobispo de Toledo D. Pedro Tenorio al cabildo de su Yglesia, con mil florines de oro más . . . ," Madrid, Biblioteca Nacional, MS. 13018, ff. 119v-120r.

[146] "Biblioteca de la Santa Iglesia de Toledo: Inventario de 1455," [ed. by José Foradada y Castán], *RABM*, 7 (1877), 321-324, 338-340, 355-356, 366-372. Agustín Millares Carlo had an edition prepared in 1935, but it was never published; cf. his *Los códices visigóticos de la catedral toledana: Cuestiones cronológicas y de procedencia* (Madrid: Ignacio de Noreña, Editor, 1935), p. 12.

[147] "Biblioteca de la Santa Iglesia de Toledo," pp. 371-372.

rhetorics in MS. 10070 of the Biblioteca Nacional in Madrid and the *Ars Dictandi* in MS. 43-3 of the cathedral library of Toledo. The former are contained in a thirteenth-century manuscript and the latter in one from the fourteenth century; so they could have been in Toledo when the library was being formed in the fourteenth century.[148]

The evidence of inventories of other thirteenth-century cathedral libraries is very similar. The 1275 inventory of the library of the cathedral of Salamanca mentions thirty-seven works, including the *Bucolics* of Virgil and a copy of Sallust, but no rhetoric.[149] There is no other information about Salamancan libraries until well into the fifteenth century. It is surprising that the university apparently had no permanent library until late in the same century.[150]

D. Fernando de Mesa, fourth bishop of Cordova after the Reconquest, donated his books to found the cathedral library, which was enlarged in 1303 with those of the dean, don Pedro Ayllón. No early inventories are known.[151] A late thirteenth-century inventory from the cathedral of Burgo de Osma notes the existence of two copies of *De Inventione*, one of which may perhaps be identified with the twelfth-century manuscript of the same work still conserved in the chapter library.[152] The inventory also mentions "una summa chica de dictar que incipit afficiendo."[153] The reference, obviously to an *ars dictaminis*, is too vague to permit more exact identification.

Catalogues of monastic libraries from the low Middle Ages are even more infrequent than those of cathedral libraries during the same period. One of the manuscripts from the library of Santo Domingo de Silos, now in the Bibliothèque Nationale of Paris, shows that the monastery had the *Etymologiae* of St. Isidore among its several hun-

---

[148] See my forthcoming "Retóricas clásicas y medievales en bibliotecas castellanas," *Ábaco*, for a fuller description of these MSS.

[149] Marcos Rodríguez, "La antigua biblioteca," p. 285; first ed. by Manuel Gómez Moreno, "Inventario de la Catedral de Salamanca (1275)," *RABM* (2ª época), 7 (1902), 175-180.

[150] Beltrán de Heredia, *Bulario*, p. 175.

[151] Luis María Ramírez y de las Cazas-Deza, *Descripción de la Iglesia Catedral de Córdoba*, 4a ed. corr. y aum. (Cordova: Imp. R. Rojas, 1866), pp. 82-83.

[152] Timoteo Rojo Orcajo, "Catálogo descriptivo de los códices que se conservan en la Santa Iglesia Catedral de Burgo de Osma," *BRAH*, 94 (1929), 660, 706.

[153] Ibid., p. 661.

dred books, but no rhetorical works.[154] The library of the monastery of Oña is represented by a thirteenth-century inventory containing about 110 works, of which one is called *Aurea Gemma*.[155] The title is ambiguous, but an *ars dictaminis* of that title is known.[156]

Illuminating for what they tell us not only about the contents of monastic libraries but also about the textual and investigative methods of Alfonso the Learned and his collaborators are two letters from the year 1270 in which the king acknowledges the loan to him of nineteen "libros de letra antigua" from the monasteries of Albelda and Santa María de Nájera. These books include a copy of the *Etymologiae* (from Albelda), the *Barbarismus* of Donatus, the *Georgics* and *Bucolics* of Virgil, the *Priscianus Magnus* (the first sixteen books of the *Institutiones Grammaticae*) and Cicero's *Somnium Scipionis* (from Santa María de Nájera).[157] The king continues: "E otorgo de vos les enviar tanto que los haya fecha [sic] escrebir."[158] It would be tempting to deduce from this, as Menéndez Pidal does, the lack of these books in either the royal library or in libraries to which the king had ready access.[159] But Alfonso's previous reference to "letra antigua," in all probability Visigothic script, provides a clue to his real purpose.[160] Books such as the *Etymologiae*, the grammars of Donatus and

---

[154] Beer, *Handschriftenschätze Spaniens*, p. 455; cited from Leopold Delisle, "Manuscrits de l'abbaye de Silos . . . ," in his *Mélanges de paléographie et de bibliographie* (Paris: Champion, Libraire, 1880), p. 75.

[155] Guillermo Antolín, *Catálogo de los códices latinos de la Real Biblioteca del Escorial*, 5 vols. (Madrid: Imprenta Helénica, 1910-1923), III, 467.

[156] E. H. Kantorowicz, "Anonymi *Gemma Aurea*," *MH*, 1 (1943), 41-57.

[157] First ed. in *MHE*, 1 (1851), 257-258; repr. by Pérez de Guzmán, "El libro y la biblioteca en España," p. 116.

[158] Ibid., p. 116.

[159] *Primera crónica general de España*, 2d ed., ed. by Ramón Menéndez Pidal, Universidad de Madrid, Facultad de Filosofía y Letras, Seminario Menéndez Pidal, 2 vols. (Madrid: Editorial Gredos, 1955), I, xx-xxi.

[160] Agustín Millares Carlo points out that Visigothic script was sometimes called "littera toletana" or "moçarava": *Tratado de paleografía española*, 2a ed. corr. y aum. (Madrid: Librería y Casa Editorial Hernando, 1932), p. 82. An example of this, coupled with the qualification "antigua," is found in the *Primera parte* of Alfonso's *General estoria*: " . . . es ala que llaman agora letra toledana, e es antigua, e non qual la que agora fazen." Ed. by Antonio G. Solalinde (Madrid:

Priscian, and even the Virgilian works were not that rare. The king was apparently trying to establish the most accurate text of these works as he assembled sources for the *Primera crónica general* and later for the *General estoria*. Therefore he was seeking out the oldest manuscripts of these works in his kingdom.

Library inventories from the fourteenth century, whether from cathedrals or monasteries, are very scarce.[161] Of these few inventories, the most important detail the expansion of the library of the cathedral of Burgos at the end of the fourteenth century and during the first years of the fifteenth. In the first of these, the library contains eighty-six codices, none of which is concerned with grammar, rhetoric, or poetics.[162] But the second inventory, of books donated by Alfonso Álvarez in 1398, contains a copy of the *Etymologiae* and two *artes dictandi*, one of which is specifically called a rhetoric and attributed to "magister Guido."[163] The *incipit*, "Quasimodo geniti infantes," makes it clear that the reference is to the *Summa Dictaminis* of Guido Faba, professor of *dictamen* at Bologna in the first half of the thirteenth century. The later Burgos inventories contain no mention of rhetorical works.

Our survey shows that references to rhetorical works in Spanish libraries in the thirteenth and fourteenth centuries are meager. Summing up, there are definite references to the classical rhetorics seven times (*De Inventione*, 4; *Rhetorica ad Herennium*, 2; Aristotle, 1), to the *artes dictaminis* six times (Bernard and Guido are the only names specifically mentioned), and to the *artes praedicandi* three times (twice to the *Summa de Arte Praedicatoria* of Alain de Lille, which is not a technical treatise, and once to an anonymous *ars*). There is one rather dubious reference to a book of versification. The *artes poetriae*

Junta para Ampliación de Estudios e Investigaciones Científicas, Centro de Estudios Históricos, 1930), p. 167a.26-28.

[161] Again whether this is a real scarcity or whether it merely reflects the lack of investigation of the historical sources of this period is a moot point.

[162] Demetrio Mansilla Reoyo, *Catálogo de los códices de la Catedral de Burgos* (Madrid: Consejo Superior de Investigaciones Científicas, Instituto Enrique Flórez, 1952), pp. 155-167.

[163] Ibid., pp. 168-173.

which have attracted so much modern attention are conspicuous only because of their absence.

MODERN SPANISH LIBRARIES

After having examined medieval Spanish education and medieval Spanish libraries, we are now in a position to look at the evidence that can be gleaned from the rhetorical manuscripts extant in Spanish libraries.[164] While it is not complete, such a study permits us to draw certain conclusions, probably valid, about the relative abundance of the various categories of rhetorical treatises. In considering these various categories I exclude manuscripts written after 1400 and those which (as near as can be ascertained) did not enter Castile until after that date. The most important omissions of the latter sort are the manuscripts from the Escurial which came from the collections of D. Antonio Agustín, archbishop of Tarragona (d. 1586), and of D. Diego Hurtado de Mendoza.

In the first place, the *artes poetriae* can probably be dismissed as an important influence in medieval Spain. I find no copies of them in the medieval libraries and only three manuscripts, all of Geoffroi de Vinsauf's *Poetria Nova*, in modern libraries. Two of these (Bibl. Nac. 3699 and 9589) are dated fourteenth or fifteenth century, the third (Seville Bibl. Cap. 82-1-19) definitely fifteenth century. None can be traced to a Castilian origin or shown to have been in Castile during the Middle Ages. In fact, the contrary is true. Bibl. Nac. MS. 3699 was written in the territories of the crown of Aragon, probably in Italy. MS. 9589 is almost certainly of Aragonese origin as well. The Seville manuscript was written by a scribe from the north of Italy and was in Padua in the year 1478. The *Breve Compendium Artis Rethorice* of Martín de Córdoba, which relies heavily upon the *Poetria Nova*, at first glance appears to contradict this conclusion. But, as we shall see in Chapter IV, this work was probably written

---

[164] The raw material for this examination will be found in my "Retóricas clásicas y medievales," which also contains descriptions of the various MSS and bio-bibliographical notes on the authors of the works found therein.

in France and therefore cannot serve as a true manifestation of the Spanish rhetorical tradition.

Second, the evidence for the influence of the *artes praedicandi* is not impressive. Only four MSS written earlier than the fifteenth century are extant. Of these, one (Madrid Bibl. Univ. 35), from the thirteenth century, contains the treatise "Ad habendum materia predicationis . . . ," which is only two folios in extension. Another thirteenth-century MS contains Alain de Lille's *Summa de Arte Praedicatoria* (Sigüenza Bibl. Cap. 63). This Sigüenza MS may possibly be identified with the one mentioned in the early fourteenth-century inventory of that library (see above, p. 38). Alain's work is not a technical treatise. Prior to the fifteenth century, Caplan and Charland list only two Spanish authors of *artes praedicandi*, the little known Arnaldus de Puig (late fourteenth century), whose work is no longer extant, and Francisco Eiximenis (1349-ca. 1412).[165] Both authors are Catalonian in origin. Even in the fifteenth century there is only one Castilian author of an *ars praedicandi*, Martín Alfonso de Córdoba, master in theology from Toulouse.[166]

Unlike the medieval libraries, the modern ones show that the most common rhetorical works are the *artes dictaminis* and the classical treatises, in that order. Of the former there are about forty copies of thirty-two different works written by fourteen authors. The most popular of these, as in the later Middle Ages,[167] is Guido Faba, with three copies of his *Dictamina Rhetorica*, two of his *Summa Dictaminis*, and one each of the *Epistole sive Litera[s]*, *Exordia*, *Exordia Continuata*, *Gemma Purpurea*, four different *Littere*, and the *Rota Nova*. Six of these works are found in a late thirteenth-century Spanish manuscript

---

[165] Harry Caplan, *Mediaeval "Artes Praedicandi." A Hand-List*, Cornell Studies in Classical Philology, 24 (Ithaca: Cornell University Press, 1934), p. 38; Charland, *Artes Praedicandi*, pp. 26, 35-36.

[166] Fernando Rubio Álvarez, in the intro. to his ed. of Martín's *Ars Praedicandi*—*CD*, 172 (1959), 327—cites Martín de Córdoba, *Jardín de nobles doncellas*, ed. by Félix García (Madrid, 1956), pp. 23-49, for a biography of this author.

[167] ". . . i *Dettati* incontrarono la stessa fortuna, che più tardi ebbe il *Formulario* di Rolandino nell'arte notaria. Essi rispondevano a un bisogno vivamente sentito nella pratica . . . Il pregio dei *Dettati* consistè in questo, che essi erano vere lettere, appropriate a tutte le circonstanze possibili della vita." Gaudenzi, "Sulla cronologia," pp. 137-138.

now in England; the other eight date from the fourteenth century. Seven of the minor works of Buoncompagno of Bologna occur in a thirteenth-century MS in Salamanca. Laurentius de Aquilegia is represented by four different works, the *Ars Dictandi Abreviata, Formula Dictandi, Practica sive Usus Dictaminis,* all in fourteenth-century MSS. There are single works of Berardus Caraccioli of Naples, Gerardus Odonis, an unidentified Hugo, Johannes Bondi de Aquilegia, Johannes de Sicilia, Laurentius Abbas, Petrus Blesensis, Poncius Provincialis, Ricardus de Pofi, and Stephanus Tornacensis, besides various anonymous works.

The school of *dictamen* represented is preponderantly the Italian of the thirteenth century. Of the eleventh- and twelfth-century Italian *dictatores* we find nothing, and of the Orléans school that reached its height in the second half of the twelfth century only single copies of works by Peter of Blois (s. XII ex.), Stephan of Tournai (s. XII ex.), and Ponce of Provence (s. XIII med.). Since the Spanish MSS are almost entirely from the fourteenth century, this is not surprising. By the end of the thirteenth century, Italian *dictamen* had almost entirely replaced the earlier French school because it used simple, clear models and insisted on following the style of the Roman Curia rather than the classical forms advocated at Orléans.

Of less interest from a purely rhetorical point of view are the various notarial treatises used primarily for drawing up legal documents. The five works which might have been in Spain before 1400 are extant in fourteenth-century manuscripts. The only ones by a known author are the *De Arte Notarie* and *Opusculum siue Sumula Edita Super Tribus Partibus Artis Notarie* of Rolandinus Rodulphus Passagerius (d. 1300) of Bologna, the most important exponent of *ars notaria* during the Middle Ages.

The classical treatises are only slightly less common, with thirty-seven copies of twelve different works. The proportion of the various authors is very similar to that found in the medieval libraries. Cicero's *De Inventione*, the *Rhetorica ad C. Herennium*, and Aristotle's *Rhetorica*, the only classical works mentioned, are the most common works in the modern libraries as well, the *Ad Herennium* being the most popular. Aristotle, by a slight margin, is the single most popular author. There are six MSS of Latin translations of the *Rheto-*

rica, divided evenly between thirteenth- and fourteenth-century MSS, and one of the *Commentarium Medium* of Averroes on the *Rhetorica* (s. XIII). There also exist one copy of the *Poetica* almost contemporary with the translation of William of Moerbeke (1278) and three of the *Commentarium Medium* on the same work.[168]

Of classical Latin treatises, by far the most common are the *Rhetorica ad C. Herennium* and Cicero's *De Inventione,* with eight copies of the former and seven of the latter. In five thirteenth-century MSS the works are found together. Both of the separate MSS of the *De Inventione* are relatively early, going back to the twelfth century; one of the *Ad Herennium* MSS goes back to the same century and the others date from the fourteenth. Brunetto Latini's *Trésor* should be considered along with the *De Inventione;* the section on rhetoric in Book III follows the former work closely. We find four MSS of the work, two of the original and two of the Spanish translation. We also find two separate commentaries on the *Ad Herennium,* a short one (Madrid Bibl. Nac. 9309) and a considerably longer one, Phillipus de Pistoia's *Elucidarium Super Nova Rethorica Tulliana,* both in fourteenth-century manuscripts.

There is one fourteenth-century MS of Cicero's *De Oratore* and *Orator ad Brutum* of Italian origin; it belonged to the Marqués de Santillana and was probably acquired for him in Italy. A thirteenth-century MS of Quintilian in Salamanca is of French origin, its provenience uncertain. There are two MSS of Horace's *Ars Poetica,* both of which belonged to the Aragonese historian Jerónimo Zurita. Of the late classical treatises based on the earlier works, the only one found in Spanish libraries is Boethius' *De Differentiis Topicis* (see Chap. III for a discussion of this work) in two thirteenth-century MSS.

To sum up the results of this inventory: By far the most common rhetorical works known to have been extant in thirteenth-century

---

[168] William F. Boggess has recently demostrated that the *Poetica* was known in the fourteenth century only through an abbreviated version of Hermannus Alemannus' translation of the *Commentarium Medium,* probably produced at the University of Paris in the late thirteenth or early fourteenth century, and points out that it was considered a logical work: "Aristotle's *Poetics* in the Fourteenth Century," *SPh,* 67 (1970), 284.

Castile are Cicero's *De Inventione* and the *Rhetorica ad C. Herennium.*
In the earliest MSS these works are separate; but from the thirteenth
century they generally occur together. This follows the trend noted
by Grosser in her study on their influence (see above, p. 38). At the
end of the thirteenth century and the beginning of the fourteenth,
there is a surge of interest in Aristotle's *Rhetorica* and *Poetica*, immediately after their translation into Latin. The enormous prestige enjoyed by "el filósofo" may account for the relative popularity of his
works.

In the fourteenth century, classical works are relatively rare, but
we find a concentration of works of *dictamen* from that century. It
is hard to say whether the paucity of earlier MSS of *dictamen* reflects
a real absence of them in thirteenth-century Spain or whether the
earlier ones simply disappeared because of the hard use they must
have received in chapters and chanceries. The latter explanation seems
more probable. We know of the existence of *artes dictaminis* in Spain
in the thirteenth century of which no MSS from that period remain
in Spanish libraries. Juan Gil de Zamora's *Dictaminis Epithalamium*
(extant only in Salamanca Bibl. Univ. MS. 2128, fifteenth century)
and Geoffrey of Everseley's *Ars Epistolaris Ornatus* (extant in the
thirteenth-century Perugia Bibl. Comunale Augusta MS. F. 62) come
readily to mind. It is possible, also, that the earlier works were superseded by more up-to-date ones. This would explain the relative
abundance of the later Italian works on *dictamen* as opposed to the
scattered texts from the earlier Italian and French schools.

The *artes praedicandi* which remain from this period are few in number and tend to concentrate on the general theory of preaching (Alain de Lille). Technical treatises setting forth the thematic sermon
are almost nonexistent. The *artes poetriae* are of even less importance.

In resumé: The external testimony for the existence of a Spanish
rhetorical tradition is rather slim. There is no evidence that rhetoric was taught in the schools. Library catalogues, both medieval
and modern, show that the classical rhetorics—principally *De Inventione* and the *Rhetorica ad C. Herennium*—hold pride of place until
almost the end of the thirteenth century. At that point the *artes dictaminis* begin to appear in increasingly important numbers. Never-

theless, we cannot assume that any rhetorical knowledge found in thirteenth-century Spanish authors reflects the influence of these two traditions alone. Documentary evidence of the type surveyed here, while important, is not the only evidence. An examination of the literary and historical works produced in the thirteenth century and earlier reveals rhetorical and cultural traditions about which the documents are silent.

CHAPTER III

REFERENCES TO RHETORIC IN
MEDIEVAL SPANISH AUTHORS

RHETORIC IN THE LATIN AUTHORS

INTERNAL EVIDENCE for the knowledge of rhetoric in medieval Spain is much more plentiful than documentary evidence. Many works both in Latin and in Castilian contain allusions to rhetoric from which the state of the art can be inferred. The most detailed of these are found in the encyclopedic compilations of the liberal arts.

Prototype of these compilations in Spain and for centuries the most important of them was the *Etymologiae* of St. Isidore. The first three books of this work contain a compact exposition of the liberal arts in the following order: Grammar (Book I), Rhetoric and Dialectic (Book II), Arithmetic, Geometry, Music, and Astronomy (Book III).[1] Rhetoric precedes dialectic. The same order is observed in the *De Divisione Philosophiae* of Dominicus Gundisalvus. In the Alfonsine corpus, however, rhetoric regularly follows dialectic as the third part of the trivium.

The chief source of Isidore's rhetorical doctrine is the discussion of the same art in Cassiodorus Senator's *Institutiones*.[2] It is highly unlikely that Isidore was acquainted with any of the Ciceronian treatises. As Grosser points out, only in sections derived from Cassiodorus does Isidore use *De Inventione*.[3] Nevertheless, the doctrines

---

[1] Isidori Hispalensis Episcopi *Etymologiarum sive Originum Libri XX*, ed. by W. M. Lindsay, 2 vols. (Oxford: E Typographeo Clarendoniano, 1911; repr. 1966); further references are incorporated into the text.

[2] For a general discussion of Isidore's dependence on Cassiodorus, see Paul Lehmann, "Cassiodorstudien. IV. Die Abhängigkeit Isidors von Cassiodor," *Philologus*, 72 (1913), 504-517.

[3] "Studies in the Influence," pp. 59-60.

[52]

that St. Isidore sets forth are essentially Ciceronian in outlook, although highly abbreviated. Following Cassiodorus, he defines rhetoric as "bene dicendi scientia in civilibus quaestionibus" (II. i. 1) and the rhetor as "vir bonus, dicendi peritus" (II. iii. 1). The Ciceronian concept of rhetoric as a moral science is apparent. The inventors of rhetoric are then named, in a section not taken from Cassiodorus (II. ii). There follow the five parts of classical rhetoric: invention, disposition, style, memory, and delivery (II. iii). Then comes a discussion of the three kinds of rhetorical speeches, deliberative, demonstrative, and judicial (III. iv). Chapter v treats the concept of *status*, the sorts of issues that must be considered in different kinds of arguments. Chapters vi, vii, and viii treat simple and complex questions, the parts of an oration, and the reactions of the audience to various kinds of arguments. All this comes directly from Cassiodorus. It is perhaps significant that Isidore suppresses the next paragraph of Cassiodorus' work, which considers the relative value of Cicero's *De Inventione*, Quintilian's *Institutio*, and Fortunatianus' *Artis Rhetoricae*.[4] Cassiodorus specifically states that these works formed part of his library. We may assume from Isidore's silence that he did not have access to them. Finally, Isidore bases his Chapter ix, on argumentation, on Cassiodorus.

Cassiodorus' comments on rhetoric end here and Isidore immediately begins to lose the admirable clarity which distinguishes the sections based on Cassiodorus. For no apparent reason Isidore breaks off his discussion of rhetoric to turn to the problem of law in Chapter x: its origins, the difference between law and custom, and the purpose of law.[5] In a note at the beginning of II. x, Lindsay cites Hermagoras as the source of this chapter; and Hermagoras also seems to be the source of the distinction between sentences and *chria* (II. xi).

The last part of the book, including the sections on figures of speech and thought, seems to have its source in some work related to Quin-

---

[4] Cf. Cassiodori Senatori *Institutiones*, ed. by R. A. B. Mynors (Oxford: At the Clarendon Press, 1937; repr. 1963), II. ii. 10.

[5] The substance of this chapter is repeated in Bk. V, iii-xxi, sometimes in exactly the same words; it is unclear why Isidore inserts it in the section on rhetoric as well.

tilian—a later commentary on the *Institutio* or possibly the lost rhetorical treatise of Celsus, one of Quintilian's own sources.[6] St. Isidore catalogues twelve figures of speech and twenty-three figures of thought, most of them illustrated from the orations of Cicero (II. xx-xxi). Other subjects mentioned in the second half of Book II include the three levels of style, the use of periods, and errors of diction and thought to be avoided (II. xvi-xx).

Isidore's work lies within the classical tradition and is indeed one of the major means of transmission of this tradition to the later Middle Ages. While not in itself sufficient for the adequate teaching of rhetoric, at least it kept some notion of the art alive.

This same brief description of rhetoric, setting forth the major points as part of a general description of the liberal arts but going into no detail, is characteristic also of the next Spanish works which treat rhetoric, a full five centuries later. The *De Consolatione Rationis* of Petrus Compostellanus and the *De Divisione Philosophiae* of Dominicus Gundisalvus date from the twelfth century, the former probably from the decade of 1140-1150, the latter from soon after 1150.[7]

The *De Consolatione Rationis* is based on Boethius' *De Consolatione Philosophiae* and employs the same mixture of prose and verse which the latter work popularized.[8] Petrus' work is an allegory in which Reason, in the form of a beautiful maiden, shows the sleeping author how to escape from the dangerous pleasures of the world through the exercise of his own faculties of reason. In the course of this demonstration she presents to him her seven handmaidens, the liberal arts, who will aid Petrus in his struggle against evil. The

[6] Grosser, "Studies in the Influence," p. 60.

[7] The *terminus a quo* of the *De Divisione Philosophiae* is 1150, date of Gundisalvus' translation of al-Fārābī's *De Scientiis*; cf. Manuel Alonso, "Traducciones del arcediano Domingo Gundisalvo," *Al-Andalus*, 12 (1947), 306. The *terminus ante quem* is 1155, date of the death of Thierry of Chartres, who used the section on rhetoric in the *De Divisione* in his own *Commentarium in Ciceronis "De Inventione"*; cf. Nicholas M. Haring, "Thierry of Chartres and Dominicus Gundissalinus," *MS*, 26 (1964), 278.

[8] *Petri Compostellani De Consolatione Rationis Libri Duo*, ed. by Pedro Blanco Soto, Beiträge zur Geschichte der Philosophie des Mittelalters, VIII, 4 (Münster: Aschendorffsche Verlagsbuchhandlung, 1912).

work falls within the most venerable Occidental tradition, for in addition to its dependence upon Boethius, it uses St. Isidore's *Synonyma* and St. Augustine's *De Libero Arbitrio*.[9]

The rhetorical source, or rather the source of all the material on the liberal arts, was probably much more recent, judging from the fact that the author calls the figures of thought and diction "colors," a usage which is not found until the eleventh century.[10] The source can be traced to the tradition springing from Martianus Capella as opposed to Isidore, since the *De Consolatione Rationis* follows the former in assigning rhetoric to the third position in the trivium instead of to the second position. The numerous verbal parallels between Petrus' description of rhetoric and that in Alain de Lille's *Anticlaudianus* indicate some relationship between the two works.[11] Since Alain (ca. 1128-1203) is younger than Petrus, either he was acquainted with the *De Consolatione Rationis* or both men used a common source. The latter explanation seems the more likely because of the numerous reminiscences of Martianus Capella found in Alain and not in Petrus. Both writers used some digest, possibly in verse (verbal parallels are frequently found as hemistichs in both works), based on Martianus Capella's allegorical presentation of the liberal arts as beautiful maidens. We may further surmise that this digest was in some way connected with the school of Chartres. The

---

[9] Ibid., pp. 35, 39.

[10] Murphy, "Chaucer, Gower," p. 26.

[11] Alain de Lille, *Anticlaudianus*, ed. by R. Bossuat (Paris: Librairie Philosophique J. Vrin, 1955). Compare the following passages:

Anticlaudianus	*De Consolatione Rationis*
"Purpureus roseo *uultum splendore colorat,*	"Tertia virgo nitens *vultum splendore colorat*
Sed partim uultus *candor peregrinus inheret*" (III, 154-155)	Quasi sertum roseum pilus arte politus honorat;
	Nullus et in facie *candor peregrinus inheret.*" (p. 62.24-26)
"Hic uelud in libro legitur quis finis et actor,	"Queritur hic *que causa, quis ordo* queque potestas,
Forma uel officium, que causa, quis ordo, quid artis" (III, 170-171)	*Forma vel officium,* vel quem demostrat honestas" (p. 62.31-32)

There are other similarities, but these are the most striking.

writers of that school were well acquainted with Martianus and the commentaries on his work.[12] Alain, moreover, while not trained at Chartres, expresses in the *Anticlaudianus* Neoplatonic views similar to those espoused by members of that school.[13] Thus one of the links between Martianus and Alain could well have been a poetic treatise on the liberal arts or even a general classification of knowledge embodying the Neoplatonic ideas of the school of Chartres. Such a treatise could have served as a source for Petrus as well.

Some thirty-five lines of verse of the *De Consolatione Rationis* (pp. 62.23-63.22) are dedicated to Rhetorica, of which the first eight describe her appearance. The rhetorical doctrines set forth in the remaining verses are so generalized that it is impossible to trace them to a given rhetorical tradition. The author mentions the *genus causae*, the necessity of determining the facts in a case of law, the colors that an orator might use to ornament his speech. But he does not say what the various kinds of causes are, nor how the facts should be determined, nor what kind of colors can be used.

If the *De Consolatione Rationis* falls within the purest western Latin tradition, the same cannot be said of the *De Divisione Philosophiae*.[14] Dominicus Gundisalvus, or Domingo Gundisalvo, was archdeacon of Segovia and one of the important translators of the school of Toledo. Twenty-two separate works, either original or translated, are attributed to him.[15] Most of these are concerned with the natural sciences or logic, but at least two address themselves to the larger problem of the organization of human and divine knowledge: the translation of the *Opusculum de Scientiis* of al-Fārābī and his own *De Divisione Philosophiae*.

The *De Divisione* is an attempt at classifying all knowledge "essentially derived from the Kitāb iḥṣā'al-'ulūm of al-Fārābī (first half of the tenth century), but [it] is *not* a translation of it; it is

---

[12] Cf. Cora E. Lutz, "Remigius' Ideas on the Classification of the Seven Liberal Arts," *Traditio*, 12 (1956), 84-86.
[13] Cf. R. Bossuat, "Introduction" to his ed. of the *Anticlaudianus*, pp. 32-33.
[14] Ed. by Ludwig Bauer, Beiträge zur Geschichte der Philosophie des Mittelalters, IV, 2-3 (Münster: Druck und Verlag der aschendorffschen Buchhandlung, 1903).
[15] Díaz y Díaz, *Index Scriptorum*, pp. 227-232.

more elaborate than the Iḥṣā'."[16] The scientific sections are derived primarily from Arabic authors. The sections on poetics and rhetoric come from Latin authors.[17] The latter also serve as the source of the schema used to present each of the individual sciences: "Circa unamquamque autem earum hec inquirenda sunt scilicet: quid ipsa sit, quod genus est, que materia, que species, que partes, quod officium, quis finis, quod instrumentum, quis artifex, quare sic vocetur, quo ordine legenda sit."[18] Hunt points out that this schema is based on one used by Boethius in *De Differentiis Topicis* and that it is essentially the same, except for order, as that used by the grammarian Petrus Helias in *Summa super Priscianum*.[19] Because the general doctrines advocated by Petrus Helias are so similar to those developed in the schools of northern France, Hunt concludes that Petrus Helias did not use Gundisalvus as a source. He points out also that "there are distinctions in Gundissalinus, which are derived from Latin sources, for example that between the *ars extrinsecus* and *intrinsecus*, and which are not found in Petrus Helias. The most probable explanation is that they were both drawing on some common school tradition."[20]

Hunt further conjectures that the school involved is that of Chartres, since Gundisalvus makes a distinction between *eloquentia* and *sapientia* unique to that school.[21] There is evidence in other works that Gundisalvus was acquainted with the doctrines of Chartres. Nicholas M. Haring suggests that "certain elements in his *De Processione Mundi*, written about or shortly after 1150, point to Thier-

---

[16] George Sarton, *Introduction to the History of Science*, Vol. II: *From Rabbi Ben Ezra to Roger Bacon*, in two parts (Baltimore: Published for the Carnegie Institution of Washington by the Williams and Wilkins Company, 1931), part i, p. 172.

[17] Ibid.

[18] Gundisalvus, *De Divisione Philosophiae*, p. 19.

[19] Richard William Hunt, "The Introductions to the 'Artes' in the Twelfth Century," in *Studia Mediaevalia in Honorem Admodum Reverendi Patris Raymundi Josephi Martin* (Bruges: Apud Societatem Editricem "De Tempel," [1948]), p. 87.

[20] Ibid., p. 91.

[21] Ibid., pp. 91-92; see below, pp. 86-88, for a more detailed discussion of this distinction as it relates to the definitions of the liberal arts given by Alfonso X in the *General estoria*.

ry" of Chartres himself.[22] Nor was influence in the other direction, from Spain to the school of Chartres, lacking either. Thierry took over Gundisalvus' section on rhetoric almost verbatim as the introduction to his own *Commentarium in Ciceronis "De Inventione."*[23] Hermann of Carinthia could have served as the specific link between the two. He studied under Thierry before going to Spain to undertake translations of Arabic scientific works. His presence is documented in various cities in the south of France and the north of Spain between 1138 and 1143.[24]

All this is indicative of rather close intellectual relations between the school of Chartres and Spain. In light of the strongly pro-French sympathies of the Castilian kings from Alfonso VI onward, and the influence of the French clergy in Spanish ecclesiastical matters, these relations are not surprising, especially since Archbishop Raymond of Toledo, the organizer of the school of translators, was of French origin.

The editor of the *De Divisione Philosophiae*, Ludwig Bauer, discusses the sources of the section on rhetoric extensively, but he concentrates on the parallels between Gundisalvus' work and that of the classical Latin rhetoricians. If our conclusions concerning medieval Spanish libraries are correct, the latter were almost certainly not known to Gundisalvus directly. He mentions both Quintilian and Cicero by name, the former as the author of a *De Instructionibus Oratoris*.[25] Gundisalvus cites Cicero's *De Inventione* sev-

---

[22] "Thierry of Chartres and Dominicus Gundissalinus," p. 280.

[23] Ibid., passim. Because of the remarkable textual agreement between the two works, a direct relationship must be posited rather than independent use of a common source. In spite of the fact that Gundisalvus is a much younger man, I am inclined to agree with Haring that Thierry used the *De Divisione Philosophiae* rather than the other way around. If so, it indicates a startling rapidity of transmission of intellectual information. As I have shown above (p. 54), the maximum length of time between the two works is only five years (1150-1155).

[24] Charles Homer Haskins, "Hermann of Carinthia," in his *Studies in the History of Medieval Science*, 3d ed. (New York: Frederick Ungar Publishing Co., 1960), p. 55.

[25] Thierry gives the correct title, *De Institutionibus Oratoriis*. In other words, he was familiar with the work and corrected the title he found in Gundisalvus,

eral times, in each citation referring to the same passage (I. v. 6), and Quintilian four times.[26] Two of the citations of Quintilian are mere repetitions of *De Inventione* I. v. 6, the third probably came through the intermediary of St. Isidore, and the fourth is little more than a reminiscence.[27] It is probable that Gundisalvus found all this material in one source, possibly Victorinus' commentary to the *De Inventione* or some work based on it.[28]

Of the later tradition, Gundisalvus specifically mentions Boethius, and finds material from both the *De Differentiis Topicis*, Book IV, and the *Interpretationes Aristotelis*.[29] As we shall see, Bauer grossly underestimates the extent of the borrowings from Boethius, both with regard to the schema used to organize the material and the material itself.[30] Although Gundisalvus does not mention St. Isidore, there are phrases throughout the section that could have come from him, and, toward the end, one whole passage on the "vir bonus, dicendi peritus" is quoted from St. Isidore verbatim.[31]

The rhetorical doctrines Gundisalvus sets forth, such as they are— and it must be remembered that he is intent only on classifying the sciences, not on teaching them—do remain within the classical tradition, although rather less so than Bauer thinks. Gundisalvus defines rhetoric as "sciencia bene dicendi" and "sciencia dicendi apposite ad persuasionem de causa proposita" from Isidore and Boethius, respectively.[32] From the standpoint of *genus* it is part of ci-

---

while the latter, ignorant of the work, preserved the incorrect title he found in his source.

[26] *De Divisione Philosophiae*, pp. 64-67.

[27] Ibid., pp. 67, 68.

[28] See below, pp. 60-61.

[29] *De Divisione Philosophiae*, pp. 65, 282.

[30] Nor does Bauer point out that the pseudo-Boethian *Speculatio de Rhetorice Cognatione* (Migne, *PL*, vol. 64, cols. 1217-1222), basically a summary of *De Differentiis Topicis* IV, could also be a source. It includes all the information that Gundisalvus presumably took from *De Differentiis Topicis* IV.

[31] *De Divisione Philosophiae*, p. 68.

[32] *De Divisione Philosophiae*, p. 64; Isidore, *Etymologiae* II. i. 1; Boethius, *De Differentiis Topicis Libri Quatuor* (Paris: Ex officina Michaelis Vascosani, 1543), f. 17r. Future citations of these works will be incorporated into the text. The *De Differentiis Topicis* is also found in Migne, *PL*, vol. 64, cols. 1173-1216.

vil science (p. 64). It is contrasted with wisdom (*sapientia*)—a distinction derived from Cicero (*De Inv.* I. i. 1) but emphasized by the school of Chartres. The *materia* of rhetoric is the hypothesis, which Gundissalvus defines as a controversy to be decided according to the circumstances of person, fact, cause, place, time, mode, and faculty (p. 65). These circumstances are drawn from Boethius (*De Diff. Top.* IV, f. 19r). The *species* of civil controversies are divided into judicial, deliberative, and demonstrative, depending on whether they have to do with what is just, what is useful, or what is honest (p. 66; Boethius, *De Diff. Top.* IV, f. 16v). Gundisalvus gives the traditional five *partes* of rhetoric: "inuencio, disposicio, pronunciacio, memoria, elocucio" (p. 66). With variations in order we find the same parts in Cicero (*De Inv.* I. vii. 9), Quintilian,[33] Boethius (*De Diff. Top.* IV, f. 17r), and Isidore (*Etym.* II. iii. 1). Like Boethius (loc. cit.), Gundisalvus points out that if one of these parts is missing, the oration will not be perfect (p. 66). The *officium* of a rhetor is to speak in a manner designed to persuade; the end is to persuade by speech (p. 67). The *instrumentum* of the rhetor is the oration, divided into five parts: "exordio, narracione, particione, confirmacione, epilogacione" (p. 67). Boethius mentions six parts, of which the first four coincide with those of Gundisalvus (*De Diff. Top.* IV. f. 17r).

The use of the term *epilogacione* instead of the more common *peroratio* might come from Victorinus' commentary on the *De Inventione*.[34] As Hunt points, out, this work was also the source for the distinction between *ars extrinsecus* and *intrinsecus* found in an earlier section of the *De Divisione Philosophiae*.[35] The example that Gundisalvus uses to illustrate the kinds of controversies treated by rhetoric, "an horestes iure occiderit matrem suam" (p. 65), occurs in Victorinus as well as in *De Inventione*.[36]

---

[33] *Institutio Oratoria*, ed. and trans. by H. E. Butler, Loeb Classical Library, 124-127, 4 vols. (Cambridge: Harvard University Press, 1920-1922; London: William Heinemann Ltd., 1920-1922; repr. *saepe*), III. iii. 1.
[34] Q. Fabii Laurentii Victorini *Explanationum in Rhetoricam M. Tulii Ciceronis Libri Duo*, ed. by C. Halm in his *Rhetores Latini Minores*, p. 194.29.
[35] "The Introductions to the 'Artes'," p. 87.
[36] *Explanationum*, p. 210.24; *De Inv.*, I. xiii. 18-xiv. 19.

Next comes a definition of the *artifex* of the rhetorical oration, the orator (p. 68). Still following Victorinus,[37] Gundisalvus distinguishes him from the rhetor: the orator uses rhetoric; the rhetor teaches it. A whole section on the attributes of the orator is taken word for word from St. Isidore (p. 68; *Etym.* II. i. 1). Finally, Gundisalvus states that rhetoric is to be taught after grammar and poetics (pp. 68-69).

Whether Gundisalvus' work is "original" or is based on some previous work—presumably of French origin because of the reminiscences of the school of Chartres—is of little importance for the history of rhetorical knowledge in Spain. The ideas it presents are entirely inadequate as a text for learning rhetoric. Nor need we attribute much rhetorical knowledge to Gundisalvus himself. Even if the section on rhetoric is "original," Gundisalvus could have extracted most of his information from Boethius and Isidore. The importance of the *De Divisione Philosophiae,* as of Petrus Compostellanus' *De Consolatione Rationis,* lies less in what it tells about rhetoric than in what it indicates about the intellectual relations between the schools of northern France and the cathedral centers of Spain, Compostela and Toledo. We shall find further evidence of these relations in the following section.

Rhetorical References in Vernacular Authors

The first appearance of the word "retórico" in Castilian occurs in the late twelfth-century text of the *Auto de los reyes magos.*[38] After talking to the three magi, Herod calls for his own wise men to explain the meaning of their visit:

---

[37] Ibid., p. 156.23-25; I am indebted to Professor Harry Caplan of Cornell for this reference.

[38] Joan Corominas, *DCELC,* Biblioteca Románica Hispánica, V, Diccionarios Etimológicos, 4 vols. (Madrid: Editorial Gredos, 1954), III, 1103-1104. It now appears that the work may not in fact be Castilian. Rafael Lapesa proposes a Gascon origin on the basis of defective rhymes in the Castilian version: "Sobre el *Auto de los reyes magos*: Sus rimas anómalas y el posible origen de su autor," in his *De la edad media a nuestros días: Estudios de historia literaria,* Biblioteca Románica Hispánica, II, Estudios y Ensayos (Madrid: Editorial Gredos, 1967), pp. 37-47.

> Herodes: Id por mios abades
>   i por mis podestades
>   i por mios scriuanos
>   i por meos gramatgos
>   i por mios streleros
>   i por mios retoricos;
>   dezir man la uertad, si iace in escripto
>   o si lo saben elos o si lo an sabido.[39]

The context makes clear that a "retórico" is considered only as one among a number of learned men, and perhaps the least learned of the lot. The anonymous author starts off with the religious and civil authorities ("abades," "podestades"), and then passes on to men expert in narrower branches of learning—notaries, grammarians, astrologers, and rhetoricians. It is surprising to note the absence of a logician from the list. This may indicate the Isidorian basis of medieval Spanish culture,[40] or merely that the balance had not yet shifted toward dialectic as it had already begun to do in France. In any event, the use of "retórico" in the *Auto* tells us nothing about the author's knowledge of rhetoric.

Corominas lists the *Setenario* of Alfonso the Learned as the first work in which the word *retórica* occurs.[41] This can only be so on the supposition that the *Libro de Alexandre* was written after the *Setenario*, which it almost certainly was not.[42] The first usage of the word occurs in the history of the Trojan war, with reference to

---

[39] *Auto de los reyes magos*, in *Crestomatía del español medieval*, ed. by Ramón Menéndez Pidal, Universidad de Madrid, Facultad de Filosofía y Letras, Seminario Menéndez Pidal, 2 vols. (Madrid: Editorial Gredos, 1965-1966), I, 75.

[40] Cf. Eleuterio Elorduy, "San Isidoro. Unidad orgánica de su educación reflejada en sus escritos: La gramática ciencia totalitaria," in *Miscellanea Isidoriana* (Rome: Typis Pontificiae Universitatis Gregorianae, 1936), pp. 293-322.

[41] *DCELC*, IV, 1103.

[42] The latest date proposed for the *Libro* is 1204; cf. Niall J. Ware, "The Date of Composition of the *Libro de Alexandre*: A Re-examination of Stanza 1799," *BHS*, 42 (1965), 252-255. Raymond S. Willis maintains the more traditional date of the second quarter of the thirteenth century in his review article of Emilio Alarcos Llorach, *Investigaciones sobre el "Libro de Alexandre,"* in *HR*, 19 (1951), 168.

the education of Paris: "Apriso de retórica, era bien razonado."[43] We shall note the use of the term "bien razonado" in both the *Setenario* and the *General estoria* of Alfonso the Learned.

A much longer reference to all the liberal arts occurs when Alexander is lamenting the uselessness of his education while Greece lies under the yoke of Darius. A significant feature of this passage is that it is original with the author of the *Alexandre*; indeed, it appears to be the longest completely original passage in the work.[44] It begins with stanza 37, in which Alexander states that he began to study with Aristotle at the age of seven; in stanza 38 he says that he now knows as much of "cleressia" as he needs to, more than anyone else except Aristotle himself, and that he now understands all the arts. The following stanzas (39-43) describe the content of his studies:

Entiendo bien gramatica, se bien toda natura,
bien dicto e versifico, conosco bien figura,
de cor se los actores, de libro non he cura,
mas todo lo oluido tanto he fiera rencura.

Bien se los argumentos de logica formar,
los dobles silogismos bien los se you [sic] falsar,
bien se yo a la parada a mi contrario leuar,
mas todo lo oluido tanto he grant pesar.

Retorico so fino, se fermoso fablar,
colorar mis palabras, los omnes bien pagar,
sobre mi aduersario la mi culpa echar,
mas por esto lo he todo a oluidar.

Apris toda la fisica, so meie natural,
conosco bien los pulsos, bien judgo orinal,
non ha fueras de ti mejor nin tal,
mas todo non lo presçio quanto vn dinero val.

---

[43] *Libro de Alexandre*, ed. by Raymond S. Willis, Elliott Monographs in the Romance Languages and Literatures, 32 (Princeton: Princeton University Press, 1934; Paris: Les Presses Universitaires de France, 1934), stanza 361.

[44] Raymond S. Willis, *The Relationship of the Spanish "Libro de Alexandre" to the "Alexandreis" of Gautier de Châtillon*, Elliott Monographs in the Romance Languages and Literatures, 31 (Princeton: Princeton University Press, 1934; Paris: Les Presses Universitaires de France, 1934), p. 61.

Se por arte de musica por natura cantar,
se fer sabrosos puntos, las bozes acordar,
los tonos como enpieçan e como deuen finar,
mas non me puede todo esto vn punto confortar.

Willis states that this passage "is really a short catalogue of the accomplishments of a completely educated man of the thirteenth century."[45] Alexander knows the three arts of the trivium, medicine, and music. (Stanza 44 briefly mentions the "calidades de cada elemento" and the "signos del sol," that is, *physica* and astrology). If we compare this list with either actual practice in thirteenth-century Spain or the theoretical situation as outlined in the *Partidas*, we find discrepancies.[46] None of the chairs Alfonso the Learned established at Salamanca has to do with rhetoric, although the other disciplines mentioned in the *Alexandre* are found. The *Partidas* specifically mention all the liberal arts along with canon and civil law, but nothing about medicine. The *Setenario* comes closest to the formulation in the *Alexandre* since it mentions all the sciences that the latter does and adds only one other, metaphysics.[47] Like the *Alexandre*, the *Setenario* is interested not in what disciplines are actually taught, but rather in what disciplines should ideally be taught.

An examination of the arts mentioned by Alexander reinforces this impression. For each he gives one or two major characteristics, enough for the educated reader to identify it. Thus grammar figures largely as the study of the accepted authors, the "actores" of the text. This study includes the composition of both prose and poetry ("bien dicto e versifico"), presumably with the aid of the rhetorical figures ("conosco bien figura"). The emphasis on the *auctores* and on composition is characteristic of humanistic studies in the twelfth century, particularly at Chartres. Turning to logic, Alexander mentions the syllogism ("los dobles silogismos"). This was one of the chief tools of the logician, particularly in formal disputation ("bien se yo a la parada a mi contrario leuar"). Of medicine

---

[45] Ibid., p. 63.
[46] See above, pp. 29-30.
[47] See below, p. 68.

Sarton states that "the two methods of diagnosis which were the most popular in our period [the twelfth century] were the examination of the patient's urine and the feeling of his pulse."[48]

As with the other arts, so with rhetoric. The author of the *Alexandre* emphasizes two characteristics: style ("se fermoso fablar, / colorar mis palabras") and the manipulation of an audience ("los omnes bien pagar, / sobre mi aduersario la mi culpa echar"). Style was a major concern of medieval rhetoric, and the appeal to an audience is usually cited in brief definitions of rhetoric as well.[49] The author of the *Alexandre* presents doctrines which are part of the common intellectual coin of late twelfth-century Europe. They apparently represent what the moderately well-educated Spaniard could be expected to know in the first half of the thirteenth century.

Gonzalo de Berceo never mentions rhetoric specifically in his works, but there is indirect evidence pointing to his knowledge of the *ars dictandi*. The last stanza of the fifteenth-century manuscript of the *Libro de Alexandre* reads as follows:

> Sy queredes saber quien fizo este ditado,
> Gonçalo de Berceo es por nombre clamado,
> Natural de Madrid, en Sant Mylian criado,
> Del abat Johan Sanchez *notario* por nonbrado.[50]

Leaving aside the question of the authorship of the *Alexandre*, Brian Dutton points out that there is every reason to suppose that the information given in the passage is correct. He shows that a Juan Sánchez was abbot of "the monastery of San Millán from 1209 to 1253. He appears in all but one of the documents witnessed by Berceo."[51] Furthermore, Berceo demonstrates a knowledge of technical legal terminology which implies some legal training. Assuming Berceo to have been the notary of the monastery, his training might well have included the study of *dictamen*. Since the notary was in

---

[48] *Introduction to the History of Science*, Vol. I, part i, p. 75.

[49] See below in the *Setenario*, p. 69, and in the *General estoria*, p. 91.

[50] Paris, Bibliothèque Nationale, MS. esp. 488; this passage was first printed by Alfred Morel-Fatio, *Catalogue des manuscrits espagnols et des manuscrits portugais de la Bibliothèque Nationale* (Paris: Imp. Nationale, 1892), p. 360.

[51] "The Profession of Gonzalo de Berceo and the Paris Manuscript of the *Libro de Alexandre*," *BHS*, 37 (1960), 139.

charge of drawing up the monastery's documents and letters, he would have had to know the appropriate legal and epistolary formulae.

A broader knowledge of the *ars dictandi*, however, is difficult to substantiate in Berceo's works. The only reference to technical rhetorical terms occurs in two passages from the *Milagros de Nuestra Señora*. In the first of these, Berceo is speaking of the services that St. Ildefonsus rendered to the Virgin: "Fizo della un libro de dichos colorados / De su virginidat contra tres renegados" (ll. 51cd). The reference is to the *De Virginitate Sanctae Mariae*. Given the highly rhetorical style of that work, the "dichos colorados" would refer specifically to the *colores rhetorici*.[52] In line 779a ("Façes peticiones locas e sin color") the author apparently uses the word in a similar sense, which here appears to be negative, that is, "without art." In both passages Berceo reflects a usage widespread at the time he was writing.[53]

The *Setenario* of Alfonso the Learned is the first work to give a formal definition of rhetoric in Castilian. Although the *Setenario* is a precursor of the *Siete partidas*, it contains material omitted from the final redaction of the latter work—for example, the eulogy of St. Fernando III, Alfonso's father, in the first ten laws.[54] The eleventh law explains why the book is called the *Setenario* and serves as the introduction proper to the work. It is in this justification of the book's title ("Por quáles rrazones pusiemos nonbre a este libro *Ssetenario*," p. 25) that the discussion of rhetoric occurs.

The work is called the *Setenario* because it is organized around the number seven. The use of this number as a principle of compo-

---

[52] 5th ed., by Antonio G. Solalinde, Clásicos Castellanos (Madrid: Espasa-Calpe, S. A., 1958). Gariano makes the same point in *Análisis estilístico*, p. 99; in her review of this book, Margherita Morreale accepts this interpretation but shows that "color" does not always refer to rhetoric even when used allegorically: "La lengua poética de Berceo: Reparos y adiciones al libro de Carmelo Gariano," *HR*, 36 (1968), 145.

[53] Cf. Faral, *Les arts poétiques*, ch. VII, "Compositions relatives aux figures de rhétorique," pp. 48-54.

[54] Alfonso el Sabio, *Setenario*, ed. by Kenneth H. Vanderford, Facultad de Filosofía y Letras de la Universidad de Buenos Aires (Buenos Aires: Instituto de Filología, 1945), pp. 8-25; subsequent citations are incorporated into the text.

sition was widespread throughout Antiquity and the Middle Ages. For Macrobius it was the universal number because of the innumerable heptads in both microcosm and macrocosm—the seven liberal arts, the seven planets, and the seven musical tones, among others.[55] For mnemonic and mystical reasons the Church organized much of its dogma around the same number: the seven sacraments, the seven virtues, the seven vices, the seven works of corporal mercy, and the seven works of spiritual mercy. We find much of this material in Hugh of St. Victor's *De Quinque Septenis*.[56] The *De Septem Septenis* attributed to John of Salisbury retains the heptad of the seven virtues described in Hugh's formulation and adds six more heptads describing the attributes of the soul.[57] The second heptad of these seven enumerates the *viae animae*, the seven liberal arts, and describes them briefly.

Alfonso's schema is more complicated than that of the *De Septem Septenis* because he breaks down some of his secondary heptads into tertiary and even quaternary ones, but it is less perfect because he fails to complete the seven primary heptads. Nevertheless, he is obviously following the same tradition, which springs from members of the school of Chartres.[58]

Alfonso starts to give seven reasons for calling the book the *Setenario* (only four are actually named) and subdivides each of these into seven more reasons. The primary heptads are "entendimiento," "natura," "ssabiduría," and "[rrazón]" (p. 26). The subdivisions of

---

[55] Vincent Foster Hopper, *Medieval Number Symbolism: Its Sources, Meaning, and Influence on Thought and Expression*, Columbia University Studies in English and Comparative Literature, 132 (New York: Columbia University Press, 1938), p. 44.

[56] Ibid., p. 109.

[57] Ed. by Migne, *PL*, vol. 199, cols. 945-963.

[58] It has also been suggested that the organization of both the *Setenario* and the *Siete partidas* was influenced by the constitution *Tanta*, in which the Emperor Justinian confirmed the Digest: ". . . et in septem partes eos digessimus, non perperam neque sine ratione, sed in numerorum naturam et artem respicientes et consentaneam eis divisionem partium conficientes"; cited by Raimundo Bidagor, "El derecho de las *Decretales* y las *Partidas* de Alfonso el Sabio de España," in *Acta Congressus Iuridici Internationalis*, Pontificium Institutum Utriusque Iuris (Rome: Apud Custodiam Librariam Pont. Instituti Utriusque Iuris, 1936), III, 305.

"ssabiduría" are the "siete ssaberes, a que llaman artes . . . " (p. 29). These arts are *not* the traditional seven liberal arts, although they include the latter. Alfonso's seven arts are: (1) "ffablar e mostrar todas las cosas" (p. 29), which subsumes grammar, logic, and rhetoric; (2) "arismética" (p. 31); (3) "geometría" (p. 32); (4) "acordança, . . . música en griego" (p. 34); (5) "astrología" (p. 35); (6) "Ffísica . . . que quier dezir tanto commo natural ssaber de melezina" (p. 36); (7) "metaffísica" (p. 38).

In fact this turns out to be the trivium, the quadrivium, medicine, and metaphysics. None of the earlier compendia on liberal arts is organized in quite this way. Nevertheless, except for the inclusion of medicine, it is a schema which Alfonso repeats in later works. In the first part of the *General estoria* we find seven liberal arts together with "fisica" and metaphysics. Here "fisica" is defined as the discipline which teaches the "naturas de las cosas," i.e., the natural sciences.[59] This is the traditional meaning of the term "physica" up until the twelfth century. There is no doubt that the *Setenario* in its listing has confused "physica" in the sense of the natural sciences and "physica" in the sense of medicine.[60] For only if we asume that such a confusion has occurred does the inclusion of "metaffísica," that which is beyond nature, make any sense.

The definition of rhetoric in the *Setenario*, while longer and more detailed than anything found before or after it in the thirteenth century, is inconclusive because of the arbitrary way it has been divided into seven sections to make it fit into Alfonso's overall plan:

Rrectórica llaman a la terçera partida destas tres, que sse entiende que enssenna a ffablar ffermoso e apuesto, e esto en siete razones:

color	fermosura	apostura	conueniente
amorosa	en buen son	en buen contenente	

---

[59] Alfonso el Sabio, *General estoria*, I, 21a. 40-45; further references will be incorporated into the text.

[60] Paul Oskar Kristeller finds that the usage of *physicus* for *medicus* started during the twelfth century in the medical schools of France and Salerno; it is not of Arabic origin: "The School of Salerno: Its Development and Its Contribution to the History of Learning," in his *Studies in Renaissance Thought and Letters*, Storia e Letteratura, Raccolta di Studi e Testi, 54 (Rome: Edizioni di Storia e Letteratura, 1956), pp. 515-517.

Ca esto conuyene mucho al que desta arte husare, que cate que la rrazón que ouyere a dezir, que la colore en manera que paresca bien en las uoluntades de los que la oyeren. Et la tenga otrosí por ffermosa, para cobdiçiarla aprender e saber-la rrazonar. Et que sse diga apuestamiente, non mucho apriessa nin mucho de uagar. Et que ponga cada rrazón allí do conuiene ssegunt aquello que quisiere ffablar. E que lo diga amorosamiente, non muy rrezio nin muy brauo nin otrosí muy fflaco; mas en buen sson mesurado, non altas bozes nin muy baxas. Et ha de catar que el contenente que touyere, que sse acuerde con la rrazón que dixiere. Et desta guisa sse mostrará por bien rrazonado aquel que rrazonare, e mouerá los coraçones de aquellos que lo oyeren para adozirlos más ayna a lo que quisiere. (pp. 30-31)

The similarity to the rhetorical comments in the *Libro de Alexandre* is immediately apparent. Style and, in the last lines, the effect of the speaker on the audience, are the elements emphasized. But as with the Latin texts on rhetoric previously studied, it is to the liberal arts compendia that we must turn for sources and analogues to this passage rather than to the classical or medieval treatises on rhetoric. In spite of Menéndez y Pelayo's assertions about the resumption of the tradition of Quintilian and Isidore, the source of this passage is certainly not one of the early compendia of Martianus, Cassiodorus, or Isidore.[61] Although extremely abbreviated, these works follow the dictates of classical rhetoric rather faithfully. Of the seven aspects of rhetoric which Alfonso mentions, four ("apostura," "amorosa," "en buen son," "en buen contenente") correspond to delivery, two ("color," "fermosura") to style, and only one ("conueniente") to invention. It is precisely the latter which is the most important part of classical rhetoric.[62]

As for delivery, St. Isidore says that it should be "aperte et suaviter" (*Etym.* II. xvi. 2). The figures should be used to avoid "fatigationem atque fastidium" in both the speaker and the audience (II. xxi. 1). We have seen that Boethius, and following him Gundisalvus, defines rhetoric as "scientia dicendi apposite ad persuasionem de causa proposita" (*De Diff. Top.* IV, f. 17r). In other words,

---

[61] *Ideas estéticas,* I, 444-445.

[62] H. M. Hubbell in the "Introduction" to his ed. of Cicero's *De Inventione,* Loeb Classical Library, 386 (Cambridge: Harvard University Press, 1949; London: William Heinemann Ltd., 1949; repr. 1960), p. ix.

there are similarities, but none so striking as to identify either Boethius or Isidore as the immediate source of this passage.

The reference to the art of rhetorical coloring at the beginning of the definition indicates a more modern source. But it is not one of the arts of poetry supposedly so well known in Spain. Had Alfonso used any of them it would probably have been John of Garland's *Poetria . . . de Arte Prosayca Metrica et Rithmica*, which is explicitly divided into seven different parts.[63] Nor can any striking parallels be found in the *artes praedicandi* edited by Charland or in the *artes dictaminis* printed by Rockinger.[64]

Alfonso probably took his information on all the liberal arts from some modern treatise. One of the few concrete clues to the identity of this unknown treatise is that it considered the arts of the trivium as a unit, the art "de ffablar e mostrar todas las cosas" (p. 29). Since I treat this at greater length in discussing the *General estoria*,[65] it will suffice here to say that the opposition or mutual dependence of the trivium and the quadrivium, *eloquentia* and *sapientia*, was one of the questions examined by various members of the school of Chartres.

The second part of the prologue to the *Siete partidas* condenses the eleventh law of the *Setenario* to such an extent that the seven

---

[63] "Primo tradetur doctrina inveniendi, deinde docebitur de modo eligendi materiam, postea de dispositione et de modo ornandi materiam, deinde de partibus dictaminis, postea de viciis vitandi in quolibet genere dictandi; consequenter constituitur tractatus de rethorico ornatu, necessario tam in metro quam in prosa, utpote de coloribus materiam abbreviantibus et ampliantibus ad scribentis electionem. Septimo et ultimo subiciuntur exempla literarum curialium et dictaminum scolasticorum, et versuum et rithmorum ornate compositorum, et diversorum metrorum." Ed. by Giovanni Mari, pp. 885-886. At a later period Alfonso was acquainted with John's *Integumenta Ovidii*, using it as a source for the *General estoria*. Cf. José Antonio Maravall, "La estimación de Sócrates y del saber clásico en la Edad Media española," *RABM*, 63 (1957), 45-46; and María Rosa Lida de Malkiel, "La *General estoria*, notas literarias y filológicas," *RPh*, 12 (1958), 115.

[64] *Briefsteller und Formelbücher des eilften bis vierzehnten Jahrhunderts*, Quellen und Erörterungen zur bayerischen und deutschen Geschichte, 9 (Munich: 1863-1864; repr. Burt Franklin Research and Source Works Series, 10, New York: Burt Franklin, 1961).

[65] See below, pp. 83-84.

arts are reduced to a single phrase.[66] But in the first *partida*, title v, law 37, Alfonso states that the prelate must be "sabidor en los saberes que llaman artes, et mayormiente en estas quatro . . . ." He then mentions and briefly defines grammar, logic, rhetoric, and music. Rhetoric is the "ciencia que demuestra ordenar las palabras apuestamiente et como conviene . . . " (I, 222). This is obviously related to the definition given in the *Setenario*. Furthermore, it is not found in the source for the passage as a whole, Raimundo de Peñafort's *Summa de Poenitentia*.[67]

The *Siete partidas*, however, contain at least three other passages on the nature of rhetoric or the importance of speaking well. One of the longest expositions of rhetorical theory in the work is the abbreviated *ars praedicandi* in title v of the first *partida*. The title as a whole is concerned with the qualities of prelates; laws 41 to 47 list those necessary to make the prelate a good preacher. This passage, a translation of Raimundo de Peñafort's *Summa de Poenitentia et Matrimonio* (Book III, title 9), "De doctrina ordinandorum, et de correctione eorum,"[68] indicates little about contemporary rhetorical theory in Spain. A comparison of law 43 with title 9, paragraph 3, of the *Summa de Poenitentia* indicates the closeness of the translation:

Pedricación para ser bien fecha ha menester que el que la feciere cate estas quatro cosas: tiempo, et lugar, et a quien et como. Et el tiempo debe catar que non sermone cotidianamiente, mas en sazones contadas et guisadas ; ca si siempre lloviese nunca	Circa tertium autem, scilicet circa actum praedicationis, quattuor sunt attendenda, scilicet tempus, locus, qualitas audientium, modus, et qualitas dicendorum. Tempus, vt non semper loquatur, sed temporibus opportunus: si enim semper plueret, terra numquam

---

[66] " . . . por este cuento de siete partieron los saberes a que llaman artes . . . ." Ed. by Real Academia de la Historia, I, 7; subsequent references are incorporated into the text.

[67] Compare the parallel passage from the *Summa* (III, t. 5): "Hoc tamen non intelligas de omnibus liberalibus artibus, sed de trivialibus tantum, scilicet. Grammatica, Dialectica, et Rethorica, quia illae specialiter ducunt, et erudiunt homines ad scientias pietatis . . . "; cited by José Giménez y Martínez de Carvajal, "San Raimundo de Peñafort y las *Partidas* de Alfonso X el Sabio," *AA*, 3 (1955), 270-271; see also ibid., p. 279n.

[68] Ibid., p. 276.

llevaría la tierra fruto: *eso mesmo se-*
ríe de la pedricación que si siempre
pedricasen recibrían los homes enojo
della, et non les entraría tanto en vo-
luntad para facer bien. Otrosí debe
catar el lugar o ha de pedricar, ca
la pedricación débela facer en la eg-
lesia o en otro lugar honesto, et ante
todos et non apartadamente por las
casas, porque non nazca ende sospecha
de heregía contra los que pedricasen
nin contra aquellos que los oyesen.
Et por esto mandó Moysen en la ley
vieja que quando el sacerdote entrase
en el templo que toviese aderredor de
su vestidura muchas campaniellas que
sonasen porque lo oyesen; ca aquello
tanto quiere decir et mostrar como que
paladinamente debe facer su pedricación.
Et por esta razón mesma dixo el rey
Salomon: departe tus aguas en las pla-
zas. [Emphasis mine; I, 228.]

germinaret. *vnde contra tales in Leuit.*
5 vir, qui fluxum seminis patitur, im-
mundus erit. item Gregorius super illum
Apost. ad Timoth. I. c. 4. Praedica
verbum, insta opportune, et importune,
ait: dicturus importune, praemisit op-
portune, quia apud auditorum mentes
ipsa sua vilitate se destruit, si habere
importunitas opportunitatem nescit. 43.
dist. sit rector. in fine. Locus attenden-
dus est, quia debet fieri praedicatio
in ecclesia, vel in alio publico loco,
et honesto, non autem in priuatis locis, vel domibus, ne nascatur ex hoc
suspicio haeresis. 30. dist. si quis extra.
vnde Moysi praecipitur in Exodo 28.
vt sacerdos ingrediens tabernaculum
tintinnabulis ambiatur, ac si dicat,
cum ingreditur tabernacula poterit am-
biri tintinnabulum, idest poterit prae-
dicare. item Salom. Prouerb. 5. In
plateis tuis aquas tuas diuide.[69] [Em-
phasis mine.]

Alfonso's changes are either interpolations designed to explain certain ideas more fully ("eso mesmo . . . facer bien") or omissions of
specific citations ("vnde contra . . . in fine") not germane to the
issue.

The comments on preaching in the *Siete partidas*, like those in
the source, the *Summa de Poenitentia*, do not constitute an *ars praedicandi* in the technical sense of the term. They are directed to the
moral qualities needed by the preacher and to the external circumstances of preaching—time, place, audience, manner—rather than to
the problems of composing an effective sermon.

Title v of the second *partida* is concerned with "qual debe ser el
rey en sus palabras" (II, 21). The prologue to the title begins: "Palabra es donayre que los homes han tan solamente, et non otra animalia ninguna" (II, 21). This goes back to Cicero's definition of man

---

[69] Ed. by Joannes de Fribvrgo (Rome: Sumptibus Ioannis Tallini, 1603; repr.
Farnborough [England]: Gregg Press Limited, 1967), p. 276.

in *De Inv.* I. iv. 5. In the first law of this title, Alfonso shows "qué cosa es palabra, et a qué tiene pro" (II, 21). The second law discusses the various manners of speaking:

Quatro maneras dixieron los sabios que son de palabras; la primera quando dice home palabras convenientes, la segunda quando las dice sobejanas, la tercera quando las fabla menguadas, la quarta quando son desconvenientes. Et convenientes son quando las dice apuestamente et con complimiento de razón, et sobejanas son quando se dicen además, o sobre cosas que non convengan a la natura del fecho sobre que se deben decir. Et sobre esta razón fabló Aristóteles al rey Alexandre como en manera de castigo, quandol dixo que non convenie a rey de ser muy fablador, nin que dexiese a muy grandes voces lo que hobiese de decir, fueras ende en lugar do conviniese, porque el uso de las muchas palabras envilece al que las dice; et otrosí las grandes voces sácanle de mesura, faciéndole que non fable apuesto. Onde por esto debe el rey guardar que sus palabras sean equales et en buen son: et las palabras que se dicen sobre razones feas et sin pro, que non son fermosas nin apuestas al que las fabla, nin otrosí el que las oye non podríe tomar buen castigo nin buen consejo, son además, et llámanlas cazurras, porque son viles et desapuestas, et non deben seer dichas a homes buenos, quanto más en decirlas ellos mesmos, et mayormente el rey. (II, 21-22)

This amalgam of moral precept and rhetorical theory is taken from a variety of sources. The reference to Aristotle comes from the *Poridat de las poridades*: "*Et* non fable mucho ny a uozes sy no quando fuere muy grant mester, *et* pocas uezes . . . ."[70] The phrase "Et convenientes son quando las dice apuestamente et con complimiento de razon . . . " agrees with the definition of rhetoric found in the *Setenario*.[71] The emphasis on *mesura* is also consonant with the formulation found in the *Setenario*.

The third law enjoins the king to explain himself fully but at the same time with brevity:

La segunda manera de mengua de fablar seríe quando dixiese las palabras tan breves et tan apriesa, que las non pudiesen entender aquellos que las oyesen: ca se-

---

[70] Ed. by Lloyd A. Kasten, Seminario de Estudios Medievales Españoles de la Universidad de Wisconsin (Madrid: S. Aguirre Torre, 1957), p. 37.

[71] "Et que sse diga apuestamiente, non mucho apriessa nin mucho de uagar. Et que ponga cada rrazón allí do conuiene ssegunt aquello que quisiere ffablar. E que lo diga amorosamiente, non muy rrezio nin muy brauo nin otrosí muy fflaco; mas en buen sson mesurado, non altas bozes nin muy baxas. Et ha de catar que el contenente que touyere, que sse acuerde con la rrazón que dixiere." Ed. by Vanderford, p. 31.

gunt dixieron los sabios, como quier que el home debe fablar en pocas palabras, por eso non lo debe facer en manera que non muestre bien et abiertamente lo que dixiere: et esto debe el rey guardar más que otro home, ca si lo non ficiese, terníen los que lo oyesen que lo facía por mengua de entendimiento o por embargo de razón. (II, 22)

Here we have a theory of style which antedates by almost seventy-five years don Juan Manuel's in the *Libro de los estados*: " . . . et poniendo declaradamente complida la razón que quiere decir, pónelo con las menos palabras que pueden seer."[72] From the similarities we might suspect a common source, or even direct dependence of don Juan Manuel on the work of his uncle Alfonso X.

Much the same counsels are repeated in title vii of the second *partida*, which deals with the education of the king's children. The seventh law discusses "como los ayos deben mostrar a los fijos de los reyes que fablen bien et apuestamente":

Onde conviene mucho a los ayos que han de guardar a los fijos de los reyes que puñen en mostrarles como fablen bien et apuestamente: ca segunt dixieron los sabios que fablaron en esta razón, estonce es buena la palabra et viene a bien quando es verdadera et dicha en el tiempo et en el lugar do conviene; et apuestamente es dicha quando non se dice a grandes voces, nin otrosí muy baxo, nin mucho de priesa, nin muy de vagar, et diciéndola con la lengua, et non mostrándola con los miembros, faciendo mal contenente con ellos, así como moviéndolos mucho a menudo, en manera que semejase a los homes que más se atreven a mostrarlo por ellos que por palabra, ca esto es grant desapostura, et mengua de razón: otrosí ha meester que la palabra sea complida, ca así como seríe mal quando fuese además, otrosí non seríe bien quando fuese menguada. (II, 49-50)

The similarity between this exposition and the definition of rhetoric given in the *Setenario* is even greater than that between the *Setenario* and *Siete partidas* II. v. 2. It is evident that all three passages have a common source. As I suggested earlier, that source is most probably a treatise on all the liberal arts.[73]

Most of Alfonso's observations on and prescriptions for *ars dictaminis* are found in the third *partida*; but, in discussing the duties of the officials of the king's court in the second *partida* (title ix, law 4), Alfonso writes about the king's *chanciller*, his notaries, and his

---

[72] Cited by Ángel Valbuena Prat, *Historia de la literatura española*, 7th ed., 3 vols. (Barcelona: Editorial Gustavo Gili, 1964), I, 167-168.

[73] See above, pp. 69-70.

scribes. The chancellor inspects all royal documents before they are sealed; the notaries take minutes concerning the legal provisions of these documents and enter them in the registers; the scribes actually draft and write the documents according to the notaries. Of the chancellor Alfonso says that he must be "de buen linage, et haya buen seso natural, et sea bien razonado, et de buena memoria, et de buenas costumbres, et que sepa leer et escrebir, también en latín como en romance; et sobre todo que sea home que ame al rey naturalmente . . . " (II, 61). Explaining the necessity of "leer et escrebir" in the same law, Alfonso says: "Et leer et escrebir conviene que sepa en latín et en romance, porque las cartas quel mandare facer sean dictadas et escriptas bien et apuestamente; et otrosí las que enviaren al rey que las sepa bien entender" (II, 61). The word "dictadas" is probably used in its technical sense of writing a letter according to the precepts of *dictamen.*

The king returns to the duties of the scribe in the third *partida* (title xix, law 2): "Et otrosí deben seer sabidores de escrebir bien et entendudos de la arte de la escribanía, de manera que sepan bien tomar las razones et las posturas que los homes posieren entre sí ante ellos . . . " (II, 634). That Alfonso is referring to *ars notaria* is evident from the fifth law of the same title, in which the king states that the scribe must be thoroughly conversant with the technical requirements of various kinds of documents:

Otrosí deben guardar que en las cartas foreras non pongan palabras por que semejen de gracia, et los previllejos que mandare confirmar el rey que valan así como valieron en tiempo de algunt rey o después fasta tiempo señalado, que non pongan en ellos otras palabras por que semejen que son confirmados sin entredicho ninguno, o que valan por todavía . . . . (II, 636)

The one hundred twenty-one laws of title xviii of the third *partida,* "De las escripturas por que se prueban los pleytos," also bear witness to the king's emphasis on the practical and legal aspects of *ars notaria.* Although Antonio C. Floriano Cumbreño calls this title a "verdadero tratado de *Ars dictandi,*"[74] it disregards the theoretical aspects of *dictamen* almost completely. Only by inference

[74] *Curso general de paleografía y paleografía y diplomática españolas* (Oviedo: Imprenta La Cruz, 1946), p. 260.

can we gain a slight knowledge of them from title xviii. Law 1
begins with a general definition of "escriptura": ". . . toda carta
que sea fecha por mano de escribano público o seellada con seello
de rey o de otra persona auténtica que sea de creer . . . " (II, 547).
In law 2 the king explains the two kinds of royal documents, "previllejos" and "cartas plomadas." The definition of the privilege follows:

Previllejo tanto quiere decir como ley que es dada et otorgada del rey apartadamente a algunt logar o a algunt home por le facer bien et merced: et débese facer
en esta manera segunt costumbre de España: primeramente débese comenzar en
el nombre de Dios, et después poner hi palabras buenas et apuestas segunt conviene a la razón sobre que fuere dado . . . . (II, 547)

Again the emphasis lies on the agreement between thought and word
found in other parts of the *Siete partidas* and in the *Setenario*.

Laws 6-25 of title xviii explain in detail the forms to be used in royal
documents. Laws 26-53 discuss the legal aspects of these documents—under whose authority they may be issued, who may judge
them, how they may be invalidated, and so on. Law 44, "Quáles
previllejos valen et quáles non," is the only one that contains material on *ars dictaminis*:

Non debe seer creído el previllejo nin la carta plomada en que non fuese escripto
el nombre del rey que lo dio, et el día, et el mes et el año en que fue fecho, et quán-
tos años ha que regna el rey que lo mandó facer, o que non fuese seellado de su seello
o firmado con el signo que usaba facer el rey de quien face mención en el previllejo. Otrosí decimos que si el previllejo desacordase del curso et de la manera
en que acostumbraban a facer los otros previllejos que solíe dar aquel rey mesmo,
que non debe seer creído . . . . (II, 571-572)

This is the first allusion in Spanish to the *cursus*, the use of rhythmi-
cal periods at the ends of clauses. Since Alfonso is here referring
to domestic documents, and since all such documents during his
reign were written in Castilian, it is clear that the *cursus* was adap-
ted from Latin for use in the vernacular. This is a development
of first importance for the evolution of Spanish prose and deserves
the immediate attention of competent scholars. The "manera" which
the law also mentions undoubtedly refers to the technical rules of
dictamen.

The rest of title xviii establishes rules for "cartas públicas," documents used in the affairs of private individuals. As with the royal

documents, Alfonso first gives the forms to be followed (in laws 56-110), then explains their legal aspects (in laws 111-121). The points emphasized are of legal and notarial interest exclusively.

Alfonso returns to rhetoric in at least one other work, the *General estoria*.[75] Here again rhetoric must be considered in context with the other arts, since the author takes his information from some compendium of the liberal arts rather than from an independent treatise. The first reference to the liberal arts in the *General estoria* is an account of their origin taken from the *Historiarum Antiquitatis Iudaicae* of Flavius Josephus: "Destos linages de Seth cuenta Iosepho, que ouieron ell ensennamiento delas cosas celestiales, dela astrologia *e* delos otros saberes liberales" (I, 20b.41-44). This is repeated in a more elaborate form farther along in the same chapter:

E los que descendieron de Seth, que assi como lo començaron a aprender de su padre Seth *e* de Adam, que gelo contaua como lo aprendiera de Dios, que fallaron el saber delas estrellas, *e* de todo el cielo, *e* de todos los siete saberes liberales, *e* del saber dela fisica, que es el saber que ensennan las naturas delas cosas, *e* dela methafisica, que es el saber otrossi que muestra connoscer a Dios *e* alas otras creaturas espirituales. (I, 21a.35-45)

Josephus at this point mentions only "disciplinam vero rerum caelestium . . . ."[76] The other usual sources of the *General estoria*— Gotifredus de Viterbo's *Pantheon*, Petrus Comestor's *Historia Scholastica*, and Lucas de Tuy's *Chronicon Mundi*—are equally laconic. The references to the liberal arts, physics, and metaphysics are Alfonso's own interpolations. These are the same disciplines found in the *Setenario*, with "física" reverting to its traditional meaning from

---

[75] I find only one reference to rhetoric in the *PCG*: "Et segund el latin nuestro et ell arte de la *rectorica*, que es .el saber de fablar apuestamientre, dictador tanto quiere dezir cuemo dezidor, que dize mucho et todauia bien et apuesto." *Primera crónica general de España*, I, 85b.42-46; cited by Antoinette Letsch-Lavanchy, "Eléments didactiques dans la *Crónica General*," *VR*, 15 (1956), ii, 237-238. The resemblance to the definition found in the *Setenario* is obvious.

[76] Flavius Josephus, *Historiarum Antiquitatis Iudaicae*, in *The Latin Josephus: I. Introduction and Text. The Antiquities: Books I-V*, ed. by Franz Blatt, Acta Jutlandica, Aarsskrift for Aarhus Universitet XXX 1, Humanistisk Serie 44 (Copenhagen: Universitetsforlaget i Aarhus; Ejnar Munksgaard, 1958), Bk. I, ch. ii, p. 132.10.

the modern meaning of "medicine." Alfonso seems to conceive of the liberal arts as an unbreakable unit. A reference to any of them in his sources elicits a reference to all of them in the *General estoria*. This same sort of automatic expansion occurs when he speaks of the longevity of the first generations of men. Such longevity was necessary in order for them to be able to learn "el saber dela astrologia, *e* dela geometria, *e* de todos los saberes liberales *e* delos otros . . . " (I, 37a.41-43). Josephus, his source, mentions only geometry and astrology.[77]

Alfonso discusses the further transmission of the arts under the reign of Nino, king of Babylonia. At that time Ham, son of Noah, was studying the seven liberal arts in Bactria and through them discovered "el arte magica—que es el saber del encantar . . . " (I,79a.49-50). Fearing another flood or the devastation of the world by fire, Ham "fizo quatorze pilares en su regno, los siete de ladriellos *e* los siete de cobre, *e* entallo en ellos por letras *e* por figuras aquellas VII artes liberales, una uez todas enlos siete pilares delos ladriellos *e* otra uez en los otros siete de cobre . . . " (I, 79b.12-18).[78]

Alfonso attributes this passage to Gotifredus de Viterbo and Paulus Orosius. Gotifredus in turn states that he is following Josephus, which cannot be true for this passage does not occur in Josephus, at least not in the Latin version attributed to Rufinus.[79] While Go-

---

[77] Ibid., Bk. I, ch. iii, p. 136.30.

[78] This same device is attributed also to Jubál and the descendants of Seth earlier in the work (I, 13b-14b, 20b-21b). Josephus, who refers only to the descendants of Seth, is the original source. Petrus Comestor, following an error of Hrabanus Maurus, attributes the device to Jubal, confusing him with Tubal, the inventor of music. Alfonso was familiar with all three texts and was apparently rather hard put to sort out the truth. He admits the possibility of the same device being used in two separate instances and attempts to resolve the problem by stating that on one set of pillars the sons of Cain wrote the mechanical arts and on the other those of Seth wrote the liberal arts. María Rosa Lida de Malkiel discusses this passage in detail in "Josefo en la *General estoria*," in *Hispanic Studies in Honour of I. González Llubera*, ed. by Frank Pierce (Oxford: The Dolphin Book Co., Ltd., 1959), pp. 179-180. For the historiographical origins of this problem cf. Cora E. Lutz, "Remigius' Ideas on the Origin of the Seven Liberal Arts," *MH*, 10 (1956), 32-49, esp. 47-49.

[79] Gotfridus Viterbiensis, *Pantheon*, in *Germanicorum Scriptorum*, ed. by Joannes Pistorius (Ratisbon: Sumptibus Joannis Conradi Peezii, 1726), Vol. II, pars

tifredus does provide the bare bones of this narration, most of the details about the fourteen pillars come from Petrus Comestor.[80] Orosius is responsible only for the mention of the arts of magic.[81]

Alfonso's biggest problem with regard to the origin of the liberal arts is explaining their transference to Egypt and thence to Greece. He does this by stating that all the descendants of the line of Shem, son of Noah, were acquainted with the arts. Thare, father of Abraham, "trabaiaua delos saberes del quadriuio, *e* sobre todo del saber delas estrellas . . . Entre todas las otras tierras, los de Caldea se trabaiauan del saber delas estrellas mas que otra yente a aquella sazon; e a Thare plogo dello mucho, *e* finco alli de morada con su conpanna" (I, 84a.35-48).[82] Presumably he taught the arts to Abraham, who then taught them to the Egyptians when famine in the land of Canaan forced him to migrate to Egypt:

> E maguer que Abraha*m* finco poco en aquella tierra, tanto ensennaua bien *e* aguda mientre, que de estonçes aprendieron los dalli las artes liberales *e* las sopieron por Abraa*m*, qui las decogio en Caldea o fueron primero, e las ensenno el en Egipto; *e* por esso dizen Josepho *e* mahestre Godofre que estos saberes primero fueron en Caldea que en otro logar, *e* dalli los ouieron los de Egipto, *e* de Egipto uinieron a los griegos, *e* delos griegos alos de Roma, *e* de Roma a Affrica o a Francia . . . .
> (I, 110b.51-111a.10)

Gotifredus de Viterbo is the primary source for this passage.[83]

The same motif of transference of the arts occurs in the allegorical interpretation of the history of Jupiter and Io which Alfonso attributes to John of Garland and "el frayre" (I, 165a.32). Mercu-

---

ii, 88. This edition, which reprints that of Joannes Heroldus (Basel: Ex officina Iacobi Parci, 1559), gives an intermediate version of the text instead of the final one. G. Waitz prints the rubrics of both versions in his edition of the latter: *Monumenta Germaniae Historica, Scriptorum*, XXII, 107-113. Judging from these there is apparently no substantive difference between the two versions in the parts that interest us.

[80] *Historia Scholastica*, ed. by Migne, *PL*, vol. 198, col. 1090.

[81] Pauli Orosii *Historiarum Adversum Paganos Libri VII*, ed. by Carolus Zangemeister (Leipzig: In aedibus B. G. Teubneri, 1889), p. 17.14-15.

[82] The circumstantial detail of this passage is found in none of Alfonso's sources: Josephus, Gotifredus de Viterbo, Lucas de Tuy, Petrus Comestor, Paulus Orosius.

[83] *Pantheon*, pars iv, 92.

ry charms Argus, Io's guard, with a pipe of seven reeds taken from the banks of the river Ledon in Greece. These reeds represent the seven liberal arts, supposedly taught on the banks of the same river to philosophers from all parts of Greece.[84] Alfonso hastens to point out that the liberal arts did have their beginning in Caldea and went from there to Egypt and finally to Greece, as he had stated previously, but that "en Grecia fueron apurados *e* acabados *e* puestos en certedumbre . . . " (I, 165b.27-29).

The perfecters of the liberal arts in Greece were Jupiter and his children Minerva and Mercury. Alfonso seizes upon Gotifredus de Viterbo's statement that it is "Juppiter ex patre Saturno natus Athenis, / A quo quadrivii, triviique scientia venit" as motive for a complete discussion of the liberal arts.[85] María Rosa Lida de Malkiel rather unjustly sees the *Pantheon* as the source of the "larga serie de noticias sobre los estudios del rey Júpiter en Atenas . . . ." She states that "mentira parece que se pudiera tomar en serio a semejante escritor . . . ."[86] Had she been aware of the existence of the *Germanicorum Scriptorum* edition of the *Pantheon*, seen what Gotifredus actually says, and noted the enormous expansion for which Alfonso is responsible, she would doubtless have modified her views.[87]

Gotifredus supplies little more than the excuse for the passage. Alfonso then adds a circumstantial exposition of the arts on the basis of information taken from some other source. This is standard technique in the *General estoria*. The work is a synthesis of the Bible, Josephus, Petrus Comestor, and Gotifredus de Viterbo for biblical history,[88] and of the last two for the correlation of biblical and

---

[84] This particular interpretation of the story, however, is not found in the *Integumenta Ovidii*; cf. Giovanni de Garlandi, *Integumenta Ovidii*, ed. by Fausto Ghisalberti, Testi e Documenti Inediti o Rari, 2 (Messina-Milan: Casa editrice Giuseppe Principato, 1933), p. 43. María Rosa Lida de Malkiel suggests that Alfonso might have used a gloss to the *Metamorphoses* based on John of Garland as well as on the unidentified "frayre": "La *General estoria*," p. 115.

[85] *Pantheon*, pars iv, 105.

[86] "La *General estoria*," p. 121.

[87] That Mrs. Malkiel was not acquainted with this ed. is evident from her remarks in ibid., p. 137n.

[88] Lida de Malkiel, "Josefo en la *General estoria*," p. 166.

secular history. Alfonso introduces information about secular matters at the points indicated by Petrus Comestor or Gotifredus, but usually takes that information from other, more detailed sources. Mrs. Malkiel describes this technique quite accurately in saying that for "puntos secundarios de la narración la fuente elegida es, sencillamente, la más extensa de que dispone en cada caso la cámara regia . . . ."[89]

The origin of the king's information on the schools of Athens and the subjects taught there remains unknown. The passage contains certain clues which are tantalizing in their vagueness. After describing the construction of the city of Athens and the seven-doored palace in its center which housed the schools, Alfonso says: "Et alli fueron primera mientre las escuelas delos saberes de Grecia, dond uino alos latinos despues el saber que ouieron, assi como uiene ell arroyo dela fuente alos quil an mester; *e* esto affirman Donat, *e* Precian, *e* Remigio *e* otros con ellos que fablauan desta razon" (I, 193a. 41-47). A little farther on the king explains why the liberal arts are so named:

. . . *e* llamauan liberales a aquellas siete artes et non alos otros saberes, segund departe Ramiro sobrel Donat, *e* otros con el por estas dos razones: la una por que non las auie a oyr si non ombre libre que non fuesse sieruo, nin om*n*e que uisquiesse por mester; la otra por que aquellos quelas oyen que auien aseer libres de todo cuydado *e* de toda premia queles otre fiziesse, ca tod esto a mester qui aprende pora bien aprender. (I, 193b.10-21)

These source references are puzzling. Donatus and Priscian were both known primarily for their grammatical works in the Middle Ages. None of these works is concerned with the liberal arts, except peripherally. Remigius of Auxerre wrote extensive commentaries on Donatus' *Ars Minor, Ars Maior,* and *Barbarismus* (the last part of the *Ars Maior*), on Priscian's *Partitiones XII Versuum Aeneidos* and *Institutio de Nomine, Pronomine, et Verbo,* and on Martianus Capella's *De Nuptiis Philologiae et Mercurii.*[90] "Ramiro sobrel Donat" is a reference to one of Remigius' commentaries on Donatus,

---

[89] "La *General estoria,*" p. 112.

[90] Remigii Autissiodorensis *Commentum in Martianum Capellam,* ed. by Cora E. Lutz, 2 vols. (Leiden: E. J. Brill, 1962-1965), p. 12.

as Solalinde has pointed out.⁹¹ None of Remigius' Donatus commentaries, however, mentions the origins of the liberal arts or the meaning of the term.⁹² The commentary on the *De Nuptiis* of Martianus Capella would seem a bit more promising, but it says nothing about the origins of the liberal arts.

The three specific reasons given to justify the name of the liberal arts offer a little more to go on. The first two—that only a free man can learn them and that a man who earns his living by a "mester" cannot—merely rephrase the traditional explanation Seneca gives in his *Epistolae Morales*.⁹³ The third—that only those who are free of all care can learn them, since only they have the concentration necessary to learn them well—is more modern, being derived ultimately from Remigius' commentary on Martianus Capella: "Quae idcirco liberales dicuntur quia liberaliter fruge veritatis animam pascunt vel quod liberam et expeditam mentem a tumultibus saeculi requirunt."⁹⁴ Similar definitions, evidently based on this passage from Remigius, appear in two of the writers of the school of Chartres, Hugh of St. Victor and John of Salisbury.⁹⁵

---

⁹¹ Antonio G. Solalinde, "Fuentes de la *General estoria* de Alfonso el Sabio," *RFE*, 21 (1934), 14-15. Solalinde seems to consider that the commentary in question is Remigii Autissiodorensis *In Artem Donati Minorem Commentum*, ed. by W. Fox, Bibliotheca Scriptorum Graecorum et Romanorum Teubneriana (Leipzig: In aedibus B. G. Teubneri, 1902). But there is nothing remotely resembling the Spanish text in this work.

⁹² The only reference to the arts occurs in Remigius' commentary on the origin of letters, where he repeats the story of their preservation by Ham, son of Noah, on pillars of brick and marble: *Commentum Einsidlense in Donati "Artem Maiorem,"* ed. by Hermann Hagen, in *Grammatici Latini*, ed. by Heinrich Keil (Leipzig: In aedibus B. G. Teubneri, 1870) VIII, 221. R[amón] Fernández Pousa states, in *Los manuscritos gramaticales de la Biblioteca Nacional* (Madrid, 1947), pp. 29-30, that Madrid's Biblioteca Nacional contains a thirteenth-century manuscript (MS. 7800 [*olim* V. 225]) of a work called *Remigius super Donatum* followed by St. Isidore's *Etymologiae*. It should be checked for possible parallels to the *General estoria*.

⁹³ "Quare liberalia studia dicta sint vides: quia homine libero digna sunt," 88.1; cited by Lutz, "Remigius' Ideas on the Classification," p. 77.

⁹⁴ Ibid.

⁹⁵ Hugh of St. Victor, *Didascalicon*, 2.20: "Sicut aliae septem liberales appellatae sunt, vel quia liberos, id est, expeditos et exercitatos animos requirunt, quia

After this presentation of the teaching of the liberal arts in Athens in general and of Jupiter's studies in particular, Alfonso explains the relationships between the trivium and the quadrivium. He then gives short definitions of each of the arts as well as of the three *saberes* that are above the seven liberal arts.

The king sets forth the reasons for the division of the liberal arts into the trivium and the quadrivium as follows:

E las tres primeras destas siete artes son el triuio, que quiere dezir tanto como tres uias o carreras que muestran all omne yr a una cosa, et esta es saber se razonar cumplida mientre. Et las otras quatro postrimeras son el quadruuio, que quiere dezir tanto como quatro carreras que ensennan connoscer complida mientre, saber yr a una cosa cierta, e esta es las quantias delas cosas, assi como mostraremos adelante. (I, 193b.46-194a.3)

In another passage Alfonso explains this categorization more fully. The trivium includes the arts which teach man the names of things and how to reason properly; the quadrivium, those which teach him knowledge of the things themselves. Even though things—the subject of the quadrivium—came before the names of things—the subject of the trivium—the arts of the trivium must be taught before the arts of the quadrivium. Only by means of the former can the latter be understood.[96] This precedence of the arts of language is

---

subtiliter de rerum causis disputant . . . "; John of Salisbury, *Metalogicon*, 1.12: "Sic et liberales dicte sunt ad hoc quod querunt hominis libertatem, ut curis liber sapientie vacet, et sepissime liberant a curis his, quarum participium sapientia non admittit"; cited by Lutz, ibid., pp. 83, 85.

[96] " . . . e fazen all omne estos tres saberes bien razonado, e uiene ell omne por ellas meior a entender las otras quatro carreras aque llaman el quadruuio.

"E las quatro son todas de entendimiento e de demostramiento fecho por prueua, onde deuien yr primeras en la orden. Mas por que se non podien entender sin estas tres primeras que auemos dichas, pusieron los sabios a estas tres primero que aquellas quatro, ca maguer que todas estas quatro artes del quadruuio fablan delas cosas por las quantias dellas, assi como diremos, e las tres del triuio son delas uozes e delos nombres delas cosas, e las cosas fueron ante que las uozes e quelos nombres dellas natural mientre. Pero por quelas cosas non se pueden ensennar nin aprender departida mientre si non por las uozes et por los nombres que an, maguer que segund la natura estas quatro deurien yr primeras et aquellas tres postrimeras como mostramos, los sabios por la razon dicha pusieron primeras las

another reminiscence of the school of Chartres. We find similar statements in Gundisalvus and Hugh of St. Victor.[97]

After a description of the arts of the quadrivium, which includes the well-known passage on the invention of the art of music by the Greeks, Alfonso again attempts to show the relationship between the trivium and the quadrivium: "Et las primeras tres artes, que auemos dicho que llaman triuio, son en estas quatro que dizen quadruuio, como en las cerraias las llaues que las abren, *e* abren estas del triuio todos los otros saberes por quelos puedan los omnes entender meior" (I, 196b.22-28). The use of the metaphor links the passage stylistically to one in the *Segunda parte* of the *General estoria* taken from an unknown *Summa de la Rectorica*.[98]

Alfonso ends his remarks on the arts with references to the "saberes que son sobre las vii artes liberales" (I, 196b.30-31). He mentions "methafisica" and "ethica" as the first and third of these disciplines and calls the second the knowledge "delas naturas por connoscer todas las cosas que an cuerpos ... " (I, 196b.44-46). He is evidently referring to *fisica*. These are the same disciplines, with the addition of "ethica," which are mentioned in the *Setenario* and earlier in the *General estoria*.[99]

---

tres artes del triuio *e* postrimeras las quatro del quadruuio; ca por las tres del triuio se dizen los nombres alas cosas, *e* estas fazen al om*n*e bien razonado, *e* por las quatro del quadruuio se muestran las naturas delas cosas, *e* estas quatro fazen sabio elle om*n*e; pues aprendet por aqui que el triuio faze razonado ell om*n*e y el quadruuio sabio" (I, 194a.33-b.11).

[97] "Ceterae prius repertae fuerant, sed necesse fuit logicam quoque inveniri, quoniam nemo de rebus convenienter disserere potest, nisi prius recte et veraciter loquendi rationem agnoverit ...." Hugonis de Sancto Victore *Didascalicon de Studio Legendi*, ed. by Charles Henry Buttimer, The Catholic University of America Studies in Medieval and Renaissance Latin, 10 (Washington, D.C.: The Catholic University Press, 1939), 19.2-4; " ... quare logica naturaliter precedit omnes partes philosophie theorice et est necessaria illis ad acquirendum uerum. Set quia logica uerum non nisi proposicione significat, omnis uero proposicio ex terminis constat, set terminos formando et componendo sibi sciencia grammatice preparat: ideo grammatica logicam et omnes alias sciencias tempore precedit ...." Dominicus Gundisalvus, *De Divisione Philosophiae*, p. 18.

[98] See below, p. 89.

[99] See above, pp. 68, 77.

At various points in his narration Alfonso calls Minerva—Pallas Athena—and Mercury children of Jupiter. Allusions to their knowledge of the quadrivium and trivium inevitably accompany their names, almost like epithets. For Alfonso that knowledge is part of their very nature, and he mentions it even where there is no such allusion in his sources. Thus, when first speaking of Athena, Alfonso explains the sciences of which she is mistress: "*E* era otrossi muy sabia *e* muy maestra enel triuio *e* enel quadriuio—, que son las siete artes liberales—, *e* sobre todo en el quadriuio, *e* en naturas . . ." (I, 71b.6-10). Another version of Minerva's birth says that "esta duenna sopo los saberes liberales, *e* fallo y muchas cosas que emendo, *e* dixo, *e* ensenno *e* ennadio; *e* llamaron la otrossi deessa del triuio, *e* del quadriuio *e* delas naturas . . . " (I, 186a.53-b.4).[100] Citing the children of Jupiter in another context, Psllas is called "deesa de los quatro saberes del quadruuio . . . ."[101]

In the same passage Mercury is called "dios de los tres saberes del triuio . . . " (II, 88a.11-12). There are at least five other references to Mercury's knowledge of the trivium.[102] In one of these Alfonso links Mercury to Hermes Trismegistus and the Egyptian origin of the liberal arts by means of the trivium: "Del philosopho Tat que ouo nombre Hermes, *e* fue fijo del otro Hermes Trimegisto, *e* fue Mercurio" (II, 34b.18-20); " . . . et dixieron le por ende este nombre Trimegisto, fascas maestro de tres saberes . . . " (II, 35a. 8-10). The immediate source of this identification is unknown. Among the classical and early Christian writers the identity of Mercury and Thoth is found in Cicero, Servius, and Lactantius.[103] Isidore links Mercury, Hermes, and Egypt in the section of the *Ety-*

---

[100] The reference to the liberal arts occurs in neither Lucas de Tuy, *Chronicon Mundi*, ed. Schottus, p. 10, nor in Gotifredus de Viterbo, *Pantheon*, pars iv, 99-100.

[101] Alfonso el Sabio, *General estoria. Segunda parte*, ed. by Antonio G. Solalinde, Lloyd A. Kasten, and Victor R. B. Oelschläger, Consejo Superior de Investigaciones Científicas, Instituto "Miguel de Cervantes" (Madrid: Imp. S. Aguirre Torre, 1957), I, 88a.14-15. Subsequent references, preceded by the Roman numeral II, are incorporated into the text.

[102] Besides the passages discussed in the text, cf. I, 90a.36-39 and I, 91b.24-32.

[103] Lutz, "Remigius' Ideas on the Origin," p. 35.

mologiae that deals with the origin of law.[104] The Arabic Hermetic tradition was also known in thirteenth-century Spain.[105]

Alfonso, too, calls Mercury god of the trivium and identifies the latter as "los tres saberes que ensennan all omne fablar *e* seer bien razonado . . ." (II, 213a.5-7). This identification of Mercury with eloquence is of remote origin, but the proximate source for most of the Middle Ages was Martianus Capella, especially as interpreted by Remigius of Auxerre. In the *De Nuptiis Mercurii et Philologiae* Mercury represents eloquence and Philologia knowledge. Miss Lutz remarks that "this must have been a common bit of mythological lore" in Martianus' time.[106] By the thirteenth century it was a commonplace. The union symbolized by the marriage of Mercury and Philologia (eloquence and wisdom) is of ancient origin, also, appearing already in a statement in Cicero's *De Inventione*.[107]

By the high Middle Ages the following interrelationship of these ideas had occurred: Mercury was linked to eloquence and the trivium, Philologia to wisdom and the quadrivium. It was perhaps inevitable that the ordering of these ideas into three parallel pairs— trivium and quadrivium, Mercury and Philologia, eloquence and wisdom—should have taken place.

We can trace the stages of this ordering in some detail. The relationship eloquence-trivium and wisdom-quadrivium is described "in a gloss of Lanfranc on I Cor. 2. 1. ' *Veni non in sublimitate sermonis aut sapientiae.* Sublimitatem sermonis vocat logicam, quia ipsa toda de artificiosa oratione est. Sapientiam vocat quadrivium et maxime libros Platonicos, speciem nomine genera designans.' PL,

---

[104] V. i. 2: "Mercurius Trimegistus primus leges Aegyptiis tradidit"; cited by Lutz, ibid.

[105] Cf. Henry and Renée Kahane and Angelina Pietrangeli, "*Picatrix* and the Talismans," *RPh*, 19 (1966), 574-593, for a discussion of this tradition in Spain with particular reference to the Alfonsine lapidaries.

[106] "Remigius' Ideas on the Origin," p. 35.

[107] "Ac me quidem diu cogitantem ratio ipsa in hanc potissimum sententiam ducit, ut existimem sapientiam sine eloquentia parum prodesse civitatibus, eloquentiam vero sine sapientia nimium obesse plerumque, prodesse nunquam." Ed. by Hubbell, I. i. 1.

150, col. 161 B."[108] William of Conches (ca. 1080-ca. 1154) elabo-rates this distinction in his *In Boetium*, a commentary on the *De Consolatione Philosophiae*.[109] Then, in his *Philosophia Mundi*, Wil-liam links the eloquence and wisdom of Cicero with the marriage of Mercury and Philologia of Martianus Capella.[110]

Thus by the late twelfth century the identification of Mercury with eloquence and the trivium on the one hand and of Philologia with wisdom and the quadrivium on the other hand is well known to students of the school of Chartres. Hugh of St. Victor refers to the liberal arts as the "septem ancillae quas Mercurius a Philologia in dotem accepit, quia nimirum eloquentiae, cui iuncta fuerit sa-pientia, omnis humana actio servit . . . ."[111] In the *De Septem Sep-tenis* attributed to John of Salisbury we find the following: "Sic igitur animus erudientis per has septem trivii et quadrivii vias elo-quentiam et sapientiam adipiscitur."[112] And a recent interpretation of John's *Metalogicon* sees the union of wisdom and eloquence as the key to the meaning of the work.[113]

Thierry of Chartres, in the introduction to his *Heptateuchon*, states that he has collected the most authoritative treatises on the se-ven liberal arts, "nam, cum sint duo precipua phylosophandi instru-menta, intellectum autem quadruvium illuminet, eius vero interpre-

---

[108] Hunt, "The Introduction to the 'Artes'," p. 92n.

[109] "Scientie due sunt species, sapientia et eloquentia, et est sapientia vera cog-nitio rerum, eloquentia est scientia proferendi cognita cum ornatu verborum et sententiarum, et dicuntur species scientie, quia in istis duobus est omnis scientia: in cognoscenda res et ornate proferendo cognita. Eloquentia tres sunt partes, sci-licet grammatica, rhetorica, dialectica"; cited by Tullio Gregory, *Anima Mundi: La filosofia di Guglielmo de Conches e la scuola di Chartres* (Florence: G. C. San-soni, 1955), pp. 272-273.

[110] "Quoniam, ut Tullius in prologo Rethoricorum, eloquentia sine sapientia no-cet, sapientia vero sine eloquentia, etsi parum, tamen aliquid, cum eloquentia au-tem maxime prodest, errant qui, postposita proficiente et non nocenti, adhaerent nocenti et non proficienti. Id namque agere est Mercurii et Philologiae coniugium, tanta cura virtutis et Apollinis quaesitum, omnium conventu deorum approba-tum, solvere"; cited by Gregory, *Anima Mundi*, p. 253.

[111] *Didascalicon*, ed. by Buttimer, p. 39.

[112] Migne, *PL*, vol. 199, col. 949.

[113] Cf. Brian Patrick Handley, "Wisdom and Eloquence: A New Interpretation of the *Metalogicon* of John of Salisbury" (unpubl. diss., Yale University, 1966).

tationem elegantem rationabilem ornatam trivium subministret, manifestum est eptatheucon totius phylosophye unicum ac singulare esse instrumentum."[114] Thierry returns to the problem of the relationship of wisdom and eloquence in his *Commentarium in Ciceronis "De Inventione,"* which has already been discussed in relation to Dominicus Gundisalvus.[115] In the introduction to the *De Divisione Philosophiae,* Gundisalvus treats the problem in much the same terms as William of Conches.[116]

For Tullio Gregory this relationship is "una delle maggiori caratteristiche della cultura di questa etá, che non fu semplicemente letteraria, ma volle congiungere trivio e quadrivio, la 'retorica' con la 'scienza' . . . ."[117] We need not belabor the point. The school of Chartres equated the trivium with eloquence, represented by Mercury, and the quadrivium with wisdom, represented by Philologia. As I noted previously, they considered the trivial arts as propaedeutic to the quadrivium. These are precisely the doctrines set forth in the *De Divisione Philosophiae* of Gundisalvus and a century later in the *General estoria.*

In the *General estoria* there is a further example touching on all these points, a quotation in Latin which Alfonso attributes to an unknown *Summa de la Rectorica.* This passage, on the trivium, occurs in the middle of the legend of Europa and the bull. The motive for its introduction is an allusion to Mercury, son of Jupiter,

[114] Cited by Gregory, *Anima Mundi,* p. 247. Unfortunately the *Heptateuchon* has never been completely edited; the work would undoubtedly prove to be a mine of information on the precepts of the school of Chartres with regard to the liberal arts.

[115] "Fragmentum Scholiastae Inediti ad Ciceronem De Invent. Rhet." ed. by W. H. D. Suringar in his *Historia Critica Scholiastarum Latinorum* (Leiden: Sumptibus S. et J. Luchtmannorum et J. C. Cyfveerii, 1834), part i, pp. 217-218, 227-231, 234, 247-248; cited by Gregory, *Anima Mundi,* p. 254.

[116] "Humana uero sciencia appelatur, que humanis racionibus adinuenta esse probatur et omnes artes que liberales dicuntur. Quarum alie ad eloquenciam, alie ad sapienciam pertinere noscuntur. Ad eloquenciam enim pertinent omnes que recte uel ornate loqui docent, ut grammatica, poetica, rethorica et leges humane. Ad sapienciam uero pertinent omnes, que animam hominis uel illuminant ad cognicionem ueritatis uel accendunt ad amorem bonitatis," p. 5.

[117] *Anima Mundi,* p. 251.

as agent for the latter in the abduction of Europa. Alfonso explains, again, that Mercury was the god of the trivium, gives a one-line explanation of each of the trivial arts, and, mentioning the *Summa*, calls the trivium "el razonamiento *e* el quadruuio el saber de las cosas" (II, 57a.14-15). This is the same formulation seen previously.

The king then states that Mercury was so wise in the trivium that the learned have ever since called these arts the "ministras mercuriales, que quieren seer tanto cuemo seruientes de Mercurio . . . " (II, 57a.19-20), and continues:

. . . pone el autor alli en aquella Summa de la Rectorica unas palabras muy buenas dell ensennamiento destos tres saberes del triuio, por so latin muy fermoso *e* muy apuesta mientre ordenado, et por que parescen muy bien aquellas palabras en el latin *e* dan muy bien ensennamiento del officio destos tres saberes, queremos uos los aqui dezir primero por aquel latin que see en el libro, et desi partir las por el lenguage de Castiella; et dizen assi:

cum ex coniugio sermonis *et* sapientie opus insolubile prodeatur, et utrumq*ue* alt*ero* comprobetur maxime indigere huic operi, gramatica prima omnium mercurialium ministrarum accomodat fundamentum, dialetica pariete erigit, rectorica totum edificium pingit et tectum siderium super ponit; prima *est* uia, secunda dux uie, tercia comes iocundus in uia; pri*m*a lingua balbucientem purgat, secunda rubiginem falsitatis elimat, tercia inde opus uariis celaturis informat; prima dat intelectum, secunda fidem, tercia persuasionem; prima docet nos recte loqui, secunda subtiliter *et* acute, tercia persuasibiliter *et* hornate. (II, 57a.21-b.16)

Mrs. Malkiel tries to make a case for the origin of this passage in a "verdadero manual de retórica según la rutina antigua y no de un *ars dictaminis* como pedían los nuevos tiempos . . . ," and suggests that the same work might be the source of the repeated references to the passage in Cicero's *De Inventione* (I. ii. 2) which treats of the civilizing influence of eloquence.[118] She bases her opinion on the "estilo muy adornado" and on the reminiscences of Martianus Capella ("ex coniugio sermonis *et* sapientie") and Publilius Syrus ("comes iocundus in uia": "comes facundus in uia pro uehiculo est").[119]

---

[118] References to this passage occur at I, 61b.24-28, 62a.5-39, 76a.50-b.15, 198b. 41-199a.4, 550b.42-51; cited in "La *General estoria*," p. 116.

[119] "La *General estoria*," p. 116; she might have mentioned another reminiscence of Martianus Capella as well: "gramatica prima omnium mercurialium ministrarum." "Mercurialium ministrarum" occurs at the beginning of Bk. III, on grammar, of the *De Nuptiis*, ed. by Dick, p. 82.10.

The only other critics who have mentioned this passage are Américo Castro and Luis López Santos. The former was unable to identify it; [120] the latter asserts that it is based on a "texto isidoriano sobre el Trivio y el Cuatrivio . . . ."[121]

We can dismiss the latter contention at once, for there is no passage remotely similar in the *Etymologiae*. Besides, the division between the trivium and the quadrivium gained currency only in the
eleventh century.[122] We cannot dismiss Mrs. Malkiel's arguments so
easily; but her identification of the *Summa* with the source of the
Ciceronian references loses much of its force if we consider that these
same references occur in the *Pantheon* of Gotifredus de Viterbo.
Alfonso might very well have been acquainted with Martianus Capella through the writings of the school of Chartres.[123] Given Alfonso's insistence that he is using a *Summa de la Rectorica*, Mrs. Malkiel's suggestion that the passage is from a "verdadero" manual
of rhetoric instead of from an *ars dictaminis* is perfectly plausible.
But since the passage explains *each* of the three arts of the trivium
metaphorically (which links it to the previous passage in which Alfonso describes the trivium as the key to the lock of the quadrivium)[124]
and then insists on the marriage of wisdom and eloquence, we should
probably conclude that the source was not a rhetorical treatise but

---

[120] *Glosarios latino-españoles de la edad media*, *RFE*, Añejo 22 (Madrid: Revista de Filología Española, 1936), p. xiii n.

[121] "Isidoro en la literatura medieval castellana," in *Isidoriana* (*Colección de
estudios sobre Isidoro de Sevilla*), ed. by Manuel C. Díaz y Díaz (León: Centro de
Estudios "San Isidoro," 1961), p. 429.

[122] Lutz, "Remigius' Ideas on the Classification," p. 75.

[123] For the influence of Martianus Capella on the school of Chartres, particularly through the commentaries of Remigius of Auxerre, cf. Lutz, "Remigius'
Ideas on the Classification," pp. 84-86.

[124] The metaphor of the edifice of the spirit was common in medieval literature.
In the twelfth century Petrus Cantor uses it in his *Verbum Abbreviatum*: "Lec-
tio autem est quasi fundamentum, et substratorium sequentium; quia per eam
caeterae utilitates comparantur. Disputatio quasi paries est in hoc exercitio et
aedificio; quia nihil plene intelligitur, fideliterve praedicatur, nisi prius dente
disputationis frangatur. Praedicatio vero, cui subserviunt priora, quasi tectum
est tegens fideles ab aestu, et a turbine vitiorum." Ed. by Migne, *PL*, vol. 205,
col. 25. Cf. Harry Caplan, "Classical Rhetoric and the Medieval Theory of Preaching," *CPh*, 28 (1933), 88. I am indebted to Professor Caplan for this reference.

a general one on all the liberal arts. None of the strictly rhetorical treatises, classical or medieval, goes into the other arts in this detail.

This treatise is still undiscovered. We can make certain broad statements about it, however. In the first place, it was probably the source of Alfonso's other comments on the liberal arts in the *General estoria* and possibly in the *Setenario*. Second, it was probably written by a member of the school of Chartres or by a person greatly influenced by that school. If the former, a likely candidate would be Thierry of Chartres himself, of whose interest in the liberal arts the *Heptateuchon* is ample evidence.[125] If the latter, it would not be surprising if he were Spanish. The use of metaphor, the fivefold repetition of the same basic ideas, the syntactical simplicity of the passage, and its short periods all recall the style of St. Isidore's *Synonyma* and of St. Ildefonsus' *De Virginitate Sanctae Mariae*.

In contrast to the information we can extract from Alfonso's comments on the liberal arts as a whole, what he says about rhetoric by itself tells us very little. The longest description of rhetoric in the *General estoria* occurs in the section on the studies of Jupiter in Athens:

La rectorica otrossi es art pora affermosar la razon *e* mostrar la en tal manera, que-la faga tener por uerdadera *e* por cierta alos que la oyeren, de guisa que sea creyda. Et por ende ouo nombre rectorica, que quiere mostrar tanto como razonamiento fecho por palabras apuestas *e* fermosas *e* bien ordenadas. (I, 194a.22-29)

Alfonso stresses the stylistic aspect and the effect on the audience. Rhetoric takes an idea and ornaments it in such a manner that those who hear it will consider it true and thus believe it. We find the same emphasis on stylistic embellishment in Alfonso's references to rhetoric in the *Setenario*.[126]

The brevity of his remarks need not surprise us. In both the *Setenario* and the *General estoria* Alfonso is interested in the content of the liberal arts only secondarily. In the former work it is the struc-

---

[125] One point of difference between the Alfonsine text and the writers of the school of Chartres is the use of "sermo" in the former as opposed to the almost exclusive use of "eloquentia" by the latter.

[126] See above, p. 69.

ture that is important: there are *seven* liberal arts. The actual doctrines Alfonso sets forth are rather arbitrarily arranged to conform
to the sevenfold scheme of the work. In the *General estoria* Alfonso is concerned primarily with the origin and development of the
liberal arts, their historical *razón de ser*. Therefore his explanations
aim only at explaining the basic ideas of the liberal arts. This concern with the origin and development of the arts explains why Alfonso emphasizes their internal relationships and the various figures, biblical, secular, and mythological, associated with them.

All this throws unsuspected light upon the intellectual resources
and relationships of Alfonsine Spain. Most striking, of course, is
the strong and continuing relationship between Spain and the members of the school of Chartres in the twelfth century and the doctrines of that school in the thirteenth. The channels of that relationship are hard to establish. In the twelfth century there is evidence of direct, two-way communication between Toledo and Chartres and possibly of contact with Compostela as well. The mutual
scientific interests of the schools of Chartres and Toledo suffice to
account for this interchange. In Spain the arts of the trivium ben-
efited as an almost unintended side effect from the more general
interest in the problem of classifying all human knowledge in a general scheme.

It is more difficult to account for the continuing influence of the
ideas of the school of Chartres in the latter half of the thirteenth
century, a hundred years and more removed from the apogee of that
school. We have no certain knowledge of the vehicles of transmission. Alfonso may have had firsthand knowledge of specific texts
of the school of Chartres. One argument in favor of direct knowledge is the heavy reliance that Alfonso places on other non-Spanish
texts of the twelfth century, such as Petrus Comestor's *Historia
Scholastica* and Gotifredus de Viterbo's *Pantheon*. We cannot dismiss the possibility of intermediary sources, although at this point
we cannot say what these sources might have been. Scholars have
yet to plunge very deeply into the tangled thickets of thirteenth-
century discussions of the liberal arts.

Unfortunately, none of the above tells us very much about the
rhetorical doctrines actually professed by contemporary Spanish teach-

ers or followed by contemporary Spanish authors. Vernacular descriptions in the thirteenth century are infuriatingly laconic. Later works in either Latin or Spanish are even less informative, with the possible exception of the translation of Brunetto Latini's *Livres dou Trésor*. However, it is impossible to form an adequate opinion of this work in the absence of an edition of it. The rhetorical portions of the original are based on the *De Inventione* instead of on the contemporary rhetorical *artes*, in keeping with the classical tradition of rhetoric as one of the sciences of civil administration.

Fourteenth-century works tell us even less. We might suppose that don Juan Manuel would touch upon formal education in his didactic works, but he does not mention it in the *Libro de los estados*, in the *Libro enfenido*, or in the *Libro del cavallero et del escudero*. His esthetic preoccupations do not seem to have extended beyond the problems of verse composition, which he treats in his *Reglas de cómo se debe trovar*, now lost.[128]

In the middle of the fourteenth century (ca. 1345), Fr. Juan García de Castrojeriz translated and glossed Giles of Rome's *De Regimine Principum*, which, in the second part of Book II, considers the upbringing of the young prince. Chapter eight discusses "Cuántas son las sciencias que deven aprender los fijos de los nobles e mayor-

---

[127] There is no good study of Brunetto Latini's relationship with Spain or of the circumstances of the Spanish translation of the *Livres*. We know that Brunetto served as Florentine ambassador to Alfonso X before 1260. Sarton speculates that his knowledge of Arabic science was acquired in Toledo and Seville: *Introduction to the History of Science*, Vol. II, part ii, p. 927. The *Livres* was apparently translated at the order of Sancho IV by Alfonso de Paredes and Pero Gómez, respectively physician and scribe to the king. Cf. Menéndez y Pelayo, *Ideas estéticas*, I, 445. The translation enjoyed a certain amount of popularity; nine manuscripts, two of them prior to the fifteenth century, are still extant. When López Estrada's announced edition appears, we shall be in a better position to evaluate the work.

[128] But in the *Libro de los estados* we find the following reference to his own *Conde Lucanor*: "Este libro fizo don Johan, en manera de fabliella. . . . es muy buen libro et muy aprovechoso, et todas las razones que en él se contienen son dichas por muy buenas palabras et por los muy [sic] fermosos latines que yo nunca oí decir en libro que fuese fecho en romance, et poniendo declaradamente complida la razón que quiere decir, pónelo con las menos palabras que pueden seer"; cited by Valbuena Prat, I, 167-168.

mente los fijos de los reyes e de los príncipes." These are the seven liberal arts, plus "filosofía moral," "metafísica," "teología," "ciencias morales," and other less important sciences like "perspectiva," "física," and "derecho civil e canónico."[129] Of rhetoric Giles says, "La Retórica fue fallada, según que dice ese mismo filósofo, para facer razones gruesas e palabras cuales son menester en las sciencias morales especulativas. Así la Retórica muestra facer razones sotiles en las sciencias prácticas, que son en las obras de los ommes, e por eso llamaba él a la Retórica Lógica gruesa."[130] Fray Juan glosses this as follows: "Lo tercero conviene a los nobles aprender la Retórica, que les muestra ser compuestos en sus razones, ca toda la Retórica es del componimiento e del descomponimiento de las razones, ca es Lógica gruesa, que muestra razonar gruesamente."[131] The "filósofo" mentioned in the translation is al-Fārābī, although

---

[129] *Glosa castellana al* Regimiento de príncipes *de Egidio Romano*, ed. by Juan Beneyto Pérez, Biblioteca Española de Escritores Políticos, 3 vols. (Madrid: Instituto de Estudios Políticos, 1947), II, 153-154. The only edition of the complete work was printed in Seville, 1494, by Meynardo Ungut and Stanislao Polono at the expense of Conrrado Aleman and Melchior Gurrizo (ibid., I, xxv). The translation was done at the order of Bernabe, bishop of Osma (1331-1351), who was named Canciller Mayor of the *infante* don Pedro in 1344 (ibid., I, xxvi-xxvii). "E fizolo trasladar de latyn en romance Don Bernabe, obispo de Osma . . . ." Mario Schiff, *La bibliothèque du Marquis de Santillana*, Bibliothèque de l'École des Hautes Études, Sciences Historiques et Philologiques, 153 (Paris: Librairie Emile Bouillon, Éditeur, 1905), p. 210.

[130] *Glosa castellana*, II, 153-154. The translation follows the original quite closely, although compressing considerably, even to the curious use of the word "gruesa": "Tertia scientia liberalis dicitur esse Rhetorica. Est autem Rhetorica, vt innuit Philosophus in Rhetoricis suis, quasi quaedam grossa dialectica. Nam sicut fiendae sunt rationes subtiles in scientiis naturalibus *et* in aliis scientiis speculabilibus, sic fiendae sunt rationes grossae in scientiis moralibus, quae tractant de agibilibus. Quare sicut necessaria fuit dialectica, quae docet modum arguendi subtilem *et* violentiorem: sic necessaria fuit rhetorica, quae est quaedam grossa dialectica docens modum arguendi grossum *et* figuralem. Haec autem necessaria est filiis liberorum *et* nobilium, *et* maxime Regum, *et* Principum: quia horum est conuersari inter gentes *et* dominari populo, qui non potest percipere nisi rationes grossas *et* figurales." Aegidii Colvmnae Romani *De Regimine Principum Lib. III* (Rome: Apud Bartholomeum Zannettum, 1607; repr. Darmstadt: Scientia Verlag Aalen, 1967), p. 307.

[131] *Glosa castellana*, II, 158.

the name appears only in the Latin text. The doctrines we encounter have virtually nothing to do with rhetoric as such. It is purely an instrumental science necessary for work in the "sciencias morales especulativas."

In both the original and the glosses the *Rhetorica* of Aristotle is cited frequently, followed with less frequency by the *Rhetorica ad C. Herennium* and Cicero's *De Inventione*. These works are used merely as sources of apothegms, exempla, or information about the psychological characteristics of people of various ages and conditions.[132] The *De Regimine Principum* contains no rhetorical material.

---

[132] The *Rhetorica* of Aristotle is cited in the glosses 16 times; the *Rhetorica ad C. Herennium*, 7; and the *De Inventione*, 3. Aristotle is cited in the *Glosa castellana* in I, 246, 292, 297, 302, 306, 311, 317, 322; II, 63, 102, 108-109, 146, 217, 223; and III, 15, 177. The *Ad Herennium* is cited in I, 83, 123, 137-138, 164, 226, 261; and III, 212. The *De Inventione* occurs in I, 124; II, 195; III, 173. Judging by the fact that Giles wrote an extensive commentary on the William of Moerbeke translation of the *Rhetorica*, we may assume that he cites the same version in the *De Reg. Princ.* See James Jerome Murphy, "The Scholastic Condemnation of Rhetoric in the Commentary of Giles of Rome on the Rhetoric of Aristotle," in *Arts libéraux et philosophie au moyen âge: Actes du Quatrième Congrès International de Philosophie Médiévale* (Montreal-Paris: Institut d'Études Médiévales-Librairie Philosophique J. Vrin, 1969), pp. 833-841. During the thirteenth and fourteenth centuries the *Rhetorica* was more often considered a moral treatise than a rhetorical one. See McKeon, "Rhetoric in the Middle Ages," p. 29; James Jerome Murphy, "Aristotle's *Rhetoric* in the Middle Ages," *QJS*, 52 (1966), 109-115.

Many of the Ciceronian passages occur along with other citations of Macrobius, Valerius Maximus, Horace, Seneca, and St. Augustine in discussions of specific moral or psychological qualities. They might all have been taken from a *florilegium* or one of the numerous *Summae de Vitiis et Virtutibus*. All the references to Aristotle's *Rhetorica*, the *Ad Herennium*, and the *De Inventione* found in Pascual de Gayango's edition of the *Castigos e documentos del rey don Sancho*, in *Escritores en prosa anteriores al siglo XV*, BAE, 51 (Madrid: Rivadeneyra, 1860; repr. saepe), occur in the forty extra chapters taken bodily from the translation and gloss of the *De Regimine Principum* and interpolated into a late MS of the *Castigos*. Cf. *Castigos*, ch. 45 (ed. cit., p. 171), and *De Reg. Princ.*, I.ii.13 (*Glosa castellana*, I, 123-24); *Castigos*, ch. 61 (p. 188), and *De Reg. Princ.* I.iii.2 (I, 246); and *Castigos*, ch. 69-75 (pp. 197-205), and *De Reg. Princ.* I.iv.1-7 (I, 292-322). For other parallels see R[aymond] Foulché-Delbosc, "Les *Castigos e documentos* de Sanche IV," *RHi*, 15 (1906), 340-371; and Agapito Rey, ed., *Castigos e documentos para bien vivir ordenados por el rey don Sancho IV*, Indiana University Publications, Humanities Series No. 24 (Bloomington, Ind.: Indiana University, 1952), p. 18.

Neither in the chronicles based on the *Primera crónica general*
nor in those originally written in the fourteenth century, such as
the *Crónica de Alfonso XI* and the various chronicles of Pero López de Ayala, do we find references to any of the rhetorical arts.
Nor are there references in any poetic work, even in that of such a
consummate artist as Juan Ruiz.[133]

To sum up, none of the evidence so far suggests that rhetoric was
studied as an independent discipline in medieval Spain. The references in the Latin works, all extremely brief, occur in the context
of the liberal arts as a whole and seem to be derived from the doctrines of the school of Chartres. The even scantier references in the
vernacular works, with the exception of the *Siete partidas*, fall within the same tradition. The *Partidas* draw upon technical treatises of *ars dictaminis* and *ars notariae*, probably Italian in origin (see
next chapter).

There seems to have been a radical division between the two traditions. Alfonso the Learned, for example, draws almost no con-
nection between the scanty fragments of rhetorical doctrine set forth
in the *Setenario* and the *General estoria* and the much more detailed technical explanations in the *Siete partidas*. In the former he

---

[133] The *Libro de buen amor* does contain one curious echo of the distinction between rhetoric and dialectic taken by Varro from Zeno and repeated by Cassiodorus and St. Isidore. In the disputation between the Greek and the Roman, carried out by means of signs, the following passage occurs: "levantóse el griego, ten-
dió la palma llana, / ë assentóse luego con su memoria sana, / levantóse el vellaco,
con fantasía vana, / mostró puño cerrado: de porfía ha gana." Ed. by Joan Corominas, Biblioteca Románica Hispánica, IV, Textos (Madrid: Editorial Gredos, 1967),
copla 57. The Greek interprets the open hand as a sign that everything is in the
hands of God and the closed fist as the Roman's answer that God has the world in
his power (vv. 60ab). The Roman sees the open hand as a slap on the ears and
responds with a blow of his fist (vv. 62d-63a). The sophisticated medieval reader would readily remember yet a third interpretation: "Dialectica et Rhetorica
est quod in manu hominis pugnus adstrictus et palma distensa: illa verba contra-
hens, ista distendens." St. Isidore, *Etymologiae* II. xxiii. 1-2; cf. also Cassiodorus,
Institutiones II. iii. 2. There is a comic contrast between the crude physical dis-
pute of the Greek and the Roman and the refined subtlety of the medieval rhetorical and dialectical disputation. And this contrast is emphasized by the choice
of the very gestures used as traditional symbols of those two disciplines. I am
indebted to Mr. Ottavio DiCamillo for this reference.

is interested in rhetoric only as one of the liberal arts; in the latter he is interested only in its instrumental value, as a useful tool in problems of administration. In neither case is the king interested in the theoretical or esthetic aspects of rhetoric.

For rhetorical theory in Spain in the Middle Ages the critic and scholar must look to other sources, principally to the treatises on *dictamen*. But, having analyzed these, as I shall do in the next chapter, he must then apply his findings to contemporary literary works in order to form an accurate estimate of the influence of rhetorical doctrine on them. He must be careful, however, not to extend comments concerning the influence of these treatises on contemporary works to the whole period of the late Middle Ages. The documents and texts I have surveyed, however briefly, show clearly that the rhetorical tradition in Spain is not monolithic, that it does vary in importance and theoretical range from one period to the next.

CHAPTER IV

RHETORICAL THEORY IN
ALFONSINE CASTILE

THE WORKS analyzed in the preceding chapter treat rhetoric summarily as one of the seven liberal arts, even less directly in referring to other matters, or in the very limited context of the practical applications of the *ars dictaminis*. For extensive discussions of rhetorical theory in Castile in the latter part of the thirteenth century and the beginning of the fourteenth, we must turn to works written in Latin. There exist at least four of these; three are *artes dictaminis* connected more or less closely with Alfonso the Learned, the *Epistolarium* of Ponce of Provence, the *Ars Epistolaris Ornatus* of Geoffrey of Everseley, and the *Dictaminis Epithalamium* of Juan Gil de Zamora. The fourth work is Martín de Córdoba's more general *Breve Compendium Artis Rethorice*, dating probably from the first half of the fourteenth century. Of these works only Geoffrey's *Ars Epistolaris Ornatus* has been studied at length.

THE *Epistolarium* OF PONCE OF PROVENCE AND THE
Ars Epistolaris Ornatus OF GEOFFREY OF EVERSELEY

Ponce of Provence was one of the itinerant teachers of *ars dictaminis* active about the middle of the thirteenth century. He is known to have taught at Toulouse, Montpellier, and Orléans.[1] Most of the manuscripts of his *Epistolarium* carry the following dedication:

Anno domine MCCLII ego magister Poncius Provincialis qui composueram summam dictaminis qui incipit de competenti doctrina dogmate ordinavi et compo-

---

[1] Paetow, *The Arts Course at Medieval Universities*, pp. 89-91.

[98]

sui presens epistolarium secundum doctrinam et ordinem summe superius nomi-
nate ad instantium viri nobilis Adefonsi discipuli predilecti . . . .[2]

Other manuscripts of the *Epistolarium* give 1259 as the date of composition.[3] The 1252 date is more likely, particularly if we can identify the "viri nobilis Adefonsi" of the *incipit* with the *infante* Alfonso before he became king in the same year. If this is so, the *Epistolarium* shows that Alfonso himself studied *dictamen* with one of
the best-known teachers of that art—which would be of enormous
significance for the study of the Alfonsine corpus. Unfortunately,
since the work has not been published, we are unable to form a
more adequate idea of its contents and possible relation to Spain.[4]

The *Ars Epistolarium Ornatus* of Geoffrey of Everseley, also unpublished, has been studied more intensively, however.[5] Along with
Juan Gil de Zamora's *Dictaminis Epithalamium*, it is of first im-

---

[2] Cited by Paul Oskar Kristeller, *Iter Italicum. A Finding List of Uncatalo-
gued or Incompletely Catalogued Manuscripts of the Renaissance in Italian and
Other Libraries*, 2 vols. (London: The Warburg Institute, 1963-1967; Leiden: E. J.
Brill, 1963-1967), I, 96.

[3] Noël Valois, "Étude sur le rythme des bulles pontificales," *BEC*, 42 (1881),
173.

[4] Many MSS of this work are known, although only one is found in a Spanish
library: Barcelona, Archivo de la Corona de Aragón, MS. Ripoll 190. Charles Homer Haskins lists seven MSS of the work, with BM MS. Arundel 514 apparently
the best: *Studies in Medieval Culture* (Oxford: At the Clarendon Press, 1929), p. 7n.
Kristeller cites at least one more in Italy: *Iter Italicum*, I, 96. J. J. Murphy points
out that Ponce is one of the last representatives of the Orléans school of *ars dictaminis*, itself a continuation in many respects of the school of Chartres. Thus
a Ponce-Alfonso relationship might help to explain the presence of doctrines of
the school of Chartres in Alfonso's work (letter dated 2 June 1971).

[5] The most recent and detailed study is that of Valeria Bertolucci Pizzorusso,
"Un trattato di *Ars dictandi* dedicato ad Alfonso X," *SMV*, 15 (1967), 3-82, which
I follow throughout. Further references are incorporated into the text. Of earlier studies, the two most important are N[oël] Denholm-Young, "The Cursus
in England," in *Oxford Essays in Medieval History Presented to Herbert Edward
Salter* (Oxford: At the Clarendon Press, 1934), pp. 68-103; and Ch[arles]-V. Langlois, "Formulaires de lettres du xiie, du xiiie et du xive siècle," *Notices et Extraits
des Manuscrits de la Bibliothèque Nationale et Autres Bibliothèques*, 35, ii (1897)
409-434. The *Ars Epistolarium Ornatus* is found in Perugia, Biblioteca Comunale
Augusta MS. F. 62 (see description in Pizzorusso, pp. 7-12). Signora Pizzorusso
promises an edition.

portance for our knowledge of rhetorical studies during the time of Alfonso the Learned. The author was an English cleric who spent some time in Rome in the late 1250's, probably with the Curia, before coming to Spain. His presence there, as notary and ambassador in the service simultaneously of Alfonso and Edward I of England, is documented for the years between 1276 and his death in February of 1283.[6] The evidence of the *Ars Epistolarium Ornatus* itself indicates that Geoffrey was in Spain earlier than this. Signora Pizzorusso dates the work, written in Spain, between 1267 and 1275 on the basis of internal evidence. Reasonably firm conjectures narrow that period down to the years around 1270 (p. 24), the date originally proposed by Langlois.[7]

Geoffrey's relations with Alfonso appear to have been close. In a letter to Edward I dated 1 April 1279, Alfonso speaks of him as follows:

... ffazemos uos saber, que por la lealdad que nos fallamos en Maestre Jofre nuestro Notario, et por que sabemos porr cierto que él ha muy grand sabor de seruir bien et leal mientre auos et a nos, et otrossi por que el sabe mucho de nuestra fazienda, tan bien del fecho del rey de Ffrancia commo de la corte de Roma, et del fecho de los moros, et del rey de Aragon, et de los naturales de nuestra tierra, touiendo por bien del embiar alla auos por cosas que uos el dira por palabra.[8]

This relationship is confirmed by Geoffrey's dedication of his treatise to Alfonso: "In hiis siquidem quinque libris octuaginta et sex capitula sunt distincta, quorum primas litteras si simul coniuncxeris, ex ipsis hec oratio resultabit: GAUFRIDUS ANGLICUS HOC FECIT OPUS IN LAUDEM DOMINI ALFONSI ILLUSTRIS REGIS CASTELLE AC ETIAM LEGIONIS . . . ." (Pizzorusso, p. 14). Other references to Alfonso, most of them highly flattering, are found throughout the work. In an example of *gradatio* the following occurs: "Alfonso, illustrissimo regi Castelle, vexatio multifaria intellectum, intellectus industriam, industria quidem virtutes, virtutes tropheos hostium triumphales, trium-

[6] Denholm- Young, p. 78.

[7] "Formulaires de lettres," p. 430.

[8] Ballesteros-Beretta, *Alfonso X el Sabio*, p. 921; London, Record Office, *Ancient Correspondence*, vol. 15, A. S. nº 6. Ballesteros thinks that this letter refers to Jofré de Loaysa, another of Alfonso's notaries, but he is undoubtedly mistaken.

phus ínsuper glóriam, gloria tandem émulos comparávit" (ibid., p. 47). And in one of *disiunctio*: "Alfonsus, invictissimus rex Castelle, circumspecta cautela incautos plurimos separavit, regem Granate suis legibus subdidit, optimates Granate devicit, et, dum esset adhuc in adolescencia constitutus, suo dominio regimen Murcie subiugavit" (ibid.). Geoffrey even takes into account the use of the vernacular in the Castilian chancery, citing *exordia* of letters from Alfonso to his Moslem vassals as examples:

> . . . salutationes per grammaticam exprimere debeant, et non est jus quare grammaticalis sermo plus debeat Hyspanis deficere quando concipiunt in vulgari quam Gallicis vel Lombardis. Et tamen Yspanici sic salutant:
> "Al muy alto *et* muy noble sen*n*or don Alfo*n*so, por la gra*c*ia de Dios Rey de Castiella, etc., yo don Mahomat Rey de Murcia beso las ves*t*ras manos *et* los ves*t*ros pies, etc." Vel e contrario:
> "De nos don Alfo*n*so, por la gra*c*ia *de* Dios Rey de Castiella, etc., a vos, don Abenmafon Rey de Niebla, salud *et* gra*c*ia."[9]

In a passage illustrating *descriptio*, Geoffrey paraphrases Matthieu de Vendôme's *Ars Versificatoria* in fourteen distichs in praise of Alfonso (Pizzorusso, pp. 38-40); and many of the sample letters are written in the king's name.

The *Ars Epistolaris Ornatus* "si presenta come uno dei più completi trattati del genere, esauriente fino alla minuzia nello svolgimento dei singoli punti pur restando didatticamente chiaro ed efficace" (ibid., p. 25). It is divided into five books, of which the first four present the theory of *dictamen* and the fifth—missing in the Perugia MS and in the extracts made by Father Burriel of one in the monastery of San Juan de los Reyes of Toledo[10]—a collection of sample letters.

Book I defines *in comuni* the traditional five parts of the letter, the *salutatio*, *exordium*, *narratio*, *petitio*, and *conclusio*. Book II deals with the three levels of style and the persons to whom they ought to be applied, stylistic vices to be avoided, the *cursus*, ways of beginning and ending periods, and various kinds of periphrases. Book III is concerned with *dignitas*, the correct use of the various

---

[9] I cite the first part of the passage, to "Et tamen . . . ," from Langlois, p. 431, and the remainder from Pizzorusso, p. 52.

[10] See my "Retóricas clásicas y medievales," no. 170.

tropes, figures of speech, and figures of thought. *Inventio* and *dispositio* are also taken up at the end of the book. Book IV returns to the five parts of the letter *in speciali*, with emphasis on the problems of the *salutatio* and the *exordium* (Pizzorusso, pp. 25-33).

Cicero is cited most frequently as a source, always in reference to either the *De Inventione* or the pseudo-Ciceronian *Rhetorica ad C. Herennium* (ibid., pp. 33-34n); but the work falls completely within the tradition of the Italian school of *ars dictandi* of the thirteenth century. Buoncompagno of Bologna and Guido Faba are specifically mentioned, and there are close parallels between Geoffrey's work and passages of the former's *Palma, Rhetorica Antiqua,* and *Rhetorica Novissima.* Signora Pizzorusso takes the latter's *Summa Dictaminis* and *Dictamina Rhetorica* to be the immediate models followed by Geoffrey (p. 36n). Priscian (*Inst. Gramm.*) is the source of the grammatical comments; Quintilian is mentioned, although it may be doubted that Geoffrey was acquainted with him directly. Tacit sources are the previously mentioned *Ars Versificatoria* of Matthieu de Vendôme and William of Conches's *Moralium Dogma Philosophorum.*

Two other presumptive sources, "Gondisalino" and "Daribundum Delfinum," present serious problems. Signora Pizzorusso surmises that the former refers to Dominicus Gundisalvus, although she is unable to locate passages cited from him in either the *De Divisione Philosophiae* or the *De Ortu Scientiarum* (pp. 37-38). At any rate, the name seems to indicate an awareness of previous Spanish work in the field. The slightly comic aspect of the second name suggests the possibility that Geoffrey may have invented it as "un idolo polemico, del tutto fittizio," particularly since no trace of any author of that name has yet been found (ibid., p. 41).

The importance of the *Ars Epistolaris Ornatus* cannot be overestimated. It shows with greater detail than any other contemporary Spanish treatise the kind of rhetorical theory available in thirteenth-century Castile. Furthermore, it is of particular interest for the history of the University of Salamanca: Salamanca is virtually the only Spanish place name mentioned in the work, and the "studio salmantino" is specifically cited (ibid., p. 20). By implication this gives us information about Alfonso's own relation to the work.

As we have seen (above, p. 29), the king was interested in Salamanca and particularly in the study of law. We may suppose, with Signora Pizzorusso, that the work was written to be used there, as an example of the latest and best Italian theory, a kind of *summa* of the art of letter-writing. That Geoffrey himself so conceived of his work is evident from the following:

Nullus enim huc usque artem compilavit complete, immo vix vel numquam ab omnibus poterit colligi complementorum. Et ideo, [in] unum cohactum in locis autenticis scriptoribus omnibus huius artis quodquisque mihi videbitur vere et artificiose percipere, id excrepam, et breviter siquidem boni mea industria propria seu mediante doctorum meorum in hac parte mihi documentata doctrina habere vel adinvenire valuero, id totum inserere presenti non opusculo postponam. (p. 25)

Going one step beyond Signora Pizzorusso's formulations, it is not unreasonable to suppose that the king himself wanted a *summa dictaminis*, based on the works of the best authors, as a counterpart to his encyclopedic works in other fields. It would not be translated into Castilian, like those works, because of the peculiar nature of the subject, the fact that it deals precisely with the rules of writing Latin letters.

Like Juan Gil de Zamora's *Dictaminis Epithalamium*, the *Ars Epistolaris Ornatus* shows that Alfonsine Spain was in process of shifting from the older, theoretically oriented French tradition to the newer, more practical Italian one. Together, these works supply a firm foundation for future studies of the style and development of literary prose during the latter half of the thirteenth century.

JUAN GIL DE ZAMORA: *Dictaminis Epithalamium*

Juan Gil de Zamora is only slightly later than Geoffrey; we know even less about him than we do about the latter. Manuel de Castro y Castro, the editor of Juan Gil's *De Preconiis Hispanie*, devotes almost a hundred pages of his introduction to the author's biography, by far the most extensive treatment ever accorded it.[11] Unfortu-

---

[11] "Gil de Zamora y la provincia franciscana de Santiago," in his ed. of *De Preconiis Hispanie* (Madrid: Universidad de Madrid, Facultad de Filosofía y Letras, 1955), pp. xxxv-cxxvi.

nately, most of his efforts are aimed at explaining the organization of the Franciscan order in Castile and León during the thirteenth century and identifying the people with whom Juan Gil probably rubbed elbows. There is very little documented information; most of the details must be supplied through conjecture.

If, as Castro y Castro believes, Juan Gil was the author of the *Vita Sancti Isidori Agricole* in 1266, he must have been born before 1241. The author of the *Vita* is a deacon and therefore, according to canon law, at least twenty-five years old.[12] If the tradition recorded by Gil González Dávila is correct, that Juan Gil served as secretary to King Fernando III, that date would have to be pushed back even farther.[13] Had he been born in 1241 he would have been only eleven years old on Fernando's death in 1252. The friar probably studied at Salamanca. One of the sample letters in the *Dictaminis Epithalamium* is directed to "P., suo amico intimo, antiquo socio Salamantice studium frequentati."[14] Castro y Castro conjectures that Juan Gil became a Franciscan about 1269 or 1270.[15] He further believes, on the basis of other sample letters in the *Dictaminis Epithalamium* which refer to Orléans and Tours and on the basis of the dedication of his *Liber Contra Venena et Animalia Venenosa* to Fr. Raimundo Gaufredi, professor at the University of Paris, that Juan Gil also studied there, probably between 1273 or 1274 and 1278.[16] In the latter year he appears in Zamora counseling the *infante* D. Sancho in a lawsuit between the bishop of Zamora and the city council. The letter from D. Sancho announcing

---

12 Ibid., p. lvi.

13 *Teatro eclesiástico de las iglesias metropolitanas*, II, 390.

14 Salamanca, Biblioteca de la Universidad, MS. 2128, saec. XV, chart., 179 ff., f. 44v.13-14. Originally part of the library of the Colegio Mayor de San Bartolomé (MS. 233), it was transferred to the Biblioteca de Palacio in Madrid (*olim* 2-L-5, II. 1369) with the suppression of the *colegios mayores* in the mid-nineteenth century. In 1954 it was returned to the University of Salamanca on the occasion of the seven-hundredth anniversary of the founding of the university. See my "Retóricas clásicas y medievales," no. 191, for a detailed description of the MS. Hereafter citations will be incorporated into the text. See the Appendix for a statement of my editorial practice.

15 "Gil de Zamora," p. lvi.

16 Ibid., pp. lxiv-lxv, lxvii.

his decision is the only document hitherto known which names Juan Gil.[17]

Little more is known about the latter part of his life. Most of it appears to have been spent in the Franciscan convent of his native Zamora as *lector* in theology.[18] He apparently occupied posts of responsibility in the Franciscan province of Santiago: custodian of the custody of Zamora (which held jurisdiction over eight convents), provincial vicar about the year 1295, and from 1300 minister of the province. The date of his death is not known, but the next person known to be minister does not appear until the year 1318.[19] Alfonso de Madrigal, *el Tostado*, records the tradition that Juan Gil reached such a great age that he lost the memory of the works he had written.[20]

During most of his long life Juan Gil probably was closely connected to the court of Castile, although again there is no documentary proof. He is said to have served as confessor to Alfonso X.[21] Ballesteros cites him as one of the companions of the king in a visit to Seville in the year 1260.[22] According to tradition, Alfonso confided to the Franciscan the education of his son Sancho IV, *el Bravo*.[23] In the prologue to the *De Preconiis Hispanie*, Juan Gil directs himself to Sancho, saying that he is "scriptor suus."[24]

---

[17] Letter dated 26 December 1278, from San Esteban de Gormaz: " . . . e auydo myo conseyo con el dean de seuylla e con el Maestre de alcántara e con pero aluarez e con frey iohan gil doctor de los frayres descalços de Çamora . . . "; printed by Cesáreo Fernández Duro in his *Memorias históricas de la ciudad de Zamora, su provincia y obispado*, 4 vols. (Madrid: Establecimiento Tipográfico de los Sucesores de Rivadeneyra, 1882-1883), I, 469; repr. by Castro y Castro, "Gil de Zamora," pp. lxvii-lxviii.

[18] María Rosa Vilchez, "El *Liber Mariae* de Gil de Zamora," *Eidos: Cuadernos de la Institución Teresiana*, 1 (1954), 10.

[19] Castro y Castro, "Gil de Zamora," pp. cv-cvi, cxix, cxix n.

[20] Ibid., p. cxxv.

[21] Tomás y Joaquín Carreras Artau, *Historia de la filosofía española: Filosofía cristiana de los siglos XIII al XV*, Asociación Española para el Progreso de las Ciencias, 2 vols. (Madrid: Real Academia de Ciencias Exactas, Físicas y Naturales, 1939-1943), I, 13.

[22] *Alfonso X el Sabio*, p. 302.

[23] Vilchez, "El *Liber Mariae*," p. 10.

[24] Ed. Castro y Castro, p. 3.

The part Juan Gil played in the literary productions of Alfonso and Sancho, if any, is also a matter for speculation. He composed an *Officium Almiflue Virginis* in honor of the Virgin for Alfonso; and it is possible that the Marian legends of Juan Gil's *Liber Marie* influenced the king's own *Cantigas de Santa Maria.*[25] For the education of Sancho he wrote the *De Preconiis Hispanie*, a sketch of Spanish history, and it is possible that he intervened in the writing of the *Lucidario* composed in Sancho's name.[26]

Juan Gil's writings can be divided into three broad groups. Among his devotional works (besides the *Liber Marie* and the *Officium*) he states that he wrote a *Liber de Miraculis Almiflue Virginis*, no longer extant,[27] and he is said to have written "Leyendas de los Santos," a *Breviloquium de Vitiis et Virtutibus*,[28] and an *Archivus seu Armarium Scripturarum.*[29] He was also concerned with certain of the liberal arts, writing an *Ars Musica*,[30] the *Dictaminis Epithalamium*, and a *Proslogion seu de Accentu et de Dubilibus Biblie.*[31] The latter combines grammatical and orthographical precepts with Biblical interpretations. It is very likely that Juan Gil also wrote the *Expositiones Quorumdam Vocabulorum Biblie* which follows this work in the Paris and Merville manuscripts.[32] There exists a series of

---

[25] Castro y Castro, "Gil de Zamora," p. lxxxi.

[26] Carreras Artau suggest, in *Historia de la filosofía española*, I, 28, that Juan Gil helped with the *Lucidario*. There are also striking similarities between the *Castigos e documentos* and the *De Preconiis Hispanie* and the *Dictaminis Epithalamium* in their use of sources. Helen L. Sears suggests the importance of the *Secretum Secretorum* for the *Castigos*: "The *Rimado de Palacio* and the *De Regimine Principum* Tradition of the Middle Ages," *HR*, 20 (1952), p. 22. The same work was a source for the *De Preconiis Hispanie* (Castro y Castro, "La obra," in his ed. of the *De Preconiis Hispanie*, p. clxxxiii) and for the *Dictaminis Epithalamium* (see below, pp. 109-110).

[27] Castro y Castro, "Gil de Zamora," p. lxxxiii.

[28] Ibid., p. cix.

[29] Ibid., p. cvi.

[30] Ibid., p. cx. Kristeller, in *Iter Italicum*, II, 429, records a MS of this work at the Archivio Capitolare Vaticano, MS. H. 29, and a copy of this MS in Bologna (ibid., I, 29).

[31] Castro y Castro, "Gil de Zamora," p. lxvi.

[32] C[elestin] Douais, "Les manuscrits du château de Merville," *AM*, 2 (1890),

historical works, of which the most important is the *De Preconiis Hispanie*. Other works, some of which are actually sections of the *De Preconiis Hispanie*, are *De Viris Illustribus, De Preconiis Civitatis Numantine*,[33] and the *Liber Illustrium Personarum*, or *Liber de Historia Canonica et Civili*.[34]

There is a concentration of this literary activity during the period 1278-1282, judging by works which can be dated. The *De Preconiis Hispanie* was probably started in 1278.[35] The *Liber Marie* was written in the same year;[36] about the same time the *Officium Almiflue Virginis* was started at the behest of Alfonso X. Since it was dedicated to the king, it must have been completed before his death in 1284.[37] By 1282 Juan Gil had finished his *De Viris Illustribus*[38] and the *Dictaminis Epithalamium*. The *Liber contra Venena*, the only work to fall outside this period, was dedicated to Fr. Raimundo Gaufredi during his term as general of the Franciscan order, 1289-1295.[39]

The *Dictaminis Epithalamium*[40] is directed to Fr. Philippus de Perugia, who was named bishop of Fiesole in 1282. Since Juan Gil

---

337. It is possible that the anonymous Latin dictionary which follows the *Dictaminis Epithalamium* in Salamanca Bibl. Univ. MS. 2128 is the same work.

[33] Castro y Castro, "Gil de Zamora," p. lxxxiii.

[34] Ibid., p. cxiii.

[35] Ibid., pp. lxxxii-lxxxiii.

[36] Ibid., p. lxxxii.

[37] Ibid., pp. lxxx-lxxxi.

[38] Ibid., p. lxxxiii.

[39] Ibid., p. lxiv.

[40] This work has hitherto been called either the *Ars Dicendi*, based on the title found on the spine, or the *Ars Dictandi*, based on a hasty survey of its contents. The first scholar to mention it, Cesáreo Fernández Duro, gives it the former name in his *Colección bibliográfico-biográfica de noticias referentes a la provincia de Zamora o materiales para su historia* (Madrid: Imprenta y Fundición de Manuel Tello, 1891), p. 419. Atanasio López uses the latter name in his "Descripción de los manuscritos franciscanos existentes en la Biblioteca de Toledo," *AIA* (1ª época), 25 (1926), 202. He prints short excerpts from the prologue and several of the sample letters, but his transcriptions are defective. The work is also mentioned by Vilchez in "El *Liber Mariae*," p. 15, and, following her, by Díaz y Díaz, *Index Scriptorum Latinorum Medii Aevi Hispanorum*, p. 29. The true title is found in Juan

does not refer to Fr. Philippus as bishop, it may be inferred that the work was written before that date.[41] How much earlier can be established on the basis of internal evidence.

A salient example is the specimen letter of consolation written by Juan Gil to Alfonso X on the death of one of his sons (f. 36r.22-v.25). Such a letter could not have been written before the fact. As it happens, the first of Alfonso's children to die was the eldest, the *infante* D. Fernando, in 1275. Another letter is directed by Pope N. to the Holy Roman Emperor R. (f. 18r.28-29). Rudolf of Habsburg became emperor in 1274 after an interregnum of almost twenty years, and in 1277 Nicholas III was elected pope. Given the correlation between these two reigns, we are perhaps justified in advancing the *terminus a quo* of the work to 1277.

But another example, in which Pope N. is petitioned by N., archbishop of Santiago de Compostela, illustrates the pitfalls of this sort of inference. There are several thirteenth-century popes whose names begin with N, but there are no archbishops of Santiago whose names begin with the same letter. What has happened is that Juan Gil has substituted the initial N, presumably standing for *nomen*, for the initials of the persons actually occupying these positions. Thus we cannot depend on such initials for purposes of dating. A sizable number of the salutations presented by Juan Gil demonstrate the same peculiarity. But enough remain with other initials or with full names to allow us to trace the genesis of the *Dictaminis*. Juan Gil mentions a Pope G. (f. 48v.3-4), and we find Gregory X wearing the tiara from 1271 to 1276. A letter from Louis, king of France, to Alfonso, king of León, Castile, Toledo, Cordova, and Seville, can only refer to the period between the accession of Alfonso X in 1252 and the death of St. Louis IX of France in 1270. There are other datable events and people which indicate an earlier period as well. I shall examine them in detail when treating the problem of sources. Provisionally, we may say that Juan Gil wrote between 1277 and 1282.

Gil's prologue: "Tractatum ergo presentem quem Ditaminis epithalamum [sic] enim titulavi . . . " (f. 1r.35-36).

[41] Castro y Castro, "Gil de Zamora," p. lxv.

In the prologue, directed to Fr. Philippus de Perugia, Juan Gil states: "Quesivisti *ergo* a me mod*um* dictandi v*er*ba *etiam* dulcia, utilia et honesta, quib*us* uti posses in *compo*sicion*e* ep*is*to*l*ar*um*, in comen*daci*on*e*m illustriu*m* p*er*son*a*rum, in detest*aci*onem viciorum, in ampliacion*e*m sermon*um*, in subtilli p*r*olacio*n*e collacionum" (f. 1r. 11-14).[42] He explains that he has divided his treatise into four parts: "antecedencia, *consequen*cia, integran*cia* et p*er*ficiencia si*ve consu*mancia" (f. 1v.1-2). The first part, *antecedentia*, treats expressions which can be used in general praise or reproof of mankind (f. 1v.2-4). *Consequentia*, the second part, considers expressions which can be applied to specific praiseworthy or blameworthy actions (f. 1v.4-5). *Integrantia*, the third part, constitutes the integral parts of letters— "salutaciones, narraciones, rogaciones, *con*clusione*s*" (f. 1v.6-8). Finally, *consumantia* considers the finished letter resulting from the judicious employment of the first three parts (f. 1v.8-10). He compares this process to the building of a house: "q*uod* pri*us* ligna *et* lapides collig*untur*, sec*undo* scind*untur et* polli*untur*, tercio in ipso hedifficio collocant*ur* dom*us* ex ipsis . . . " (f. 1v.10-12).[43] There follows a detailed table of contents (ff. 1v.16-2v.6).

The treatise proper begins with *antecedentia*, an example of how great men may be praised for their spiritual and moral qualities (ff. 2v.25-3r.33), followed by one showing how they may be praised according to their physical qualities (f. 3r.34-v.15). Juan Gil specifically points out the utility of such expressions "in descripcio*n*ib*us* cronicor*um et* in titulum p*r*econiarum" (f. 3v.16-17). He then speaks of the ways in which kings can be praised, remitting the reader to the pseudo-Aristotelian *Secretum Secretorum*, which he calls "libro de strenuitatib*us* regallib*us* sive de ingenio ordinacionis re*gis*" (f. 3v.22-23). From the wording used it is evident that Juan

---

[42] See the Appendix for transcriptions of the entire prologue.

[43] The comparison of writing a letter or making a speech to the building of a house was a common one. Cf. Guido Faba, *Summa Dictaminis*, ed. by Augusto Gaudenzi, in *Il Propugnatore* (N. S.), 3 (1890), i, 297. This may be the direct source for Juan Gil, although there are no exact parallels. Juan Gil later copies several sections from the *Summa* of Guido almost verbatim. Cf. also the formulation of this comparison in Martín de Córdoba, *Breve Compendium Artis Rethorice* (below, p. 128).

Gil follows the western version of the work instead of the longer eastern one. He may even have been familiar with the Spanish translation of that version, the *Poridat de las poridades.*[44]

The chapter on praiseworthy *antecedentia* ends with examples of panegyric of the physical and moral qualities of a king or noble (ff. 3v.35-4v.4) and then of prelates of the church (ff. 4v.5-5r.8).

The second chapter is concerned with the commendation of noble persons according to the diverse gifts of the Holy Spirit. This corresponds to the second part of Juan Gil's treatise, *consequentia.* There are short paragraphs in praise of *caritas, simplicitas, patientia, paupertas, pax, obedientia, verecundia, fortitudo, sapientia, doctrina, solicitudo, misericordia, contemptus mundi, oratio,* and *contemplatio* (ff. 5r.15-7v.12).

The author reverts to *antecedentia* with the "vices of the iniquitous" (f. 7v.19), first offering examples of general reproof of church-

---

[44] Cf. the following example of *gradatio.* I cite the *Poridat de las poridades* from the Kasten ed.—there is no ed. of the Latin original—and the eastern version of the *Secretum Secretorum* from the ed. of Robert Steele in his *Opera Hactenus Inedita Rogerii Baconi* (Oxford: E Typographeo Clarendoniano, 1920), fasc. v.

Poridat de las Poridades	*Dictaminis Epithalamium*	*Secretum Secretorum*
"*Et* quando demandare el seso el regnado por su derecho, uiene ende la uerdad, *et* de la uerdad uiene temor de Dios, *et* la uerdad es rayz de todas las cosas loadas; *et* por temor de Dios uiene iusticia, *et* por la iusticia uiene conpannia, *et* de la conpannia uiene franqueza, *et* de la franqueza uiene solaz, *et* del solaz uiene amiztad, *et* de la amiztad uiene defendimiento, *et* por esto firmasse el iuyzio *et* la ley *et* pueblas el mundo . . . " (p. 35)	"Opportet ut rex obseruet veritatem, quia ex veritate timor divinus, et ex timore divina iusticia, *et* ex iusticia societas, *et* ex societate franqueza, *et* ex franqueza solacium, et ex solacio amicicia, et ex amicicia proteccio sive defendimentum et inde firmantur delicie regum et leges *et* populatur mundus . . . " (f. 3v.24-28)	"Stude igitur et dilige bone fame, quoniam racio per desiderium bone fame elicit veritatem. Et veritas es radix laudabilium et materia omnium bonorum, quia est contraria mendacio, et desiderium justicie generat. Justicia generat confidenciam: confidencia largitatem: largitas facit familiaritatem: familiaritas amiciciam: amicicia generat consilium et juvamen. Per hoc siquidem orbis fuit constitutus et leges hominibus constitute . . . " (p. 46)

Note the use of "franqueza" and "defendimentum" in Juan Gil's text, very likely a reminiscence of the Spanish translation instead of the Latin text.

men and secular magnates (ff. 7v.15-9v.33) before passing to *conse-quentia*, detailed censure of specific vices: *contra adulatores, ebrio-sos, otiosos, negotiatores clericos, malos divites, invidos, superbos, gu-losos, avaros, detractores, prodictores, induratos,* and *venatores cleri-cos* (ff. 9v.34-17v.17). The good Juan Gil devotes approximately four times as much space to the reproval of the vicious as to the approval of the virtuous.

These examples, constituting slightly more than a fourth of the treatise, should be considered as raw material for letters rather than as precepts for the organization of that material. The style is comparable to that of St. Ildefonsus' *De Virginitate Sanctae Ma-riae.* Periods are short, repetitious, and highly parallelistic in form.[45]

Juan Gil turns next to *integrantia*, technical questions of *dicta-men*, if only briefly. He enumerates the four parts of the letter: *sa-lutatio, narratio, petitio,* and *conclusio* (f. 17v.20-23). The fifth part traditionally found in *artes dictaminis*, the *exordium*, is subsumed under the narration. The salutation must be appropriate for the estate, age, and dignity of the person to whom the letter is direct-ed (f. 17v.24-25). Thus, "unusquisq*ue secundem* suam vivat eta-te*m*; alit*er enim* religioso stabim*us,* aliter secu*lari;* senib*us enim* de-be*mus* reve*renciam,* iuvenibus correccio*n*em et amiciciam; alius eci-am honor det*ur* sumo pontifici, alius diocessano seu pr*esuli . . .* " (f. 17v.25-28). There follow sample salutations from the pope to archbishops and abbots, emperors, kings, and counts; and to the pope from the emperor and the archbishop of Santiago de Compos-tela (ff. 17v.30-18r.37). Juan Gil then works his way systematical-ly through the lower ecclesiastical and secular ranks (ff. 18r.38-19r.21), terminating with a selection of phrases to be used in salutations "according to the wit given you and the nobility of your spirit."[46]

---

[45] Cf. the following passage, taken from the section on the general praise of church-men: "Sis in iudiciis rect*us,* in loquendo modest*us,* in iubendo discret*us,* in dispen-sacione indust*rius,* in agendo strenu*us,* in auxiliando solicit*us,* in *con*siliis fid*us,* in responionib*us* circumspect*us.* Exibe te maiorib*us* devotu*m,* minorib*us* blan-du*m,* equalib*us* ma*n*suetu*m,* rigid*um* superbiis, benignu*m* humilib*us,* misericorde*m* penite*n*tib*us,* infflexibilem obstinatis" (ff. 4v.36-5r.5).

[46] ". . . *secundu*m data*m* ti*bi* adeo gr*aciam et* nobilitate*m* tui ingenii" (f. 19r. 31-32).

Many of these examples apparently come from an earlier source. Pope Alexander, mentioned in some of them, can only be Alexander IV (1254-1261). From the same period are references to F., Holy Roman Emperor (f. 18r.31-32), and to Johannes, archbishop of Toledo and primate of Spain (f. 18v.19-21). Frederick II was emperor from 1220 to his death in 1250. The only archbishop of Toledo named Johannes in the thirteenth century was Juan de Medina Pomar, who followed Rodrigo Jiménez de Rada in February of 1248 and died in July of the same year.[47]

Spanish place names predominate, particularly in the kingdom of León: Zamora (ff. 18v.1, 5-6, 10-11, 15, 19r.6), Santiago de Compostela (ff. 17v.36, 18r.38), León (f. 18v.6), and the abbey of Moreruela, in the province of Zamora (f. 18r.3). We have already seen one sample letter from St. Louis of France to Alfonso of Castile; Alfonso is mentioned again in showing how he should address "fideli baroni Viscaye" and the "duci seu comiti Barchinone" (ff. 18v. 35-19r.1). But if Spanish names predominate, foreign ones are by no means lacking. Italian sites mentioned are Ferrara (f. 18r.23) and Modena (f. 20r.23). Even farther afield are salutations for the wife of the king of Bohemia (f. 20r.14), complaints from the "nobilis mulieris A. de Boemia" (f. 20r.21), and the beginning of a letter to the archbishop of Esztergom in Hungary (f. 20r.10). We may assume that Juan Gil took sample salutations from a work written in the 1250's, probably Italian, and added examples of his own.

After instructing the notary to use "altam literam" in writing the names of men, women, cities, and castles (f. 19r.35-37), Juan Gil seems to feel it necessary to pay his respects to the traditional rhetorical doctrines, if only in passing:

Ideo ut magis rethorice procedamus, cum[48] dictio desinit in vocalem, sequens vero incipiat a vocali. Collores autem recthorici quibus uti possumus tam in epistolis quam in metris sunt isti, s[cilicet]: repeticcio, ut cum dicitur "te collo, te laudo, te glorifico, tibi g[ratulor] [?] plaudo"; converssio, ut cum dicitur "pluries sciencia superavit bonitate superante eloquencia superavit"; complexio, quia compre-

---

[47] Conradus Eubel, *Hierarchia Catholica Medii Aevi*, ed. altera (Monasterii: Sumptibus et typis librariae Regensbergianae, 1913; repr. Padua: Typis et sumptibus domus editorialis 'Il Messaggero di S. Antonio,' 1960), I, 487.

[48] MS reads "est"; I am indebted to Professor E. T. Silk for the emendation.

hendit duos primos colores, v[erbi] g[racia]: "Quis testamenti verus traslator? Ieronimus. Quis trium lingarum peritus fuit? Ieronimus. Quis destructor heresis fuit? Ieronimus."

Alii autem collores rethorici: tradicio, contencio, exclamacio, ratiocinacio, sentencia, contrarium, articulus, concordia, agnominacio et plures alii numerantur, de quibus tractare non intendimus. Eo quod plus sapiunt curiossitatem quam utilitatem. (f. 19r.37-v.10)

The only rhetorical colors that Juan Gil specifically advocates are those based on repetition: anaphora (*repetitio*), epiphora (*conversio*), and the combination of these two into symploce (*complexio*).[49] The author puts these figures into vigorous practice in his sample commendations and censures. As for the other rhetorical figures and tropes, Juan Gil names a few and dismisses the rest with the statement that they are "more curious than useful" (f. 19v.10).

Juan Gil's discussion of the narration is largely an enumeration of the ways that one can begin it. He takes each part of speech in turn and gives examples of its use in the exordium of the narration. Nouns and pronouns can be used in each of their cases at the beginning of a clause (ff. 19v.24-20v.33). The same thing is done with verbs, starting with the present indicative of *amo* and working systematically through the indicative and subjunctive (ff. 20v.34-21v.13), and with participles (f. 21v.14-31). Geoffrey of Everseley goes through the same process in Book II of the *Ars Epistolaris Ornatus*.[50]

Most of this material is drawn verbatim from the *Summa Dictaminis* of Guido Faba, although nowhere does Juan Gil cite him by name.[51] Compare the following passages:

Exemplum: 'Petrus lator presentium honorabilis civis noster, nobis conquerendo monstravit.' Genitivus: 'Petri querelam recepimus continentem.' Da-

Petrus lator presencium honorabilis civis noster, nobis conquerendo monstravit quod tales *etc.* Petri querelam recepimus continentem etc. Petro con-

---

[49] Richard A. Lanham, *A Handlist of Rhetorical Terms: A Guide for Students of English Literature* (Berkeley and Los Angeles: University of California Press, 1968), pp. 26, 28, 86.

[50] Signora Pizzorusso (p. 29) does not indicate the source of this passage.

[51] The section on nouns (ff. 19v.24-20r.1) comes from *Summa Dictaminis*, ed. by Gaudenzi, p. 378; part of the section on pronouns (f. 20v.15-33), from p. 381; most of the section on verbs (ff. 20v.36-21r.37), from pp. 379-380; all of the section on participles (f. 21v.15-31), from pp. 380-381.

tivus: 'Petro conquerenti litteras nos-
tras duximus necessario concedendas.'
Accusativus: 'Petrum nuper admisimus
conquerentum.' Vocativus: 'O Petre,
tua lamentabili querela coram nobis
sepius exponere procurasti.' Ablativus:
Petro cive nostro honorabili ac dilecto
intelleximus conquerente.[52]

querenti *litt*eras *n*os*t*ras dux*imus* nec-
*cessari*o *co*nce*dendas etc.* Petrum nup*er*
misim*us* co*n*querente*m etc.* O Petre,
tua lame*n*tabili querella cora*m* nob*is*
expon*ere* sep*ius* p*r*ocurasti q*uod* t*a*lis
etc. Petro cive nostro honorab*i*li ac
dilecto intellex*imus* co*n*querente q*uod*
t*a*lis *etc.* (f. 19v.24-30)

Juan Gil quotes Guido extensively further on as well. The material quoted all comes from the same place in the *Summa Dictaminis*, toward the end of the work, but Juan Gil distributes it quite
differently from Guido and intercalates passages not found in
the *Summa*. This might indicate that Juan Gil is following an intermediary rather than the *Summa Dictaminis* itself.

Before going on to the minor parts of speech, Juan Gil interjects
a discussion of general and mixed *exordia*—"descripci*ones* p*a*p*a*les,
imp*er*iales aliasq*ue* com*unes* s*e*cundu*m* diversitate*m* personar*um* aut
temporum" (f. 21v.33-34)—to give the reader some idea of how the
individual techniques he is describing are combined in practice
(ff. 21v.32-25r.26). Again part of this material is drawn word for word
from Guido's *Summa Dictaminis*.[53]

Juan Gil states that adverbs, prepositions, conjunctions, and inter-
jections are "colligame*n*ta parciu*m* oraci*o*nis p*r*incipaliu*m*, sic*ut* pix,
resina, stupa et claui in compos*i*ci*o*ne naviu*m*" (f. 25r.28-29). The
simile seems to be Juan Gil's own, but many of his examples—of
words which are particularly useful at the beginning of the narration—are taken from Guido Faba (ff. 25r.27-26v.38).[54]

He then takes up the next major division of the letter, the petition. Juan Gil also calls it the *libellus*, a technical term from canon
and Roman law which refers to the brief presented by the plaintiff
to the court as well as to the petition directed to an ecclesiastical
superior.

---

[52] *Summa Dictaminis*, p. 378.
[53] The section from f. 22r.7 to f. 22v.9 is taken from *Summa Dictaminis*,
pp. 388-389; that from f. 22v.9 to f. 22v.30, from pp. 391-392.
[54] The passage from f. 25r.34 to f. 25v.4 comes from *Summa Dictaminis*, p. 382.

That Juan Gil was familiar with canon law is evident from his decision to discuss the peculiar problems involved in petitioning the pope for approval of the election of a bishop or archbishop. He says that elections can be conducted in three ways: "Elecciones autem aut fiunt communiter per compromissionem aut per scrutinii inquisicionem aut per divinam inspiracionem" (f. 27r.8-10). This is a close paraphrase of Decr. I 6.42 from the Decretals of Gregory IX, collected by Raimundo de Peñafort and promulgated in 1234: "Per aliquam de tribus formis hic contentis, scilicet scrutinii, compromissi et inspirationis, procedi debet ad electionem in ecclesiis cathedralibus."[55] Juan Gil presents the proper forms to be followed in each case and refers the reader to various chapters of Book I, title 6, of the Decretals, *De Electione et Electi Potestate.*[56] Several of these forms follow the Decretals almost word for word.[57]

A whole series of letters refers to disputed archiepiscopal elections in Rouen. In one T. is elected as archbishop by the "maioris et sanioris partis capituli" (f. 27v.26-27). In 1221 Thibaut d'Amiens,

[55] *Corpus Iuris Canonici. Pars Secunda: Decretalium Collectiones,* ed. by Aemilius Friedberg (Leipzig: bei B. Tauchnitz, 1879; repr. Graz: Akademische Druck- u. Verlagsanstalt, 1959).

[56] I have been able to identify the *initia* of Decr. I 6. 3, 21, 35, 42, and 53 (ff. 27v.17-28r.18). Juan Gil attributes Decr. I 6. 3 to Alexander III instead of to its rightful author, Gregory III. The *incipit* "Dudum" (f. 27v.39) may refer to Decr. I 3. 7. I have not been able to identify the *initia* "Ad audienciam" (f. 27v.39), "Olim" and "Cum anter" (f. 28r.1).

[57] Cf. the following passages:

Decr. I 6.42: " . . . praesentibus omnibus, qui debent, et volunt et possunt commode interesse, assumantur tres de collegio fide digni, qui secrete et sigillatim vota cunctorum diligenter exquirant, et in scriptis redacta mox publicent in communi, nullo prorsus appellationis obstaculo interiecto, ut is collatione habita eligatur in quem omnes, vel maior et sanior pars capituli consentit."

Dictaminis epithalamium: " . . . presentibus omnibus qui debuerunt, voluerunt et potuerunt commede [sic] interesse, ellecti de collegio fide digni qui per formam scrutinii procedentes examinantis dilligunt votis singulorum secretim et sigillatim redatis in scriptis et mox publicatis in communi collacione habita dominus Iohannes vice maioris et sanioris partis capituli .T. in archiepiscopum rathomagensem elegit" (f. 27v.21-27).

The same passage is reproduced, with some changes, in sample letters found at f. 27r.25-29 and 27v.1-8.

treasurer of the cathedral, was elected archbishop in a disputed election.[58] The same thing happened on Thibaut's death in 1231; Thomas de Fréauville, dean of the chapter, received the majority of the votes, but his election was later set aside by the pope.[59] Juan Gil's sample letter might refer to either of these two elections. Similarly, a reference to the election of G. as archbishop (f.27v.11-14) probably points to the 1235 election of Guillaume de Dunelme.[60] There are other references to elections in Beauvais (f. 28r.6-15).

These references are not found in the Decretals themselves. The obvious implication is that Juan Gil was using a commentary on the Decretals written in Normandy, probably in the 1240's. The date in any case must be later than 1234. Since the same section, in commenting on the proper method of addressing cardinals, cites the Dominican Ugo de S. Caro, cardinal presbyter of St. Sabina (f. 27r.13-15) from 1244 to 1263,[61] and Otto de Monteferrato, cardinal deacon of St. Nicholas *in Carcere Tulliano* (f. 27r.15-17) from 1227 to 1244,[62] it seems likely that it was written in 1244, the only year in which both men held these titles.

The author of this commentary is probably the "magister Artal- dus" mentioned by Juan Gil at the end of the section on episcopal elections: " . . . q*uod* ita *concipien*d*um* sit libell*um* dic*it* *capitulo* 'uni que' m*agister* Artald*us* et ex*tra*. De Elec*c*ione 'quia p*ropter* diver- ssas'" (f. 28r.17-18).[63] I have not been able to identify him among the decretalists of the thirteenth century.

After this rather technical *excursus*, Juan Gil returns to the forms used "in aliis peti*ci*onib*us* comm*un*ibus" (f. 28r.18-19). These are principally petitions for redress of damages suffered from the violent invasion of churches, the encroachments of one monastery on the lands of another, the withholding of tithes, and so on (f. 28r.

---

[58] Leon Fallue, *Histoire politique et religieuse de l'église métropolitaine et du dio- cèse de Rouen*, 4 vols. (Rouen: A. Le Brument, Libraire-Éditeur, 1850-1851), II, 48-49.

[59] Ibid., II, 60.

[60] Ibid., II, 73-74.

[61] Eubel, *Hierarchia Catholica Medii Aevi*, I, 46.

[62] Ibid., I, 52.

[63] The reference is to Decr. I 6. 42 again.

18-v.6). The author then states that "in rogac*i*onib*u*s et *co*ndicio-
nib*u*s dicta*n*di pulc*h*ritudo magna lucescit, eo quod i*b*i captat*u*r am-
pli*u*s benivole*n*cia*m* . . . " (f. 28v.7-8). He presents a series of conclusions and subscriptions suitable for "capturing the good will" of
the various classes of people to whom his letters are directed: to "maiores," in the dative case (f. 28v.12-24), to those whom one does not
know (f. 28v.24-30), and to "maiores," in the accusative case (ff. 28v.
31-29r.10).[64] Naturally the expression of gratitude forms an important part of this section. Certain phrases are to be used for giving thanks to an equal (f. 29r.15-21), and other phrases for someone
of higher status (f. 29r.21-33).[65] There follows a series of phrases,
"generaliter amicabile*m*" (f. 29r.33) drawn verbatim from the *Summa Dictaminis* of Guido Faba (ff. 29r.33-30v.13).[66]

The theoretical part of the *Dictaminis Epithalamium*, the first
three of Juan Gil's four parts, ends here: "Intenc*i*o fuit t*r*actare de
p*a*rtib*u*s antece*de*ntib*u*s ut scire*mus co*mposic*i*onem toci*u*s, in quo
*co*nsistit finis t*r*actat*u*s *et* utilitas, reduce*n*tes *er*go ad uni*u*s armonie consona*n*cia*m* epis*t*olar*um* diffusam materia*m*" (f. 30v.14-17).
Juan Gil devotes the remaining twenty-seven folios, not quite half
of the treatise, to a series of model letters in illustration of *consumantia* or *perficientia*, organized under thirteen rubrics: *De epistolis amatoriis* (ff. 30v.22-35v.6), *de consolatoriis* (ff. 35v.7-37v.37), *de
desolatoriis* (ff. 38r.1-42r.11), *de exortatoriis* (ff. 42r.12-44v.9), *de in-
vitatoriis* (ff. 44v.10-46r.25), *de laudatoriis* (ff. 46r.26-47v.20), *de obe-
dientiariis* (ff. 47v.21-48r.8), *de querulosis* (ff. 48r.9-50r.29), *de re-
prehensoriis* (ff. 50r.30-53r.26), *de recommendatoriis* (f. 53r.27-v.38), *de
suplicatoriis* (ff. 54r.1-56v.28), *de testamentoriis* (ff. 56v.29-57r.21),
de venditoriis (f. 57r.22-37). Juan Gil's classification is alphabeti-
cal, as he himself states (f. 46r.26), and the categories are self-evi-
dent, with a few exceptions: *Epistolas amatorias* are letters of friendship, not of love; *epistolas invitatorias* are letters of invitation to
join the Franciscan order.

---

[64] This is a paraphrase of Guido Faba, *Summa Dictaminis*, pp. 385-386.
[65] The five lines from f. 29r.21 to 29r.26 are a paraphrase of the *Summa Dictaminis*, p. 384.
[66] Taken from pp. 385-386.

Eighteen of these letters are supposedly written by Juan Gil to other Franciscans (ff. 32v.19-33r.21, ff. 33v.10-34v.9), to members of other religious orders ("N., monacho sancti Facundi," f. 44r.4-v.9; the abbess of "talis monasterii," f. 46r.27-v.30), to members of the secular clergy (N., archdeacon of Zamora, ff. 35v.9-36r.21; N., archbishop of Santiago de Compostela, ff. 41r.29-42r.11), to members of the nobility (B. and D., counts of Marsano, f. 33r.21-v.9; Alfonso X, f. 36r.22-v.5), and to friends and relatives ("P., uterino et uno fratri suo," f. 51r.28-v.24). A few letters are addressed to Juan Gil (from N., Franciscan minister of the province of Santiago, f. 47v.30-39; from N., Franciscan minister of the province of Tours, ff. 47v.39-48r.8).

Other letters deal with the business of the Franciscan order in Spain (from Fr. N., requesting transfer to the convent of Zamora for reasons of health, ff. 38r.1-39r.25; permission to Fr. M. to travel from Zamora to Salamanca and back, f. 47v.22-29; to Fr. N., guardian of the convent of Salamanca, from Fr. D., guardian of that of Saragossa, f. 53r.29-v.12). The affairs of the secular clergy in Spain also receive attention (series of three letters on the election of N., bishop of Zamora, f. 56r.13-v.28; to Pope A. from N., "Tolletane ecclesie humilis minister," ff. 49v.24-50r.29; to Archdeacon eucensis [?] from N., canon of León, ff. 51v.25-53r.11). There are only three extrapeninsular references. In one the Franciscan minister of Tours gives Juan Gil permission to go to Paris on business (ff. 47v.39-48r.8). A second includes a request to Fr. Th. from the guardian and convent of Orléans for the pardon of N., a repentent sinner (f. 55r.33-v.26). The third is a plea to Pope N. from the clergy of Sicily and Apulia complaining that N., king of Sicily "a Frederici radice," has taken ecclesiastical justice into his own hands (f. 48r.10-v.2).

This letter, an echo of the struggle between Guelph and Ghibelline, is one of the few to which a date can be assigned. It must refer to the period between the death of the Emperor Frederick II in 1250 and that of his grandson Manfred, last of the Hohenstaufen dynasty to rule Sicily, in 1266. Juan Gil's letter of consolation to Alfonso X on the death of his son Fernando in 1275 has already been mentioned. There is also a letter of condemnation of a dangerous book from Alexander IV (1254-1261). Of the same period are the only two explicitly dated letters in the whole *Dictaminis Epithalamium*. In a sample will and a sample sale contract we find the dates 1262 (expressed in terms of the "anno ab incarnacione domini" f. 57r.2-3) and 1300 (expressed in terms of the *era española*, f. 57r. 29-30). In the sale contract the date is further specified: "regnante F. rege Castelle" (f. 57r.30-31). This is a curious juxtaposition, since Fernando III died in 1252. It might be explained as a partial updating of a real letter written under the reign of St. Fernando.

Most of these sample letters are concerned with the affairs of either the regular or secular clergy. Even the apparent exceptions— a request to a cardinal for the sanction of a marriage (f. 54r.4-40); the complaint to the pope from a wife whose husband has turned her out of the house (f. 48v.3-38); formulae for wills and contracts of sale (ff. 56v.31-57r.37)—involve the interaction of the secular and ecclesiastical estates.

These sample letters of part four of the *Dictaminis Epithalamium*, approximately sixty in number, seem to be original with Juan Gil. The reference to the death of the *infante* D. Fernando shows that they were written in the late 1270's, although Juan Gil probably had access to earlier records—perhaps the cartulary of the Franciscan convent of Zamora—which would explain the anachronisms,

In the course of this description of the *Dictaminis Epithalamium*, I have mentioned some of its immediate sources, particularly Guido Faba and "Artaldus." Juan Gil also cites a great many classical authors. In the prologue he writes that he has organized his treatise "secundum Quintilianum De Oratoris Institucionibus" (f. 1r.5-6). And at the beginning of the text he quotes the following passage, ostensibly from the same work: "Laudamus verba bene rebus acomodata; usitatis pocius utimur, nova verba non sine periculo fingimus. Nam si recepta sunt, modicum lucrum afferunt, repudiata vero in iocos exeunt" (f. 2v.9-12). This is actually a conflation of two widely separated passages from Book I of Quintilian: "Laudamus . . . acomodata" is found at I. v. 3-4; "usitatis . . . exeunt" (with *laudem* instead of Juan Gil's *lucrum*) is found at I. v. 71-72. This suggests that Juan Gil was using a *florilegium* rather than the *Institutio Oratoria* itself. The other citations of classical authors confirm this supposition. They are all found in the sections on the censure of vices and the commendation of virtues at the beginning of the work. Within a space of ten lines Juan Gil cites Cicero's *De Inventione* (II. lix. 178), the *Eunuchus* of Terence, Seneca, and Cicero's *De Officiis*, on the subject of rightful censure (f. 9v.19-29). Ovid (*Metamorphoses, Fasti*) and Sallust (*De Catilinae Coniuratione*) condemn avarice (f. 14r.33-38). Cicero (*De Amicitia*) is quoted on the perils to friendship (f. 10r.4-9), Claudianus (*In Rufinum* II) on those of envy (ff. 11v.37-12r.1), Ovid on patience (f. 12r.33-34), Prudentius (*Psychomachia*) on pride (f. 13v.36-38), and Pompeius Trogus on gluttony (f. 14r.1-3). One further citation of Quintilian (XI. iii. 176) appears at the beginning of the general section on censure (f. 7v.19-23). All this indicates a *florilegium* organized in the manner of the *summae* of vices and virtues, with appropriate quotations from classical and Christian authors. We need not assume much classical knowledge on the part of Juan Gil, not even of classical rhetoric.

The preceding analysis has shown a tripartite work, not the quadripartite one Juan Gil said he was writing: (1) the section on praise and censure; (2) the technical material on the *ars dictaminis*; (3) the sample letters. The first and last sections comprise the bulk of the work. The technical section has been reduced to the bare minimum. Furthermore, it is precisely the technical section which has been copied from earlier sources (principally Guido Faba's *Summa Dictaminis*). The section on vices and virtues and the sample letters are probably original with Juan Gil.

The structure and proportions of the work make it obvious that it was not intended for the practicing notary. In this respect it differs markedly from the technical *artes dictaminis* of the Italian school. It is, for the period in which it is written, unique. Late thirteenth-century *artes dictaminis* in other parts of Europe, particularly in Italy, are becoming much more technical, as we have seen in the example of Geoffrey of Everseley; they are increasingly directed toward the professional notary. This is not true of the *Dictaminis Epithalamium*. Juan Gil intends it for his friend Philippus of Perugia in particular and for the ecclesiastical man of letters in general: " You sought from me a method of writing sweet, useful, and honest words which you could use in the composition of letters, in the commendation of illustrious persons, in the condemnation of vices, in the expansion of sermons, and in subtle speeches in meetings" (f. 1r.11-14). Sermons, speeches, letters, and chronicles are the genres in which the ecclesiastic must be expert. In the *Dictaminis Epithalamium* Juan Gil attempts to provide the cleric with some of that expertise, not so much by precept as by example. This is obviously so in the section on vices and virtues. But even in the sample letters of the second half of the work, those which record purely routine matters are in a distinct minority. Instead, Juan Gil treats the general themes of friendship, of consolation, and of exhortation which the ecclesiastical man of letters must know how to handle in his dealings with the world of affairs.

Juan Gil de Zamora occupies an important place in the history of Spanish letters as the first author since St. Isidore to discuss, however briefly and if only by example, the problems of literary composition. The *Dictaminis Epithalamium* should serve as the point of departure for future studies in this field. Comparisons must be made between the practices advocated in it and those followed by Juan Gil in his own historical works. The same approach should be followed in studies on the composition of the vernacular histories, particularly the Alfonsine chronicles. An edition of the *Dictaminis Epithalamium*, upon which I am presently working, would greatly facilitate such comparative studies.

THE *Breve Compendium Artis Rethorice* OF MARTÍN DE CÓRDOBA

If our knowledge of Juan Gil de Zamora is slight, our knowledge of Martín de Córdoba is nonexistent. The name occurs in the *incipit* of the *Breve Compendium Artis Rethorice* in the following form: "Incipit breve *compendium* artis rethorice magi*st*ri M. Cordubensis." For reasons unknown to me the initial is resolved in the printed description of the manuscript as follows: "M[artini] Cordubensis breve compendium artis rhetoricae."[67] This is the only evidence we have

---

[67] *Catalogue générale des manuscrits des bibliothèques publiques de France* (Paris: Librairie Plon, 1886), I, 258. M. C. Simonnet of the Bibliothèque Municipale

concerning the identity of the author of the *Breve Compendium*. It is convenient to refer to him as "Martín," but all we really know is that the author was from Cordova and that his Christian name began with "M."

Díaz y Díaz, following the reference in the printed catalogue, identifies this "Martín" with the author of an *ars praedicandi* found in the Biblioteca Capitular of Pamplona.[68] The author of the latter, however, is Martín Alfonso de Córdoba, a theologian who died in 1476.[69] Both manuscripts of the *Breve Compendium* date from the fourteenth century.[70]

Nicolás Antonio refers to another Martín de Córdoba (or perhaps the same) as follows: "Martinus de Corduba, magistri ornatus titulo, scripsit librum *Diversarum Historiarum*, quem laudat Ferdinandus Mexia in suo Nobiliario lib. I. cap 76."[71] Far from praising, Fernando Mexía merely says that "maestro Martin de Cordoua enel lib. llamado de diuersas istorias, dize que marques en Latin dizen mar-

---

of Rouen was unable to explain why the *Breve Compendium* is attributed to Martín de Córdoba in the catalogue (letter dated 30 June 1969).

[68] *Index Scriptorum*, p. 409. Díaz y Díaz is the only scholar to mention this work in any way.

[69] The *Ars Praedicandi* of Martín Alfonso de Córdoba has been edited by Fernando Rubio in *CD*, 172 (1959), 327-348. A. D. Deyermond suggests the possibility that the same man may have written the *Ars Praedicandi* and the *Breve Compendium Artis Rethorice*, but that this would not have been the fifteenth-century Martín Alfonso de Córdoba but rather his virtually unknown fourteenth-century homonym (letter dated 25 March 1970).

[70] Besides the fourteenth-century Rouen MS. 0 52 of the Bibliothèque Municipale, there is a version comprising slightly less than the first half of the text in Madrid Bibl. Nac. MS. 9309, which dates from the first half of the fourteenth century: Martín de la Torre y Pedro Longás, *Catálogo de códices latinos*, Vol. I: *Biblicos*, Patronato de la Biblioteca Nacional (Madrid: Tipografía de Blass, 1935), p. 183. See my "Retóricas clásicas y medievales," nos. 118 and 119, for a complete description of both MSS. I refer exclusively to the Rouen MS and incorporate citations into the text. See the Appendix for a statement of editorial practice.

[71] *Biblioteca Hispana Vetus, sive, Hispani Scriptores qui ab Octaviani Augusti Aevo ad Annum Christi MD. Floruerent*, 2d ed., ed. by Franciso Pérez Bayer, 2 vols. (Madrid: Apud viduam et heredes D. J. Ibarrae, 1788), II, 372-373.

chio*n.*"⁷² Although Martín Alfonso de Córdoba is not known to
have been a historian, he may well have been. In any event, there
is no reason to link the author of *De diversas historias* with that of
the *Breve Compendium.*

Writing in 1847 on medieval popular poetry, Edélstand du Méril asserts that "le Coronica general de España . . . ne peut être pos-
térieur à la fin du xiiiᵉ siècle, puisque don Martin de Cordoue l'écri-
vit par ordre d'Alphonse le Savant . . . ."⁷³ Amador de los Ríos
states that he does not know "en qué fundamentos, [du Méril] se
apoya; pero según verán los lectores, su opinión no puede ser más
peregrina."⁷⁴ Ramón Menéndez Pidal likewise passes over in silence
the supposed participation of a Martín de Córdoba in the *Primera
crónica general*: "No tenemos para qué discutir los fundamentos, siempre muy escasos, con que se cuenta para citar, entre los colabora-
dores, nombres como los de Jofré de Loaysa, fray Juan Gil de Zamora, Bernardo de Brihuega, Martín de Córdoba y otros."⁷⁵ It is
regrettable that du Méril did not see fit to cite his source. I have
been unable to find any other information about this Martín de Córdoba. Other persons of the same name are mentioned in ecclesiastical documents of the fourteenth century, but there is no way of
knowing whether they had anything to do with the *Breve Compendium.*⁷⁶

The text offers no information about the author and very little
about the date of the work. If Torre and Longás are correct in their
assertion that the Madrid manuscript dates from the first half of
the fourteenth century, we have a *terminus ante quem* of roughly

⁷² *Libro intitulado nobiliario* (Seville: Pedro Brun Juã Gentil, 30 June 1492),
f. d iii r. [Hispanic Society of America, copy 6].

⁷³ *Poésies populaires latines du moyen âge* (Paris: Firmin Didot Frères, 1847;
Leipzig: A. Franck, Libraire-Éditeur, 1847), p. 290.

⁷⁴ *Historia crítica*, III, 567n.

⁷⁵ In the introduction to his ed. of the *Primera crónica general*, I, xx.

⁷⁶ Beltrán de Heredia, in *Bulario*, pp. 407, 501, records a Martín Martínez, cleric of Cordova, in 1366, and a Martín López, also a cleric of Cordova, in 1393. González Dávila states that a Martín Fernández de Córdoba accompanied D. Diego
de Anaya (founder of the Colegio Mayor de S. Bartolomé of Salamanca) to the
council of Constance in 1414: *Teatro eclesiástico de las iglesias metropolitanas*, II,
64.

1350. The *terminus a quo* is supplied by a reference to William of
Moerbeke's translation of the *Rhetorica* of Aristotle: "Nam ab A*ris-
tote*le p*rimo* Rethoricorum sic notifficatur: 'Rethorica est assecutiva dya*lectice*'" (f. 107v.20-21). This, the first sentence of William's
translation, varies from the wording found in the *vetus* translation
and in Hermannus Alemannus' translation of Averroes' *Commentarium Medium* on the *Rhetorica*.[77] William finished his translation
sometime before 1270 (although probably not much before that date;
his translation of the *Poetica* was finished in 1278).[78] So the *Breve
Compendium* was composed sometime during the period from before
1270 to about 1350.

There is no other incontrovertible evidence, but certain indications
point to the latter part of that period. In the prologue Martín states:
"Clarissimor*um* t*amen* quor*umdam* summ*a* ingenuitas adolescenciu*m*
rigidam michi c*on*fert audaciam, ut qui orator*um* exiguus emulator hac in celeberrim*a* resideo universitate . . . " (f. 106r.5-8).
The use of the word "university" to indicate a school is rather
late. The usual expression in the thirteenth century is "studium generale." During the early period the word "universitas" refers to
any legally organized corporation such as a cathedral chapter, a monastery, or a guild. On the basis of this evidence, admittedly slight,
I would put the date of the *Breve Compendium* between 1300 and
1350.

The *Breve Compendium* contains no sample letters like those in
the *Dictaminis Epithalamium* which would help to locate the city
in which the work was written. In fact, there are few geographical
references of any kind. In an example of amplification, Martín says:
"Ut Bononia sum ventur*us*. Dic: 'Bononiam h*abe*o p*ro*positum ve-
niendi'" (f. 113r.23-24). In an example of synecdoche, he says: "Ter-
cius apto*m*nus involuit me curis stu*d*ii p*ar*isien*sis*" (f. 116r.25-26).
This example is the more significant in that Martín's apparent source,
Geoffroi de Vinsauf's *Poetria Nova*, does not mention Paris.[79]

---

[77] *Aristoteles Latinus, Pars Prior*, pp. 167, 212.

[78] Ibid., pp. 77-78; *Pars Posterior*, p. 788.

[79] "In studio me tertia comperit aestas,/Tertius involvit autumnus . . . ." Ed.
by Faral in *Les arts poétiques*, ll.1025-1026; further references will be incorporated into the text.

There is a reference to the death of St. Thomas à Becket, archbishop of Canterbury (f. 117v.9-11). An example of asyndeton taken from Nicholas Graecus alludes to France: "Arvus milicia, rebus pietate, sobria Francia sulcitur odium vel ibi reperitur" (f. 118r.5-6). The most interesting reference occurs (predictably) just at the point where the Rouen manuscript breaks off through loss of a folio: "Unde ego sepe numero vidi oratores et domini nostri et regis Francie qui quando erant oraturi conscilio medicorum talibus utebantur alimentis . . . " (f. 123v.30-32). The reference to "domini nostri" is tantalizing. Since it is coupled with the name of the king of France, it may be supposed that it refers to another king and, further, to a king of Castile and León, since the author is in fact a Cordovan. But there is no way of knowing. However, we should not overlook the fact that the author is *also* acquainted with the king of France, and that he has been in his presence or at his court. Since Paris was the traditional seat of the French court, we may assume that our author was in Paris.

As with the date, the evidence is slight; but cumulatively it points to a French origin for the *Breve Compendium*, even though the author was Spanish. This is borne out, as we shall see later, by the analysis of the sources used in the work, as far as they can be determined. Concretely, then, the *Breve Compendium Artis Rethorice* was written by a Cordovan, whose first name may have been Martín, probably in the first half of the fourteenth century and probably in France, possibly in Paris.

The author states in a prologue that he is composing his work for youths who have completed the "rudimenta elementarum gramaticalium" and are ready to study the "ornatum lingue quam dulcissima propinat rethorica" (f. 106r.21-33).[80] For it is not good that learned men should proffer their "theosoficas profunditates" in "inculto stilo" (f. 106r.26-27). Martín cites the Greek and Latin doctors of the Church as users of rhetoric and points out the discipline's use to professors of both civil and canon law (f. 106r.30-v.21). Even the greatest philosophers have deigned to cultivate it: "Nec Aristoteles apex philosophorum eam deseruit cum opus rethorice ar-

---

[80] See the Appendix for a transcription of the prologue.

tis elegantissimum conficeret, a quo et nostri rethores Latini habundantissimam frugem colegerunt" (f. 106v.24-27).

Martín emphasizes the importance of rhetoric with a variety of comparisons. He picks up Cicero's contention (in *De Inv.* I. iv. 5)—which we have also seen in the *Siete partidas* (see above, p. 72)—that man differs from beasts in his ability to speak, and that the man most worthy of praise is he who excels others in that ability in which man excels the beasts (f. 106v.30-32). Again, many people ornament their houses richly, wear beautiful clothes, and enjoy the best in food and even shoes (f. 107r.1-22), but how much better to ornament one's speech (f. 107r.23-29). Finally, there are those who lack a hand or a foot and are crippled in body and are caused much pain thereby (f. 107r.29-32). "Quanto ergo singulariter dolendum est si lingua cespitet aut barbarizet et verba inexplanata sua ruditate loquatur" (f.107r.32-v.2).

Rhetoric helps one to polish up "rubiginem lingue quam a natura traximus" (f. 107v.6). To aid the student in learning this art, Martín has composed a "brevem et compendiosum tractatum pedestri sermone quo intelligibilior esset . . . " (f. 107v.8-9). This is a revealing commentary on the practice of composing technical treatises in verse. Apparently they were less than comprehensible to the young student.

Martín then lists the thirteen chapters of his treatise:

I. Quid est rethorica et unde dicatur.
II. De triplici negocio rethorice.
III. De inventione.
IV. De dispositione.
V. De materie prolongamine.
VI. De abreviatione.
VII. De coloribus [transumptionum].
VIII. De coloribus verborum.
IX. De coloribus sententiarum.
X. De elegancia.
XI. De viciis.
XII. De memoria.
XIII. De pronunciatione.

Except for the chapters on abbreviation and amplification we might be looking at the table of contents of a classical treatise. Included are the three kinds of causes, the five parts of rhetoric (invention, disposition, style, memory, pronunciation), and the division of rhetorical figures into tropes, figures of speech, and figures of thought.

In Chapter I Martín gives three different definitions of rhetoric, taken from three different sources. Following the passage from Aristotle's *Rhetorica* already cited, the distinction between dialectic and rhetoric is developed on the basis of their varying purposes.[81] Dialectic helps one to know the truth; rhetoric inclines one to seek the good: " . . . rhetoric ought to find ways of inflaming the listener to the love of the just and equitable. Whence the end of dialectic is to increase the conviction that disposes [one] toward knowledge. The end of rhetoric, however, is to increase the faith that leads to a certain good-will (*quandam affectionem*)" (f. 108r.15-19). This is quite unlike the traditional definitions of rhetoric as derived from Cicero and repeated by theorists from Cassidorus and Isidore to Geoffroi de Vinsauf and John of Garland. It indicates a concern for the place of rhetoric in the total organization of human knowledge which hitherto has been found only in treatises dealing with that particular question: Dominicus Gundisalvus and his *De Divisione Philosophiae*, the *Metalogicon* of John of Salisbury, and the

---

[81] I cite this passage in full because of its importance for the development of medieval rhetorical theory: "Nam ab Aristotele primo Rethoricorum sic notifficatur: 'Rethorica est assecutiva dyalectice.' Pro cuius diffinitionis determinatione advertandum est quod tota hominis perfectio in duobus consistit, s[cilicet]: in cognicione veritatis et in amore virtutis. Hinc est quod sunt alique sciencie speculative que nos iuvant ad veritatis cognicionem, sicut phisica, mathematica et methaphisica. Et alique sunt que nos inducunt ad amorem virtutis; sicut sunt sciencie morales, de quibus dicit Philosophus secundo Ethicorum quod presens negocium accepimus non ut sciamus sed ut boni fiamus.* Est verum quod noster modus cognoscendi tam in speculativis quam in moralibus est discursivus, s[cilicet] ratiocinando et arguendo; et propter hoc fuit neccessarium invenire duas artes que essent quidam modi sciendi et que nos dirigerent in huiusmodi discursibus et argumentationibus. Iste sunt dialectica et rethorica. Unde dyalectica deseruit scienciis speculativis in arguendo et sillogizando. Sicut habetur primo Thopicorum, est enim utilis ad obviationes, ad excercitaciones et ad philosophales disciplinas. Rethorica vero deseruit negocio politico et scienciis moralibus. Unde sicut illa disponit nos ut sciamus verum, ita ista nos inclinat ut velimus bonum. Est ergo rethorica assecutiva, id est inmitativa, dyalectice. Unde relictis subtilioribus huius diffinitionis declarationibus quia non multum ad rem pertinet. Ista michi videtur sufficiens: quod sicut dyalectica invenit rationes et argumenta ad cognoscendum, ita rethorica debet invenire vias ut inflammet auditores ad amorem iusti et equi. Unde finis dyalectice est augmentare oppinionem que disponit ad sciencias. Finis vero rethorice est augmentare fidem que inducit quandam affectionem. Et sic istis modis et multis aliis rethorica est assecutiva dyalectice, id est inmitativa" (ff. 107v.20-108r.21).

thirteenth-century *De Ortu et Divisione Philosophiae* of Robert Kilwardby. The concept of rhetoric is changing; it is beginning to recover its ancient dignity.

Martín does not neglect the traditional definitions of rhetoric, however. He quotes an unidentified "Alanus": "Rethorica est sciencia apposite di(s)cendi ad persuasionem sive quod idem est sciencia bene et recte dicendi. Unde sicut gramatica docet recte loqui quantum ad congruitatem, sic rethorica quo ad ornatum et decenciam" (f. 108r.22-25). The first part of the definition echoes that found in Cassiodorus (*Institutiones* II. ii. 1) and repeated by Isidore (*Etymologiae* II. i. 1) and later authors. The second part brings to mind the end of the passage on rhetoric in the *General estoria*: " . . . prima docet nos recte loqui, secunda subtiliter *et* acute, tercia persuasibiliter et hornate" (II, 57b.13-16). The resemblance is strengthened by Martín's use (still following "Alanus"?) of the following simile: "Sicut prius edifficatur domus et postea pingitur . . . " (f. 108r. 29-30). The same simile is found in the *General estoria*: " . . . gramatica prima . . . accomodat fundamentum, dialectica pariete erigit, rectorica totum edificium pingit . . . " (II, 57a.35-b.5).

A commentary on the *Rhetorica ad C. Herennium* (one of Martín's chief sources), in which the commonplace "prima docet . . . et hornate" is found, was written by an "Alanus" in the late twelfth century.[82] The author has been identified with Alain de Lille.[83] The only other time Martín refers to an "Alanus" in the *Breve Compendium* occurs in a citation of Alain de Lille's *De Planctu Naturae* (f. 117r.22-24). It seems probable, then, that the "Alanus" cited here may be the same person; and it is at least possible that the work

---

* The MS reads "fiamur"; the Madrid MS reads "eficiamur" (f. 129r.9). I am indebted to Professor Silk for the emendation.

[82] I am indebted to Professor Harry Caplan for this information (letter dated 15 February 1969). For a more detailed description of this text see Caplan, "A Mediaeval Commentary on the *Rhetorica ad Herennium*," in his *Of Eloquence: Studies in Ancient and Mediaeval Rhetoric*, ed. by Anne King and Helen North (Ithaca: Cornell University Press [1970]), pp. 247-270.

[83] Marie-Thérèse d'Alverny, while agreeing with Professor Caplan that it is not certain, is inclined to accept Alain as the author of the commentary. Alain de Lille: *Textes inédits, avec une introduction sur sa vie et ses œuvres*, Études de Philosophie Médiévale, 52 (Paris: Librairie Philosophique J. Vrin, 1965), pp. 52-55.

cited is the commentary on the *Ad Herennium* attributed to him.[84]

A third definition of rhetoric is cited, ostensibly from Cicero: "Rethorica est sciencia docens de quocumque persuasibilem invenire materiam et ipsius particulas congruenter disponere; disposita, in colore verbi et sentencie exornare; postea presentare memorie et ultimo auribus hominum pronunciatione ydonea intimare" (f. 108r.32-v.5). While this is thoroughly Ciceronian in doctrine, I have been unable to locate such a citation in either the *De Inventione* or the *Rhetorica ad C. Herennium*, the only two works to which Martín could possibly be referring.[85]

At the end of Chapter I, Martín gives the etymology of the word "rhetoric": "Dicitur autem rethorica a 'resis' Grece, quod est 'ornatus' Latine, et 'ycos,' quod est 'sciencia'; quia est sciencia de ornatu. Vel secundum alios dicitur a 'copia loqucionis,' quia 'resis' apud Grecos 'locutio' dicitur" (f. 108v.7-11). The second etymology is the one given by Isidore (*Etym.* II. i. 1-2). I have been unable to find a source for the first one.

Chapter II defines the three kinds of rhetorical causes—judicial, deliberative, and demonstrative—according to their purposes. Since the general end of rhetoric is "suadere bonum" (f. 108v.14), the specific causes address themselves to three kinds of "good." The judicial cause seeks what is just and equitable and is composed of accusation and defense; the deliberative cause seeks what is useful; the demonstrative cause seeks the praiseworthy and virtuous and is composed of preaching and persuasion to the love of virtue

---

[84] Whether this same work is the source of the passage in the *General estoria* is more debatable. As I pointed out in Chapter III, the probabilities point toward a general treatise on the liberal arts. A "family" resemblance would not be unusual, given the fact that both the unknown treatise used by Alfonso and the commentary on the *Ad Herennium* are products of the school of Chartres. Mlle. d'Alverny shows the close resemblance of the *accessus* of the "Alanus" commentary to that of Thierry of Chartres on the *De Inventione* (Alain de Lille, pp. 53-54). We have already seen the resemblances between the latter and Dominicus Gundisalvus' *De Divisione Philosophiae*.

[85] Similar statements are found in *De Inventione* I. vii. 9; and in *Rhetorica ad C. Herennium* I. ii. 3, ed. by Harry Caplan, Loeb Classical Library, 403 (Cambridge: Harvard University Press, 1954; London: William Heinemann Ltd., 1954; repr. 1964); further references will be incorporated into the text.

(ff. 108v.16-109r.4). Each of these causes can be either special or individual. If it is special, it applies to the state; if it is individual, it applies to a private person (f. 109r.9-10).

Martín continues with the proposition that the body politic is divided into three groups: judges (including princes and prelates), counselors, and people. The orator must adjust his speech to his audience: "Cum *ergo* orator loqui*tur* ad iudices debe*t* semp*er* fundare suos locos et maxi*m*as in iusto et equo eo modo quo *i*ncipit liber sapie*n*cie: 'Diligite iusticia*m* qui iudicatis terram' (Book of Wisdom I. 1)" (f. 109r. 25-29). When speaking to counselors the orator must base his argument on the useful and beneficial; when speaking to the populace he must laud virtue and condemn vice (f. 109r.30-v.3).

In further developing the doctrine of the three genres of causes, Martín shows that they correspond to the several kinds of good which exist: "bona a*n*ime" and "bona corporis" (f. 109v.8-9). The demonstrative cause is concerned with spiritual good—the virtues. The deliberative cause is concerned with corporal or temporal good. The judicial cause is concerned with both kinds of good combined, "quia totus homo est pars civilitatis et debet cu*m* aliis co*n*vive*r*e in iusticia et equitate" (f. 109v.14-15). The chapter ends with a series of rules to be followed in each of the three kinds of causes. For example, in a judicial cause the accuser begins his case with an appeal to justice; the defendant, with an appeal to clemency. The accuser seeks to demonstrate the seriousness of the crime by an examination of the crime itself or of the circumstances under which it was committed. The defendant seeks to extenuate the crime by means of the same methods (ff. 109v.16-110r.9). Similar precepts are given for the deliberative and demonstrative causes (f. 110r.9-19).

I have not found anything which resembles this in earlier treatises. Presumably it is based on *Ad Her.* I. ii. 2 or *De Inv.* I. v. 7., but it is developed far more extensively. A possible source would be a commentary on one of these works such as the "Alanus" commentary on the *Ad Herennium*.[86]

---

[86] Compare the following passage from Thierry of Chartres' commentary on the *De Inventione*: "Civiles autem controversiae aut de iusto ante iudices esse solent et tunc illae controversiae *causae iudiciales* dicuntur: aut de utili apud r. p.

Chapter III discusses *inventio*, which, following *Ad Her.* I. ii. 3, is defined as follows: "Rerum verarum vel verissi*milium* excogitacio ad hoc q*uod* intenditur suadendum" (f. 110r.23-24). Martín develops the two parts of this definition, concerning true and conjectural cases, and gives a series of rules to help the orator select his arguments. First, the orator should meditate at length on his proposed subject. Martín backs this up with a quotation from Geoffroi de Vinsauf: "Si quis h*abet* fundare domu*m*, non curret ad actu*m* impetuosa man*us*" (f. 110v.6-7; *Poetria Nova*, ll.43-44). From this point onward the organization of the *Breve Compendium Artis Rethorice* follows that of the *Poetria Nova*, and many specific examples are derived from the latter work—making even more apparent the originality of Martín's previous definitions of rhetoric and treatment of the three rhetorical genres.

The second rule of invention is to read much, and "precipue hystorica, quia ut plurimu*m* ea de quibus dicturi sumus sunt similia eis que ante nos fuerunt. Et hoc sive in libris s*anct*is sive in libris gentiliu*m*" (f. 110v.9-12). Similarly, the orator must read also in the book of nature, seeking images and arguments in the four elements and the beasts associated with them (f. 110v.12-27). The fourth rule requires the orator to pay attention to the accidents of the subject on which he is speaking. Much benefit can be derived from the application of the Aristotelian categories to the theme, "et maxime i*sta* reg*ula* proficit in arte predicandi *et* harangandi" (f. 111r.3-4). Fifth, the orator must pay attention to the attributes of the person and of the affair of which he is speaking. Personal attributes are name, surname, fortune, habit, and so on (f. 111r.7). Attributes of an affair—and here Martín specifically rejects those given by Cicero[87]—are "quis, q*uid* [?], ubi, p*er* quos, quociens, cur, quomo*do*, q*uando*" (f. 111r.11-12).

---

aut privati procuratores et tunc *causae deliberativae* dicuntur: aut de honesto apud populum in concionibus et tunc *causae demonstrativae* dicuntur. Sunt igitur hae tres res i. e. justum, utile, honestum, fines omnium causarum ex quibus omnes causae nascuntur i. e. civiles controversiae." Ed. by Suringar, p. 220.

[87] The particular attributes of the affair to which Martín here refers seem to be those found in *De Inv.* I. xxvi. 37-xxviii. 43: *causa, locus, tempus, occasio, modus, facultas*. Martín again is following a tradition based on dialectic rather than

Chapter IV deals with *dispositio*, and again Martín takes his definition from *Ad Her.* I. ii. 3. He pauses briefly to present a metaphor based on the building of a house. Just as a house requires materials, a form, and decoration, so does a speech. Invention finds the materials, disposition gives them form, and style decorates them (f. 111r. 26-v.1). The main thrust of Martín's comments on disposition is directed at the two kinds of order, natural and artificial. Natural order presents a history in the same way it happened, from the beginning to the end. Artificial order "est quando narratur non eo ordine, sed per artem ordinatur hystoria" (f. 111v.15-16). Here he is referring not to the "in medias res" of Horace's *Ars poetica*, which apparently was unknown to him, but rather to the practice of organizing a speech around certain categories. Thus a confession may be ordered by simply starting at the beginning of the repentent sinner's life and going through his sins one after the other. Or it may be organized artificially, according to the sins of the five senses, the seven deadly sins, or the ten commandments (ff. 111v.24-112r.2), as, indeed, Pero López de Ayala's is in the *Rimado de Palacio*. As a further example Martín cites from the *Poetria Nova* the history of King Minos of Crete and his son Androgeus, showing how it can be organized in various ways (f. 112r.2-v.13).[88]

Since "prolixitas vel brevitas ad disposicionem pertinet" (f. 111v.6), Martín then takes up amplification and abbreviation in Chapters V and VI. This material belonging to the medieval *ars poetria* has been grafted on to the classical schema in the most appropriate location. There are eight methods of amplification: (1) *interpretatio* (the presentation of the same idea in other words), (2) *circuitio* (circumlocution), (3) *comparatio* (the use of comparisons), (4) *apostrophe*, (5) *prosopopoeia*, (6) *digressio*, (7) *descriptio*, and (8) *oppositio* (the expression of the same idea in two contrasting ways), (ff. 112v.23-

---

rhetoric, possibly Aristotle's *Topics*, which he has cited earlier, or Boethius' *De Differentiis Topicis* IV. In the latter work the attributes of the affair are defined as follows: "Reliquas uero circunstantias, quae sunt quid, cur, quomodo, quibus auxiliis, ubi, quando, in attributis negocio ponit." Ed. Paris, 1543, f. 19r.

[88] *Poetria Nova*, ll. 156-202. Geoffroi's *Documentum de Arte Versificandi* contains the same example (ed. by Faral, *Les arts poétiques*, II. i. 3-8), but verbal parallels show that Martín used the *Poetria Nova*.

114r.14). The various methods are presented in exactly the same order as in the *Poetria Nova* (ll. 220-689), but specific examples are either original with Martín or taken from some other source which I have been unable to identify.[89]

The eight methods of abbreviation are treated in much less detail and less clearly—reflecting the treatment accorded them in the *Poetria Nova*. To balance the eight methods of amplification, Martín adds one more to the seven ways of abbreviation found in Geoffroi's work: (1) *emphasis* (the use of an abstraction for a concrete example—"envy," not an "envious man"), (2) *articulus* (suppression of conjunctions between words), (3) *absolutum* (ablative absolute), (4) *suspensio* (suppression of part of the material), (5) *intellectio* (implicit understanding of something not said), (6) *dissolutum* (suppression of conjunctions between clauses), (7) *clausum* (not found in the *Poetria Nova*; the use of general categories rather than specific examples),[90] (8) *compendium* (the narration of a long story briefly), (f. 114r.16-v.26).

In Chapter VII Martín takes up the third part of rhetoric, *elocutio*, or style. The definition is again taken from *Ad Her.* I. ii. 3. Style is subdivided into "dignity" and "elegance" (f. 114v.30-31). Dignity consists of the use of figures of speech and thought (*Ad Her.* IV. xii. 18); elegance is divided into Latinity and clarity (*Ad Her.* IV. xii. 17). Latinity consists of an abundance of vocabulary and the elimination of hackneyed expressions. Therefore it is useful for the rhetorician "ponere omnia vocabula exquisita in quodam libello ut promptius reperiat" (f. 115r.4-5). The discovery of such a manual of "exquisite words" would indeed be interesting. Clarity consists of the elimination of turgidity of expression, of all faults, and the correct placement of words.

In accordance with this definition of style, Martín then turns to the elements of *dignitas*—the tropes (*colores transumptionum*),

---

[89] Two parallels are found in Geofroi's *Documentum de Arte Versificandi*: "Viam universe carnis est ingressus" occurs at f. 113r.6-7 and II. ii. 15; a less conclusive example is found at f. 113v.25-29 and II. ii. 20.

[90] "7us modus vocatur clausum, quia si vellem dicere, 'eadem est sciencia sani et agri, virtutis et vicii,' dicerem brevius claudendo, 'omni contrariorum eadem est disciplina'" (f. 114v.16-19).

figures of speech (*colores verborum*), and figures of thought (*colores sententiarum*), which occupy the rest of Chapter VII and all of Chapters VIII and IX. Before listing the tropes, Martín presents five "rules" for their use, which are nothing more than the first five examples of "figurative meaning" of Geoffroi de Vinsauf's *ornatus difficilis* (*Poetria Nova*, ll. 765-885), followed by the ten tropes proper (ff. 115r.7-116v.17). Chapter VIII lists thirty-four figures of speech (ff. 116v.18-119v.13); Chapter IX, nineteen figures of thought (ff. 119v.14-121v.7). Although most of these figures are taken from *Ad Herennium IV* (figures of speech and thought follow *Ad Herennium* exactly), it is clear that the immediate source is the *Poetria Nova*. Like Geoffroi, Martín begins with the tropes rather than with the figures of speech; the *Ad Herennium* begins with the former. Furthermore, many of the examples are taken from the *Poetria Nova*.

Chapter X of the *Breve Compendium* takes up the second part of *elocutio*, elegance. Martín begins with *latinitas*, which he further divides into *commutatio* and *determinatio*. *Commutatio* refers to the conversion of one part of speech into another for the sake of variety. *Determinatio* is the combination of various parts of speech, one of which defines the other, as in the following example: "Unum fixum determinatur per reliquum, ut 'Hic est Paris facie, Tullius ore, Catho mente'" (f. 122v.25-27). Here the common noun is defined by the proper noun. Again the specific doctrines and examples are taken from Geoffroi de Vinsauf (*Poetria Nova*, ll. 1588-1841), but the subordination of these doctrines to the schema of classical rhetoric as set forth in *Ad Herennium* is original with Martín.

The author examines briefly the second part of elegance, *explanatio*, in Chapter XI. *Explanatio* is "abstraccio orationis a viciis" (f. 123r.7). Such faults are the too frequent repetition of a vowel, consonant, or word.[91] Others are the repetition of the same case

---

[91] Cf. f. 123r.13-15: " . . . nimia diccionis repeticio, ut 'cum sit racio racionis de racione, hinc non est racio prebere fidem rationi.'" This is taken from *Poetria Nova*, ll. 1930-1931, and ultimately from *Ad Her.* IV. xii. 18: "Nam cuius rationis ratio non extet, ei rationi ratio non est fidem habere admodum." Cervantes satirizes the same fault (using almost the same example) in *Don Quijote* I. i: "La razón de la sinrazón que a mi razón se hace, de tal manera mi razón enflaquece, que con razón me quejo de la vuestra fermosura."

ending, incongruency of expression ("celebravit furtu*m*"), and the use of monosyllables and words of more than four syllables at the end of a sentence (f. 123r.15-20). At the end of the chapter Martín defines the various parts of a rhetorical clause—comma, colon, and period—and shows the punctuation marks which indicate them.

Chapter XII briefly discusses the fourth part of rhetoric, memory, which, as in *Ad Her.* III. xvi. 29, can be natural or artificial. In either case "iuvat aut*em* memoriam p*au*citas cibi et potus et assiduitas legendi et audiendi et retinendi iuvat *et* leccio nocturna qua*n*do tempus est quietu*m* . . . " (f. 123v.4-6).

In Chapter XIII Martín takes up delivery, the fifth and final part of rhetoric. This is the "ulti*m*a et optima pars rethori*c*e. Nam teste Damasceno potissimu*m* in or*a*tione est pronu*n*ciacio" (f. 123v.23-25). "Damesceno" is apparently Demosthenes, who is cited by Quintilian (XI. iii. 6) as an exponent of the importance of delivery. The particular source quoted by Martín, however, is unknown to me.

The *Breve Compendium Artis Rethorice* breaks off as Martín is relating a story of the orators of "d*o*mini n*o*s*t*ri et regis Francie" (f. 123v.31). According to the catalogue description, one folio is missing between ff. 123 and 124 of the manuscript. So the work as we have it is almost complete. The missing part contains the end of Chapter XIII and in all probability a brief epilogue as well.

I have been assuming throughout that the *Breve Compendium* is based on Geoffroi de Vinsauf's *Poetria Nova*, yet that assumption may need qualification. The whole question of sources is quite complicated. Underlying everything, of course, is the *Rhetorica ad C. Herennium*, which Martín probably knew directly. He was probably familiar also with the late twelfth-century commentary on that text attributed to "Alanus." The discussion of the three kinds of rhetorical causes, for example, probably comes from this commentary.

Among more modern works Martín seems to be most familiar with the *Poetria Nova*. He cites less frequently a Nicholas Graecus, a Lambertus, a Guido, and takes isolated examples from the *Disticha Catonis*, Evrard de Béthune's *Graecismus*, and Boethius' *De*

Consolatione Philosophiae.[92] On one occasion he cites Guido but gives
an example which is found also in the *Poetria Nova* (f. 121r.22,
ll. 1545-1547). On another he cites an example from Geoffroi and
adds a definition from Guido (f. 116v.24-26, l. 1098). In other words,
Guido (whom I have not been able to identify; it does not seem to
be the *dictator* Guido Faba) may have followed the *Poetria Nova*,
and Martín, who is writing approximately a century after that work,
may be following Guido.

I have been unable to identify Lambertus and Nicholas Graecus.
Fabricius cites a "Nicolaus Graecus Albanensis, clarus in Anglia circa a. 1249, qui Roberto Lincolniensi traditur operam suam praes-
titisse in transferendis scriptoribus Graecis . . . ."[93] Cosenza mentions another Nicholas Graecus, Nicolaus de Deopropio, who served
Charles II and his son Roberto, kings of Sicily, as royal physician
in the first half of the fourteenth century. He did a certain amount
of translation of Greek medical works.[94] Neither of these authors
is known to have written on rhetoric, however. Of the two examples cited from Nicholas, one refers to France, which may be a clue
to his identity (f. 118r.5-6).

I have found no reference to a rhetorician named Lambertus. He
is cited eight times in the *Breve Compendium*; three of those citations
are found also in Evrard the German's *Laborintus de Miseriis Rectorum.*[95] Four other parallels to the *Laborintus* occur for which no

---

[92] Martín takes two of Evrard's examples of rhetorical figures as illustrations
of *conversio* (f. 116v.31-32) and *agnominatio* (f. 118r.28-29). Cf. Eberhardi Bethuniensis *Graecismus*, ed. by Ioh. Wrobel, Corpus Grammaticorum Medii Aevi, 1
(Breslau: In aedibus G. Koebneri, 1887), III.6 and III.41. He cites *De Cons.* I.
met. vii. 1-2 as an example of *compar*. Ed. and trans. by H. F. Stewart, Loeb Classical Library, 74 (Cambridge: Harvard University Press, 1918; London: William
Heinemann Ltd., 1918; repr. *saepe*), p. 168.

[93] Johannes Albertus Fabricius, *Bibliotheca Latina Mediae et Infimae Aetatis*,
6 vols. (I-V, Hamburg: Sumtu viduae Felgineriae, ex officina piscatoria, 1734-1736;
VI, Hamburg: Sumtu Joannis Caroli Bohn, 1746), V, 342.

[94] Mario Emilio Cosenza, *Biographical and Bibliographical Dictionary of the
Italian Humanists and of the World of Classical Scholarship in Italy, 1300-1800*,
2d ed. rev., 6 vols. (Boston: G. K. Hall, 1962-1967), V, 1250-1251.

[95] Cf. f. 118v.1-5, which corresponds to *Laborintus*, ed. by Faral, *Les arts poétiques*, ll. 479-480; f. 119r.28-31 to ll. 511-514; f. 120v.19 to ll. 531-532.

source is cited.[96] Whether Martín was acquainted with both works, whether Lambertus drew on the *Laborintus*, (or whether "Lambertus" is simply a deformation of "Laborintus") are questions that cannot be answered.

Undoubtedly other parallels could be found in many of the *artes poetriae* and treatises on rhetorical colors. However, it is difficult to decide how significant such parallels would be. Most of the *exempla* used in these treatises are commonplaces found in many different works; this makes the problem of identifying sources virtually insoluble. It is highly unlikely that Martín had at his disposal all the treatises he cites explicitly or implicitly. More probably he had two or three basic works—*Ad Herennium* with its commentary, the *Poetria Nova*, Lambertus—which he then collated with Nicholas Graecus and Guido. Scattered parallels to other works would have entered the *Breve Compendium* through these intermediaries.

If the material Martín uses is not original, the same cannot be said for the way in which he organizes it. While not breaking completely with the medieval *ars poetria*, he does attempt—and on the whole successfully—to reconcile it with the classical theories found in *Ad Herennium*. Thus the basic outline of the work— the three kinds of causes, the five parts of rhetoric—is classical. Into this outline Martín fits the specific precepts of amplification and abbreviation, *commutatio* and *determinatio*, taken from Geoffroi. Furthermore, there is a new awareness of rhetoric as a spoken art as well as a written one. Preaching and *ars arengandi*—civil speaking—have a part as well as composition.

The fragmentation which McKeon (in "Rhetoric in the Middle Ages") affirms to be the major characteristic of medieval rhetoric is beginning to disappear in the *Breve Compendium Artis Rethorice*. This marks a major step in the recovery of classical rhetorical theory.

---

[96] F. 115v.16 corresponds to *Laborintus*, l. 367; f. 118v.20-21 to ll. 489-490; f. 120v.12-14 to l. 544; f. 120v.19 to ll. 545-546. In the last example the *Laborintus* takes a passage from Ovid, citing him "teste Ovidio"; the *Breve Compendium* cites him "teste Nasone."

Conclusion

The *Ars Epistolaris Ornatus* and the *Dictaminis Epithalamium* on the one hand and the *Breve Compendium Artis Rethorice* on the other hand are very disparate works. Separated in time by perhaps fifty years, they are separated in concept by an immeasurably wider gulf. The former are still medieval works. Although there are obvious differences between them, they both fall easily within the tradition of the *ars dictandi*. the *Breve Compendium Artis Rethorice* is no longer medieval. It breaks out of the fragmented medieval categories in an attempt to compass the full meaning of rhetoric in one work.

The significance of these works for the study of medieval Spanish literature is disparate as well. The *Ars Epistolaris Ornatus* and the *Dictaminis Epithalamium*, while lying completely within the medieval Latin rhetorical tradition as exemplified by thirteenth-century Italian *dictamen*, are also completely in tune with the Spain of the late thirteenth century. The *Breve Compendium*, equally indebted to the Latin rhetorical tradition, has almost nothing to do with Spain, although it was probably known in the peninsula.[97] It reflects more properly the cultural ambience of the schools of northern Europe. Thus it is the *Ars Epistolaris Ornatus* and the *Dictaminis Epithalamium* which should be the referents in future investigations by Hispanists.

These works represent the entering wedge of Italian influence in Spain during the late medieval period. And this occurs at a time when the influence of French models—the school of Chartres, for example is—on the wane. Furthermore, Spain takes up *dictamen* just at the point when the latter is beginning to evolve into humanism in Italy.[98] The different orientation of Juan Gil and of Geof-

---

[97] In Madrid Bibl. Nac. MS. 9309, the gloss, almost contemporary with the text, is indisputable evidence that the MS was in Spain in the fourteenth century. Cf. "choça" for "tugurio," f. 127v.16.

[98] For an exposition of this thesis, still under discussion, see Paul Oskar Kristeller, "Humanism and Scholasticism in the Italian Renaissance," *Byzantion*, 17 (1944-1945), 346-374.

frey in this respect is illuminating: Geoffrey looks back to the great *dictatores* of the early thirteenth century; Juan Gil looks ahead to humanism, eliminating the technical notarial aspects of *dictamen* and concentrating on those which are likely to be of most use to the quasi-professional writer. In so doing he influences the development of Castilian prose, particularly historical prose. Furthermore, the *Dictaminis Epithalamium* and the *Ars Epistolaris Ornatus* give rise to imitations in the vernacular languages. We have already examined one of these imitations in the *Siete Partidas* of Alfonso the Learned.

CHAPTER V

CONCLUSION

THE EVIDENCE brought forward in this study has been necessarily fragmentary and of varying usefulness. Nothing was found to indicate the teaching of rhetoric in Spain at either the elementary or the university level before the beginning of the fifteenth century. Medieval and modern libraries suggest the presence of the classical rhetorics (*De Inventione* and *Rhetorica ad C. Herennium*) in the thirteenth century, and of the Latin translation of Aristotle's *Rhetorica* and the Italian *artes dictaminis* in the fourteenth century. The examination of rhetorical references in both vernacular and Latin literature indicates that treatises on the liberal arts are a source of the majority of these references and, more specifically, treatises based on the doctrines of the school of Chartres. The works of Ponce of Provence, Geoffrey of Everseley, and Juan Gil de Zamora are proof that the *ars dictaminis* was known and studied in Spain in the second half of the thirteenth century. And the glosses in the Madrid manuscript of Martín de Córdoba's *Breve Compendium Artis Rethorice* disclose that the *artes poetriae* were in all probability known in the fourteenth century.

Synthesizing the above, we arrive at the following schema of rhetorical knowledge for the thirteenth and fourteenth centuries:

1. In the period extending roughly through the first half of the thirteenth century, the dominant rhetorical sources are classical: *De Inventione* and the *Rhetorica ad C. Herennium*. Of lesser importance, because less complete, are treatises on all the liberal arts taking their inspiration from Chartres.

2. During the latter half of the thirteenth century, the period of liveliest scientific and didactic activity in medieval Spain, the *artes dictaminis* begin to assert their presence. This is not to say that the classical treatises are neglected. The evidence shows that during this period both kinds of works were available.

3. Distinctly fewer clues are found for the fourteenth century. Provisionally it may be said that the whole range of rhetorical theory accessible in other parts of contemporary Latin Europe was probably known in Spain as well. The *artes poetriae* and *artes praedicandi* were, however, of less importance than the classical works and the *artes dictandi*.

This schema has obvious implications for future studies of the relationships between rhetoric and medieval Spanish literature. It is clear that the various genres and individual works can no longer be studied merely in relation to one particular source (the *artes poetriae*). The early *mester de clerecía*, for example, grounded thoroughly in rhetorical technique, should be compared in first instance with the doctrines advocated in *De Inventione* and the *Rhetorica ad C. Herennium*.

The Alfonsine works must be studied in the light of the *ars dictandi*, particularly for concrete evidence of the use of technical devices of *dictamen*. Nor can the importance of the *cursus* be overlooked. Its influence must be traced both in the literary works and in royal documents. Its use has long been considered a principal factor in establishing the authenticity of papal and imperial documents; it is not too much to expect that it will prove of equal value in determining the authenticity of royal privileges and letters. Another point to be investigated is the correspondence between theory and practice in the letters occasionally introduced in the Alfonsine historical works, of which perhaps the most famous is Dido's letter to Aeneas (based on Ovid's *Heroides*) in the *Primera crónica general* (I, 38-43). Further problems are the stylistic differences among Alfonso's legal, historical, and scientific works and the relationship of other didactic works of the thirteenth century to the Alfonsine corpus on the one hand and the rhetorical treatises on the other hand. In translations from the Arabic the latter problem becomes of even keener interest.

The artistic prose of don Juan Manuel and the parodistic verse of Juan Ruiz allow comparison with any of the rhetorical treatises extant in the fourteenth century. Of particular importance, however, would be an examination of the possible influence of the Latin translation of Aristotle's *Rhetoric*, which, as far as I can ascertain, enjoyed a vogue in the first half of the fourteenth century.

Some of the questions raised in my Introduction can be answered more fully and categorically than others. Most important: rhetoric in Spain shows an unbroken unity with European Latin culture (given the necessary qualifications for the trajectory of the rhetorical genres). The critics who have affirmed this unity subjectively and used it as the basis for comparative studies have not been in error. But they have almost uniformly interpreted this unity too narrowly, taking as a basis for comparison only the *artes poetriae*, which constituted but a small part of the total rhetorical sources available to the Middle Ages. Worse, they have tended to make comparisons between the *artes poetriae* and works written before the *artes poetriae* were known in Spain, e.g., the thirteenth-century *mester de clerecía*.

Menéndez y Pelayo's affirmation that Spain produced nothing of importance in rhetorical theory holds true for vernacular literature, but not for works written in Latin by Spaniards or for Spaniards. The *Dictaminis Epithalamium* of Juan Gil de Zamora, the *Ars Epistolaris Ornatus* of Geoffrey of Everseley, and the *Breve Compendium Artis Rethorice* of Martín de Córdoba are sufficient rebuttal. The former are more important for Spain ; the latter is a major witness for the state of the rhetorical art in Europe in the first half of the fourteenth century and deserves the attention of all students of medieval literary theory.

This essay cannot hope to be more than a beginning, a clearing of the ground so that the real work can be undertaken. Borrowing a metaphor utilized by some of the authors examined in it, we have begun to study the foundations of the edifice of medieval Spanish rhetoric. Now we can proceed to examine the structure itself and the finer details of ornamentation.

ABBREVIATIONS

AA	*Anthologica Annua*
AEM	*Anuario de Estudios Medievales*
AIA	*Archivo Ibero-Americano*
AM	*Annales du Midi*
BAE	Biblioteca de Autores Españoles
BEC	*Bibliothèque de l'École des Chartes*
BHS	*Bulletin of Hispanic Studies*
BISI	*Bullettino dell'Istituto Storico Italiano*
BM	British Museum
BRAH	*Boletín de la Real Academia de la Historia*
CD	*Ciudad de Dios*
CHE	*Cuadernos de Historia de España*
CPh	*Classical Philology*
CT	*Ciencia Tomista*
DCELC	Juan Corominas. *Diccionario crítico etimológico de la lengua castellana*
EM	*La España Moderna*
ES	*España Sagrada*
HR	*Hispanic Review*
HS	*Hispania Sacra*
MH	*Medievalia et Humanistica*
MHE	*Memorial Histórico Español*
MS	*Medieval Studies*
PL	*Patrologia Latina*
QF	*Quellen und Forschungen aus italienischen Archiven und Bibliotheken*
QJS	*Quarterly Journal of Speech*
RABM	*Revista de Archivos, Bibliotecas y Museos*
RBN	*Revista de Bibliografía Nacional*
RE	*Revista de España* (Madrid)
RET	*Revista Española de Teología*
RF	*Romanische Forschungen*
RFE	*Revista de Filología Española*
RFH	*Revista de Filología Hispánica*
RHi	*Revue Hispanique*
RPh	*Romance Philology*
RUM	*Revista de la Universidad de Madrid*
RUO	*Revista de la Universidad de Oviedo*
RyF	*Razón y Fe*
SMV	*Studi Mediolatini e Volgari*
SPh	*Studies in Philology*
VR	*Vox Romanica*
YULG	*Yale University Library Gazette*
ZRPh	*Zeitschrift für romanische Philologie*

APPENDIX

THE FOLLOWING SELECTIONS from Juan Gil de Zamora's *Dictaminis Epithalamium* and Martín de Córdoba's *Breve Compendium Artis Rethorice* include the prologues to both works, which explain the purposes of the authors, and the longest passages cited from them in Chapter IV.

For convenience in reading, tall *s* and sigma *s* are both reproduced as normal *s*; similarly, both long and short *i* are reproduced as *i*. I have used *u* as a vowel and *v* as a consonant; there is no consistency in the MSS. Abbreviations are resolved on the basis of the readings of the same words found elsewhere in the text, and the resolutions are indicated by italics. Capitalization and punctuation are mine. Brackets indicate material that I have supplied; parentheses, material found in the manuscript that should be deleted. Significant variants for the *Breve Compendium Artis Rethorice* are given from Madrid Bibl. Nac. MS. 9309, which is designated as M. (Note that line numbers *do not* correspond to those actually found in the MSS and cited in the text.)

JUAN GIL DE ZAMORA

Dictaminis Epithalamium

f. 1r   [S]uo *fra*tri Philipo de P*e*rusio, su*us frate*r Egidii Zamoren*sis*: Amare fide-
liter et amari felicit*er*. Multo labore, assiduo studio, varia exercitacione,
pl*u*rimis exp*e*rime*n*tis, altissima prude*n*cia, prude*n*tissim*o* co*n*silio stat ars
dicendi s*ecundu*m Qui*n*tilianu*m* De Oratoris Institucionib*us* et p*re*mictit
5 notabile v*er*bum: "Plerumq*ue*," inq*uid*, "evenit ut aliq*ui*d grande inveniat,
qui se*mper* q*ue*rit q*uod* minimu*m* est." Quesivisti *ergo* a me in Ih*e*su ka-
ris*si*me aliq*ui*d *et* grande *et* mi*ni*mum; grande q*ui* de ingenii mei capacitati,
porro mi*ni*mu*m* karitati, quia in miru*m* vires q*u*as imp[er]itia denegat, caritas admi*ni*strat. Quesivisti *ergo* a me modu*m* dictandi v*er*ba *etiam* dulcia,
10 utilia et honesta, quib*us* uti posses in co*m*posicio*n*e ep*isto*lar*um*, in come[n]-

[144]

dac*io*nem illustriu*m* p*erso*n*a*ru*m*, in detest*a*cion*em* vicior*um*, in ampliac*io*ne*m* sermonu*m*, in subtilli p*ro*lac*io*ne collac*io*nu*m*. Hec, inquam, quesivisti que m*ichi* fuere dificilia, dilecc*io*ni t*amen* facilia, maxi*me* cum videram q*uod* sic aqua*m* postulat fons a rivo, sc*ien*ciam m*agiste*r a discipulo, *con*templativ*us* ab
15 activo, sp*irit*ualis a carnali, s*an*ctus a p*ecca*tore, sapiens ab ignaro. Deside-rium quid*em* huiu*s* operis in me parturivit devota affecc*io*, set sic p*ro*phe*t*a *com*memorat, "vires no*n* h*abet* p*ar*turiens." Racio quid*em* q*uod* possu*m* et si citra limites facultates suspendat*ur* affect*us* voc*is* tam*en* exuberan*s* acumu-lata caritate volu*n*tas meu*m* supleat inp*er*fectum, utar i*t*aq*ue* vice cotis
20 q*ue* obtussa e*st* e*t* tam*en* ferrum accuit ymo ut v*er*bo sapie*n*tis ut mi-*n*us sapie*n*s utar q*uod* si*n*e ficc*io*ne dedisti tue sine invidia co*m*unico caritati. Nucas e*n*im collegi q*ue* de menssa d*o*minor*um* meor*um* ceciderunt et cu*m* Ruth Moabitide in agro Booz spicas coadunavi q*ue* manu*us* evasere me*n*teciu*m* si forte in earu*m* excussione inveniat*ur* ephi me*n*sura de qua
25 in valle dictac*io*nis, arengac*io*nis ornat*us*, quoq*ue* rethorici peregrina*n*tes et d*o*mino s*er*vie*n*tes p*er* t*em*p*us* possint conficere l*i*t*er*aru*m*. Incipio *er*go et ut artificialit*er* p*ro*cedam, totu*m* op*us* distinguo p*er* capitula ut q*uod* *con*fussum, rude, ineptu*m* quoq*ue* e*t* diffussum iacebat ad uni*us* armonie *con*sona*n*ciam redigat*ur* et inve*n*ire quil*ibet* ad manu*m* queat q*uod* ante
30 disp*er*ssum ap*re*hendere no*n* valebat. Tractatu*m* *er*go p*re*sentem que*m* Di-
f. 1v tam*in*is Epithalamu*m* e*n*im titulavi in / quatuor p*ar*tes divisi, s[cilicet]: in antecede*n*cia, *con*seque*n*cia, integra*n*cia et p*er*ficiencia s*i*v*e* *con*sumancia. Antecede*n*cia voco generalia tractatu*m* s[cilicet] vocab*u*lor*um*, q*ui*bus ge-neralit*er* laudabiles e*t* vituperabiles act*us* ho*m*inum describu*n*tur. *Con*seque*n*-
5 cia voco tractatu*m* vocabulor*um* q*ui*b*us* sp*ecialiter* act*us* ho*m*ini sp*e*ciales laudabiles sive vitup*er*abiles describu*n*tur. Integra*n*cia voco p*ar*tes inte-gra*n*tes sive institue*n*tes ipsas lit*er*as utpote su*n*t salutac*io*nes, narrac*io*nes, rogac*io*nes, *con*clusio*n*es. Co*n*ssuma*n*cia sive p*er*ficie*n*cia voco illa q*ue* ex p*re*-dictis *con*stituu*n*tur et ex ip*s*is resulta*n*t. Utpote su*n*t ip*s*e p*er*fecte ep*is*t*o*le,
10 sic*ut* e*n*im in artificio videm*us*, q*uod* pri*us* ligna *et* lapides colligu*n*tur, se-cu*n*do scindu*n*tur e*t* polliu*n*tur, t*er*cio in ipso hediffic*io* collocant*ur* dom*us* ex ip*s*is. Sic ordinatis totu*m* resultat compossitu*m* iam *com*pletu*m*. Sic *et* ego in ordina*n*do p*ro*cedo ex*emplu*m assume*n*s ex na*tu*ralib*us* et artifi-cialib*us* ut p*er* distinc*io*ne*m* capitulor*um* pat*er*e pot*er*it intende*n*ti:
15   Descripc*io* generalis s*uper* ext*er*iores dis-
                                  po*si*c*io*nes.
     De v*er*bis laudatoris sive comen-   Descripc*io* generalis qu*o* ad principes

---

17 IV Kings 19.3; p*ossum*] *MS unclear.*   23 Ruth] n͞uch *MS*; Booz] bos *crossed out in text|* and Booz *added in margin.*   24 ep*h*i] ep͞hi *MS*; mensura *added from margin.*   27 p*ro*cedam *added from margin.*
5 sp*ecialiter*] spualit*er* *in MS, with* u *underpointed.*   17 ad principes] ad ad principes *MS*.

datoris in generali: P*rimu*m ca-
p*itulu*m:

20

De verbis come*n*datoris in spe-
c*i*ali: 2ᵐ ca*pitulu*m.

30

25

35

secundu*m* ex*t*eriores op*e*raciones.
Descripcio principu*m* g[eneralis] s[uper]
ex[teriores] dispo*sicio*nes.
Descripcio ge*n*eralis i*n* amo*nicio*nib*us*
pr*e*lator*um* ge*n*eraliter, *etc.*

De karitate.
De simplicitate.
De pac*ie*ncia.
De paup*e*rtate.
De pace.
De obedie*n*cia.
De v*e*recu*n*dia.
De fortitudi*n*e.
De sap*ie*ncia.
De doct*r*ina.
De solicitudi*n*e.
De mis*e*ricordia.
De co*n*te*m*ptu mu*n*di.
De or*ati*one.
De co*n*te*m*placi*o*ne.

* * * *

f. 19r Dillecto seu ka*riss*imo s*ib*i in Ch*rist*o totisq*ue* anime virib*us* amplecta*n*do
cordisq*ue* visce*rib*us alliga*n*do eccl*e*sia ex m*e*ritis intimis oriendo N. cano-
nico civi seu burge*n*si zamoren*s*is seu militi talis castri, N. canonic*us* civis,
burg*ensis* vel miles t*a*lis castri, t*a*lis civitat*is*, opidi seu castri salut*em et*
5 dileccionis vinculu*m* p*e*rhonorare, salut*em et* illius h*a*bere p*a*rticipium cui*us*
es*t* p*a*rticipacio in idips*um*; salut*em et* a Ch*rist*i semita nullaten*us* deviare;
salut*em* et vita*m* bona*m* s*et* exitum melior*em*; salut*em et* vera*m* in eo qui
es*t* ipsa v*e*ritas amiciciam *con*se*r*vare; salut*em* et dilecc*io*nis vinculu*m* in-
delebilit*er* custodire.
10 Viro ven*e*rab*i*li ac discreto d*o*mino N. decan*o* tolletano, compostellano
archidiacono, thesaurario zamorensi, f*rate*r N. Egidii s*u*b b*ea*ti Francisci
h*a*bitu milita*n*s, Ih*es*u Ch*rist*o salut*em et* prosper*os* advota success*us*; salu-
t*em* et de bono i*n* meli*us* profici[s]ci; salut*em* et grac*ia*m in pr*e*senti *et* gloria*m*
i*n* futur*o*; salut*em* et si quid meli*us* est, salute.
15 Viro religiosso pr*o*vido et honesto N., indign*us* decan*us* vel archidiacho-
n*us* eccl*e*sie zemorensis salut*em et* tota erga Deu*m* g*e*rere volu*n*tatem *et* sanc-
tu*m* proposit*um* fine *con*cludere sanciori; salut*em et* de virtute in virtute*m*
ascendere quousq*ue* videam*us* Deu*m* Deoru*m* in Sion; salut*em et* prospere

---

13 prosperos *deleted after 1st* et.

agere in adverssis; salutem et temptacionibus non subcumbere quoquomodo;
20 salutem et celeste bravium adipisci; salutem *et* pugnare Deum prelia in cas-
tris seculi huius; salutem *et* sic transire per bona temporalia ut non amitamus
eternam; salutem *et* nudum Christum in cruce positum nudum sequi; salutem amplecti stigmata Ihesum Christi. Hiis et aliis modis pluribus potes
procedere in salutacionibus secundum datam tibi adeo graciam *et* nobilitatem
25 tui ingenii quo clarescis. Et quia in compilacione literarum fere omnibus
epistolis salutaciones premituntur, ideo has paucas principio operis prepos-
sui ut per premissas viam habeas, per preposteras habitum sciencie obtineas
indicando. Nota autem quod nomina virorum seu mulierum, civitatum seu
castrorum principia ecciam clausularum scribi debent in epistolis per al-
30 tam literam. Ideo ut magis recthorice procedamus, [cum] dictio desinit in
vocalem, sequens vero incipiat a vocali. Collores autem recthorici quibus /
f. 19v uti possumus tam in epistolis quam in metris sunt isti, s[cilicet]: repeticcio,
ut cum dicitur "te collo, te laudo, te glorifico, tibi g[ratulor] plaudo"; converssio, ut cum dicitur "pluries sciencia superavit bonitate superante eloquencia superavit"; complexio, quia comprehendit duos primos colores, v[erbi]
5 g[racia]: "Quis testamenti verus traslator? Ieronimus. Quis trium ling[u]arum
peritus fuit? Ieronimus. Quis destructor heresis fuit? Ieronimus." Alii
autem collores rethorici: tradicio, contencio, exclamacio, ratiocinacio, sentencia, contrarium, articulus, concordia, agnominacio; *et* plures alii numerantur
de quibus tractare non intendimus eo quod plus sapiunt curiossitatem quam
10 utilitatem. Item in peticionibus domino pape ista [. . .] vocabulla que se-
cuntur non debent literis exarari *set* pocius evitari, s[cilicet]: idcirco, ideoque,
ea propter, quo circa, quamobrem, quantum ipse, propterea; precipue uti-
tur istis verbis, hoc tamen hodie non servatur.

Narracionum exordia subnectentes circa ipsa taliter procedemus. Primo
15 namque premitemus exordia incipiencia a nominibus, 2º a pronominibus,
3º a verbis, 4º a participis, 5º ab utrisque, 6º ab adverbiis, coniuncionibus,
preposicionibus huius. Hoc autem ideo facimus quia nullus ornate composi-
taque dictare potest prout experimento didiscimus magnifesto nisi noc-
ciciam habeat per quas dicciones incipere valeat et per quas sua dictamina
20 debeat terminare. Et quia de prioribus prior est speculacio, ideo de nomine
quod prius est in ordinacione parcium orationis, per omnes cassus exempla
utillia proponemus; verbi gracia sic procedemus.

---

30 [cum] *suggested by Professor Silk; the MS reads* est.
2 g[ratulor] *suggested by Professor Jenaro-MacLennan.* 3 superante] sape-
rante *MS.* 10 *Two letters have been crossed out following* ista. 16 ab
adverbiis] ad abverbiis *MS.*

MARTÍN DE CÓRDOBA

Breve Compendium Artis Rethorice

f. 106r   Incipit Breve *Compendium* Artis Rethorice ma*gis*tri M. Corduben*sis*.
Et si mei exilitas ingenii plenius obfuscata nebulis facu*n*die suavitate*m*
i*n* hiantib*us* hanc sap*er*e ut artis exposcit dignitas nequeat lucidare. Cla-
rissimo*rum* ta*me*n quo*rum*d*am* su*m*ma ingenuitas adolescenciu*m* rigidam
5 michi co*n*fert audacium. Ut qui orato*rum* exiguus emulator hac i*n* celeber-
rima resideo uni*ve*rsitate id paululu*m* q*u*od artis huius tenuissime sencio
insudare volentib*us* effundere cupia*m* *et* reserare. Tanta e*n*im vis orna-
tissimis rethorice sualis suppe*r*i forma*rum* dato*rum* largic*i*one tributa. Et
ut no*n* paru*m* theoricis atq*ue* praticis subs*er*viat discipulis. No*n*ne quide*m*
10 sacris eloquiis aut s*c*ripto lucidandu*m* v[o]ceq*ue* p*ro*mulgandis cu*m* suos
affert lepidos ornatus comode atq*ue* iocunde famulat*ur* clarius liquet. Si
ordi*n*e q*u*am su*m*m*us* opifex i*n* universi p*ro*ductione tenuit inspiciam*us*,
primo siquide*m* maiores mu*n*di partes utpote celum et elementa creavit.
Deinde circa celo*rum* et eleme*n*to*rum* orname*n*ta optima dedit. Hoc pro-
15 fecto, iuvenes in doct*ri*na tenendu*m* q*u*od postq*u*am adolescentes circa rudimenta elemento*rum* gramaticaliu*m* complecte vaccassent rursum ad ornatu*m* lingue q*u*am dulcissima p*ro*pinat rethorica habenas suo*rum* labo*rum*
debere refferre. Hoc ritu s*an*ctissimi doctores quo*rum* memoria in be*ne*-
dictione est sua facondissima dogmata ampliaru*n*t. Noluer*un*t hii proba-
20 tissima theosoficas profunditates scrutando in incultu stilo p*ro*palare ne
rusticano lectu, dictu ve ge*n*tiliu*m* arrogancia ponpatico detractionis emulo
sp*er*ner*en*tur. Consid*er*emus oro Basilii maxi*m*i et Iohan*ni*s os aurei, Gregorii facundiam, Augustini, Hilarii, Iheronimi, Ambrosii, Gregorii dicendi
f. 106v gravitate*m* nec nim*us* fructuosa*m* sua/vitate*m* quib*us* sua referta sunt volu*m*i*n*a. Quo sit ut tam lecto*rum* q*u*am audito*rum* conceptib*us* gratissima
sunt p*er*petua quada*m* auctoritate mane*a*nt stabilita. Reliquo*rum* vero
doctrina*m* qui aut eloque*n*ciam contempseru*n*t aut ea caruere. Et si eorum
5 dogmata fuere florifera aliqua*n*to tempore flosculo*rum* tande*m* more emar-
cueru*n*t. Se*t* ne utriusq*ue* viris omitta*m* neccessitate*m* cui*us* professores
i*n* alioru*m* utilitate*m* patroci*n*io fungentes deffend*er*e solent vel accusare.

---

1 Incipit . . . Corduben*sis*] *M om.*   2 plenius] *M* pl*u*ribus.   8 sualis] *M*
suadelis.   11 lepidos] *M* lapidos.   14 optim*a*] *M* opera*m*.   20 in-
culto] *M* culto.   22-23 Gregorii] *M* Greco*rum*.   23 Hilari . . . f. 106v.1
quib*us*] *M om.*
6 vir*is*] *M* iuris.

Profecto hec efficientibus nil eloquencia vel admirabilius audiencium res-
pectu vel eorum qui tutantur gracia aut qui iusta querela accusatoris pro-
10 clamatione culpantur. Quid dicam si Grecos legum conditores Solonem Athe-
niessem, Demossenem et Euchinem Macedonicos huius rei testes adducam,
maximam siquidem cum leges conderent facundiam tenuere quorum ca-
ratheres dum legimus disertum leporem ostendunt. Neque Latinos relinquam
Ci(n)ceronem eloquencie Romane principem, Quintum Hortencium, Mar-
15 cum Marcellum qui sub Gaii Cesaris imperio incredibili quodam ornatu leges
scripserunt. Quorum codices nobis relicti id fuisse certissimum signant.
Philosophorum enim omittando sectam prolato eminentissimus hac arte
claruit. Nec Aristoteles apex philosophorum eam deseruit cum opus rethorice artis elegantissimum conficeret, a quo et nostri rethores Latini habun-
20 dantissimam frugem collegerunt. Et nos non nulla huic nostro operi et si
pauca inseremus. Adi[s]ce quod precipuus orator Cicero in facundie pre-
conium expressit. "Cum," inquit, "homines a bestiis differamus quod loqui
possumus qua laude ille dignus est qui in ea re ceteros superat in qua homines
f. 107r bestias excellunt." Sunt / quorum cothidiana sollicitudo ad cultum rei fami-
liaris insudat et cum possent rudibus ac grossis exigere vitam in unaquaque
superlectili ornatum apponunt. Sat foret palustri culmo, terreo cespite,
ymbrium impetus necnon solis estus et alia neccessitas comoda exiguo vi-
5 tasse tugurio. Set habitacula curiosis ornamus picturis, eciam saxo quadrato
abiete ac pinopolitis parietes pingimus atque tecta aliquid voluptatis ultra
conferens intuencium luminibus autem ponimus. Sic dicam de vestium
tegumentis quorum est officium nuditatem tegere. Quoniam curioso studio
ad eorum inscisionem advocamus sartores adeo ut crassiores eos iudicemus
10 qui indumentorum novitatis aut invenire nesciunt aut nolunt. Adde no-
ticiam: Hii purpuram pro cotidiano utuntur vestitu; hii longinqui maris
luserant lictora ut pretiosiora induant vellera. Alii colore se induunt san-
guineo; alii in vestibus camporum viriditatem imitantur. Et in summa
ille apud vulgares occulos magnipanditur qui aut pallio aut pretexta novi-
15 tatem pertendit. Nec aliter de cibis et potibus loquar aut calciamentis.
Horum inanis cura et supervacua est. Quia circa moribunda occupantur
membra que nobis et aliis animantibus fore comunia liquet. Et quam salubrius

---

11 Demossenem] *M* Demostenem.   14 Ci(n)ceronem] *M* Ciceronem; Hor-
tencium] *M* Ortensium.   14-15 Marcum] *M* Marchum.   15 Gaii] *M* Gay.
17 prolato] *M* Plato.   22-24 Cicero, *De Inventione*, I. iv. 5: "Ac mihi quidem
videntur homines, cum multis rebus humiliores et infirmiores sint, hac re maxime
bestiis praestare, quod loqui possunt. Quare praeclarum mihi quiddam videtur
adeptus is qui qua re homines bestiis praestent ea in re hominibus ipsis antecellat."
24 excellunt] *M* anncelunt.
3 apponunt] *M* oponunt.   4 ymbrium] *M* nimborum; comoda] *M* incomoda.
10-11 noticiam] *M* materiam.

sibi consulerent si lingue decorem et sermonis cuius velue sunt expertes
summo studio perquirerent et perditissimum tempus quod lacivia sibi in
20 moribus vendicant melliflua rethorica reperiret. Iam si quis aut pede clau-
dicet aut manu mancus non palpet aut toto corpore suum non possit iuvare
f. 107v gressum dolet et erubescit. Quanto ergo singulariter / dolendum est si lingua
cespitet aut barbarizet et verba inexplanata sua ruditate loquatur. Hu[n]c
ergo strenui proparate adolescentes et claritudinem quam exproavit acce-
pistis subtili ingenio, culto sermone et morata indole duplicate. Rubiginem
5 lingue quam a natura traximus arte rethorica poliamus. Que ut facilius
faciatis brevem et compendiosum tractatum pedestri sermone quo intelligibilior esset composui quem per capitula divisi: Primum capitulum: Quid
est rethorica et unde dicatur. Secundum: De triplici negocio rethorice.
Tertium: De inventione. Quartum: De dispositione. Quintum: De materie
10 prolongamine. Sextum: De abreviacione. Septimum: De coloribus tussump-
tivis. Octavum: de coloribus verborum. Novum: De coloribus sententiarum.
Decimum: De elegancia. Undecimum: De viciis. Duodecimum: De memoria. Tridecimum: De pronunciatione.

---

20 moribus] *M* iunioribus.   21 1st non] *M* nunc.
3 exproavit] *M* expanis.   10-11 tussumptivis]   *M*   transumcionum.

BIBLIOGRAPHY

I. Unpublished Sources

A. TEXTS

Juan Gil de Zamora. *Dictaminis Epithalamium.* Salamanca. Biblioteca de la Universidad. MS. 2128. saec. xv. chart. 179 ff. Occupies ff. 1r-57v.

Martinus Cordubensis. *Breve Compendium Artis Rethorice.* Rouen. Bibliothèque Municipale. MS. 0 52. saec. xiv. membran. et chart. 135 ff. Occupies ff. 106r-123v.

Versus ad Pueros. Madrid. Biblioteca de la Real Academia de la Historia. cod. 46. saec. xii. membran. Occupies ff. 170v-171r.

B. DOCUMENTS

"Copia del testamento y codicilio de D. Gil de Albornoz, cardenal arzobispo de Toledo." Madrid. Biblioteca Nacional. MS. 13023 (*olim* Dd. 42). saec. xviii. chart. Occupies ff. 159r-175v.

"Donación que hizo de su librería el Arzobispo de Toledo D. Pedro Tenorio al cabildo de su Yglesia, con mil florines de oro más, para comprar tres obras que la faltavan, a saber, el Nicolás de Lira, Henrique Boyt, y el diccionario, año 1383." Madrid. Biblioteca Nacional. MS. 13018 (*olim* Dd. 37). saec. xviii. chart. Occupies ff. 117r-120v.

"Inventario de Ropas, Alahajas, Libros, y otras cosas que se hizo por los Años de 1260 [?], [illegible] al Thesorero dn. Rodrigo Iuañez para entregarle el thesoro de la Santa Iglesia de Toledo." London. BM. MS. Egerton 1881. saec. xviii. chart. Occupies ff. 118r-122r. [copy of the original found in *Liber Secundus Privilegiorum Ecclesiae Toletanae*, Madrid, Archivo Histórico Nacional.]

II. Published Sources

A. TEXTS

1. Historical and Literary Texts

a. Latin Texts

Aegidii Colvmnae Romani *De Regimine Principum Lib. III.* Rome: Apud Bartholomeum Zannettum, 1607; repr. Darmstadt: Scientia Verlag Aalen, 1967.

Alain de Lille. *Anticlaudianus.* Edited by R. Bossuat. Paris: Librairie Philosophique J. Vrin, 1955.

Boethius. *De Consolatione Philosophiae.* Edited and translated by H. F. Stewart. Loeb Classical Library, 74. Cambridge: Harvard University Press, 1918; London: William Heinemann Ltd., 1918: repr. *saepe.*

——. *De Differentiis Topicis Libri Quatuor.* Paris: Ex officina Michaelis Vascosani, 1543.

——. ——. Edited by Migne. *PL.* Vol. 64, cols. 1173-1216.

Cassiodori Senatori *Institutiones.* Edited by R. A. B. Mynors. Oxford: At the Clarendon Press, 1937; repr. 1963.

Chronica Adefonsi Regis. Edited by Antonio Ubieto Arteta. Textos medievales, 3. Valencia: Gráficas Bautista, 1961.

Commentum Einsidlense in Donati "Artem Maiorem." Edited by Hermann Hagen. In: *Grammatici Latini.* Edited by Heinrich Keil. Leipzig: In aedibus B. G. Teubneri, 1870. VIII, 219-266.

Corpus Iuris Canonici. Pars Secunda: Decretalium Collectiones. Edited by Aemilius Friedberg. Leipzig: bei B. Tauchnitz, 1879; repr. Graz: Akademische Druck- u. Verlagsanstalt, 1959.

Dominicus Gundisalvus. *De Divisione Philosophiae.* Edited by Ludwig Bauer. Beiträge zur Geschichte der Philosophie des Mittelalters, IV, 2-3. Münster: Druck und Verlag der aschendorffschen Buchhandlung, 1903.

Eberhardi Bethuniensis *Graecismus.* Edited by Ioh. Wrobel. Corpus Grammaticorum Medii Aevi, 1. Breslau: In aedibus G. Koebneri, 1887.

Flavius Josephus. *Historiarum Antiquitatis Iudaicae.* In: *The Latin Josephus. I: Introduction and Text. The Antiquities: Books I-V.* Edited by Franz Blatt. Acta Jutlandica. Aarsskrift for Aarhus Universitet XXX 1. Humanistisk Serie 44. Copenhagen: Universitetsforlaget i Aarhus; Ejnar Munksgaard, 1958.

Giovanni de Garlandi [John of Garland]. *Integumenta Ovidii.* Edited by Fausto Ghisalberti. Testi e Documenti Inediti o Rari, 2. Messina-Milan: Casa editrice Giuseppe Principato, 1933.

Gotfridus Viterbiensis. *Pantheon.* In: *Germanicorum Scriptorum.* Edited by Joannes Pistorius. Ratisbon: Sumptibus Joannis Conradi Peezii, 1726. II, 1-392.

Historia Silense. Edited by Justo Pérez de Urbel and Atilano González Ruiz-Zorrilla. Escuela de Estudios Medievales. Textos, 30. Madrid: Consejo Superior de Investigaciones Científicas, 1959.

Hugonis de Sancto Victore *Didascalicon de Studio Legendi.* Edited by Charles Henry Buttimer. The Catholic University of America Studies in Medieval and Renaissance Latin, 10. Washington, D.C.: The Catholic University Press, 1939.

Isidori Hispalensis Episcopi *Etymologiarum sive Originum Libri XX.* Edited by W. M. Lindsay. 2 vols. Oxford: E Typographeo Clarendoniano, 1911; repr. 1966.

John of Salisbury. *De Septem Septenis.* Edited by Migne. *PL.* Vol. 199, cols. 945-963.

Juan Gil de Zamora. *De Preconiis Hispanie.* Edited by Manuel de Castro y Castro. Madrid: Universidad de Madrid, Facultad de Filosofía y Letras, 1955.

Lucas de Tuy. *Chronicon Mundi.* In: *Hispaniae Illvstratae sev Rervm Vrbivmq. Hispaniae, Lvsitaniae, Aethiopiae et Indiae Scriptores Varii.* Edited by Andreas Schottus. 4 vols. Frankfurt: Apud Claudium Marnium, et Haeredes Iohannis Aubrij, 1603-1608. IV, 1-116.

Martianus Capella. *De Nuptiis Mercurii et Philologiae et de Septem Artibus Liberalibus.* Edited by Adolf Dick. Leipzig: In aedibus B. G. Teubneri, 1925.

Pauli Orosii *Historiarum Adversum Paganos Libri VII.* Edited by Carolus Zangemeister. Leipzig: In aedibus B. G. Teubneri, 1889.

Petri Compostellani *De Consolatione Rationis Libri Duo.* Edited by Pedro Blanco Soto. Beiträge zur Geschichte der Philosophie des Mittelalters, VIII, 4. Münster: Aschendorffsche Verlagsbuchhandlung, 1912.

Petrus Cantor. *Verbum Abbreviatum.* Edited by Migne. *PL.* Vol. 205, cols. 23-370.

Petrus Comestor. *Historia Scholastica.* Edited by Migne. *PL.* Vol. 198, cols. 1053-1722.

Pseudo-Aristotle. *Secretum Secretorum.* In: *Opera Hactenus Inedita Rogerii Baconi.* Edited by Robert Steele. Oxford: E Typographeo Clarendoniano, 1920. Fasc. v.

Raimundo de Peñafort. *Summa de Poenitentia et Matrimonio.* Edited by Joannes de Fribvrgo. Rome: Sumptibus Ioannis Tallini, 1603; repr. Farnborough (England): Gregg Press Limited, 1967.

Remigii Autissiodorensis *Commentum in Martianum Capellam.* Edited by Cora E. Lutz. 2 vols. Leiden: E. J. Brill, 1962-1965.

—. *In Artem Donati Minorem Commentum.* Edited by W. Fox. Bibliotheca Scriptorum Graecorum et Romanorum Teubneriana. Leipzig: In aedibus B. G. Teubneri, 1902.

    b. Spanish Texts

Alfonso el Sabio. *General estoria. Primera parte.* Edited by Antonio G. Solalinde. Madrid: Junta para Ampliación de Estudios e Investigaciones Científicas, Centro de Estudios Históricos, 1930.

—. *General estoria. Segunda parte.* Edited by Antonio G. Solalinde (†), Lloyd A. Kasten, and Victor R. B. Oelschläger. Consejo Superior de Investigaciones Científicas. Instituto "Miguel de Cervantes." Vol. I. Madrid: Imp. S. Aguirre Torre, 1957.

—. *Primera crónica general de España.* 2d ed. Edited by Ramón Menéndez Pidal. Universidad de Madrid. Facultad de Filosofía y Letras. Seminario Menéndez Pidal. 2 vols. Madrid: Editorial Gredos, 1955.

—. *Setenario.* Edited by Kenneth H. Vanderford. Facultad de Filosofía y Letras de la Universidad de Buenos Aires. Buenos Aires: Instituto de Filología, 1945.

—. *Las siete partidas del rey don . . . .* Edited by La Real Academia de la Historia. 3 vols. Madrid: Imprenta Real, 1807.

Auto de los reyes magos. In: *Crestomatía del español medieval.* Edited by Ramón Menéndez Pidal. Universidad de Madrid. Facultad de Filosofía y Letras.

Seminario Menéndez Pidal. 2 vols. Madrid: Editorial Gredos, 1965-1966. I, 71-77.

Berceo, Gonzalo de. *Milagros de Nuestra Señora.* 5th ed. Edited by Antonio G. Solalinde. Clásicos Castellanos. Madrid: Espasa-Calpe, S. A., 1958.

—. *La "Vida de San Millán de la Cogolla" de . . . .* Edited by Brian Dutton. Colección Támesis. Serie A. Monografías, IV. London: Támesis Books Limited [1967].

—. *Vida de Santo Domingo de Silos: Edición crítico-paleográfica del códice del siglo XIII.* Edited by Fr. Alfonso Andrés. Madrid: Padres Benedictinos, 1958.

Castigos e documentos del rey don Sancho. In: *Escritores en prosa anteriores al siglo XV.* Edited by Pascual de Gayangos. BAE, 51. Madrid: Rivadeneyra, 1860; repr. *saepe.* Pp. 79-228.

Castigos e documentos para bien vivir ordenados por el rey don Sancho IV. Edited by Agapito Rey. Indiana University Publications. Humanities Series No. 24. Bloomington, Ind.: Indiana University, 1952.

Glosa castellana al Regimiento de príncipes *de Egidio Romano.* Edited by Juan Beneyto Pérez. Biblioteca Española de Escritores Políticos. 3 vols. Madrid: Instituto de Estudios Políticos, 1947.

Libro de Alexandre. Edited by Raymond S. Willis. Elliott Monographs in the Romance Languages and Literatures, 32. Princeton: Princeton University Press, 1934; Paris: Les Presses Universitaires de France, 1934.

Menéndez Pidal, Ramón, ed. *Crestomatía del español medieval.* Universidad de Madrid. Facultad de Filosofía y Letras. Seminario Menéndez Pidal. 2 vols. Madrid: Editorial Gredos, 1965-1966.

Mexía, Fernando. *Libro intitulado nobiliario.* Seville: Pedro Brun Juã Gentil, 30 June 1492. [Hispanic Society of America, copy 6.]

Pseudo-Aristotle. *Poridat de las poridades.* Edited by Lloyd A. Kasten. Seminario de Estudios Medievales Españoles de la Universidad de Wisconsin. Madrid: S. Aguirre Torre, 1957.

Ruiz, Juan. *Libro de buen amor.* Edited by Joan Corominas. Biblioteca Románica Hispánica. IV. Textos. Madrid: Editorial Gredos, 1967.

—. —. *Selección.* Edited by María Rosa Lida. Colección de Textos Literarios. Buenos Aires: Editorial Losada, S. A., 1941.

c. Classical Rhetorical Texts

Cicero. *De Inventione.* Edited and translated by H. M. Hubbell. Loeb Classical Library, 386. Cambridge: Harvard University Press, 1949; London: William Heinemann Ltd., 1949; repr. 1960.

Halm, Carolus, ed. *Rhetores Latini Minores.* Leipzig: In aedibus B. G. Teubneri, 1863; repr. Frankfurt am Main: Minerva GMBH, 1964.

Q. Fabii Laurentii Victorini *Explanationum in Rhetoricam M. Tullii Ciceronis Libri Duo.* Edited by C. Halm in his *Rhetores Latini Minores.* Leipzig: In aedibus B. G. Teubneri, 1863; repr. Frankfurt am Main: Minerva GMBH, 1964. Pp. 153-304.

Bibliography 155

Quintilianus. *Institutio Oratoria.* Edited and translated by H. E. Butler. Loeb Classical Library, 124-127. 4 vols. Cambridge: Harvard University Press, 1920-1922; London: William Heinemann Ltd., 1920-1922; repr. *saepe.*
Rhetorica ad C. Herennium. Edited and translated by Harry Caplan. Loeb Classical Library, 403. Cambridge: Harvard University Press, 1954; London: William Heinemann Ltd., 1954; repr. 1964.

d. Medieval Rhetorical Texts

Alfonso de Cartagena. *La Rethorica de M. Tullio Cicerón.* Edited by Rosalba Mascagna. Romanica Neapolitana, 2. Naples: Liguori, 1969.
Evrard the German. *Laborintus de Miseriis Rectorum.* Edited by Edmond Faral in his *Les arts poétiques du XIIᵉ et du XIIIᵉ siècle: Recherches et documents sur la technique littéraire du Moyen Age.* Bibliothèque de l'École des Hautes Études, 238. Paris: Librairie Honoré Champion, 1924; repr. 1962. Pp. 337-377.
Faral, Edmond. *Les arts poétiques du XIIᵉ et du XIIIᵉ siècle: Recherches et documents sur la technique littéraire du Moyen Âge.* Bibliothèque de l'École des Hautes Études, 238. Paris: Librairie Honoré Champion, 1924; repr. 1962.
Geoffroi de Vinsauf. *Documentum de Modo et Arte Dictandi et Versificandi.* Edited by Edmond Faral in his *Les arts poétiques du XIIᵉ et du XIIIᵉ siècle: Recherches et documents sur la technique littéraire du Moyen Âge.* Bibliothèque de l'École des Hautes Études, 238. Paris: Librairie Honoré Champion, 1924; repr. 1962. Pp. 265-320.
—. *Poetria Nova.* Edited by Edmond Faral in his *Les arts poétiques du XIIᵉ et du XIIIᵉ siècle: Recherches et documents sur la technique littéraire du Moyen Âge.* Bibliothèque de l'École des Hautes Études, 238. Paris: Librairie Honoré Champion, 1924; repr. 1962. Pp. 197-262.
Guido Faba. *Summa Dictaminis.* Edited by Augusto Gaudenzi in *Il Propugnatore* (Nuova serie), 3 (1890), i, 287-338, ii, 345-393.
John of Garland. "Poetria Magistri Johannis Anglici de Arte Prosayca Metrica et Rithmica." Edited by Giovanni Mari in *RF*, 13 (1902), 883-965.
Martín de Córdoba. "*Ars Praedicandi* de Fray . . . ." Edited by Fernando Rubio [Álvarez] in *CD*, 172 (1959), 327-348.
Pseudo-Boethius. *Speculatio de Rhetoricae Cognitione.* Edited by Migne. *PL.* Vol. 64, cols. 1217-1222.
Rockinger, Ludwig. *Briefsteller und Formelbücher des eilften bis vierzehnten Jahrhunderts.* Quellen und Erörterungen zur bayerischen und deutschen Geschichte, 9. Munich: 1863-1864; repr. Burt Franklin Research and Source Works Series, 10. New York: Burt Franklin, 1961.
[Thierry of Chartres. *Commentarium in Ciceronis "De Inventione."*] "Fragmentum Scholiastae Inediti ad Ciceronem de Invent. Rhet." In: *Historia Critica Scholiastarum Latinorum.* Edited by W. H. D. Suringar. Leiden: Sumptibus S. et J. Luchtmannorum et J. C. Cyfveerii, 1834. Part i, pp. 213-253.

B. STUDIES

1. Medieval Education

Ajo G. y Sáinz de Zúñiga, C. M. *Historia de las universidades hispánicas: Orígenes y desarrollo desde su aparición hasta nuestros días.* 6 vols. Madrid: Imprenta La Normal, 1957-1966. In progress.

Amador de los Ríos, José. "Del estado y educación de las clases sociales en España durante la Edad-Media: Medios científicos que labran la educación de la clerecía española," *RUM* (2ª época), 3 (1874), 481-501.

—. "Estudios sobre la educación de las clases privilegiadas de España durante la Edad Media," *RE*, 10 (10 Oct. 1869), 389-415.

Beltrán de Heredia, Vicente. *Bulario de la Universidad de Salamanca (1219-1549).* Acta Salmanticensia. Historia de la Universidad, XII. Vol. I. Salamanca: Universidad de Salamanca, 1966.

—. *Cartulario de la Universidad de Salamanca (1218-1600).* Acta Salmanticensia. Historia de la Universidad, XVII. Vol. I. Salamanca: Universidad de Salamanca, 1970.

—. "La formación intelectual del clero de España durante los siglos xii, xiii y xiv," *RET*, 6 (1946), 313-357.

—. "La formación intelectual del clero según nuestra antigua legislación canónica (siglos xi-xv)," *Escorial*, 3 (1941), 289-298.

—. *Los orígenes de la Universidad de Salamanca.* Acta Salmanticensia. Historia de la Universidad, I, 1. Salamanca: Universidad de Salamanca, 1953.

Esperabé y Arteaga, Enrique. *Historia pragmática e interna de la Universidad de Salamanca.* 2 vols. Salamanca: Imp. Francisco Núñez Izquierdo, 1914-1917.

Fuente, Vicente de la. "Estudios y enseñanza en España: Escuelas regias y clericales en los siglos x y xi," *RUM* (2ª época), 4 (1874), 18-37.

—. *Historia de las universidades, colegios y demás establecimientos de enseñanza en España.* 4 vols. Madrid: Imprenta Viuda de Fuentenebro, 1884-1889.

—. "Historia de los establecimientos de enseñanza en España: Universidad de Palencia," *RUM* (2ª época), 4 (1874), 513-522.

Galino, María Ángeles. *Historia de la educación.* Vol. I: *Edades antigua y media.* Biblioteca Hispánica de Filosofía. Madrid: Editorial Gredos, 1960.

Kristeller, Paul Oskar. "The School of Salerno: Its Development and Its Contribution to the History of Learning." In his: *Studies in Renaissance Thought and Letters.* Storia e Letteratura. Raccolta di Studi e Testi, 54. Rome: Edizioni di Storia e Letteratura, 1956. Pp. 495-551.

Paetow, Louis John. *The Arts Course at Medieval Universities with Special Reference to Grammar and Rhetoric.* University of Illinois. The University Studies, III, 7. Urbana-Champaign: University Press, 1910.

Rashdall, Hastings. *The Universities of Europe in the Middle Ages.* 2d ed. Edited by F. M. Powicke and A. B. Emden. 3 vols. Oxford: At the Clarendon Press, 1936.

San Martín, Jesús. *La antigua universidad de Palencia.* Madrid: Afrodisio Aguado, 1942.

Sancho, H. "La enseñanza en el siglo xii," *CT*, 9 (1914), 52-76.

2. Medieval Libraries

Alonso Alonso, Manuel. "Bibliotecas medievales de los arzobispos de Toledo," *RyF*, 123 (1941), 295-309.

Becker, Gustavus, ed. *Catalogi Bibliothecarum Antiqui.* Bonn: Apud Max. Cohen et filium (Fr. Cohen), 1885.

Buttenweiser, Hilda. "The Distribution of the Manuscripts of the Latin Classical Authors in the Middle Ages." Unpublished Ph.D. dissertation, University of Chicago, 1930.

Fernández Pousa, Ramón. "Catálogo de una biblioteca española del año 1331: El monasterio de San Clemente, de Toledo," *RBN*, 1 (1941), 48-50.

[Foradada y Castán, José, ed.] "Biblioteca de la Santa Iglesia de Toledo: Inventario de 1455," *RABM*, 7 (1877), 321-324, 338-340, 355-356, 366-372.

Gómez Moreno, Manuel, ed. "Inventario de la Catedral de Salamanca (1275)," *RABM* (2ª época), 7 (1902), 175-180.

Marcos Rodríguez, Florencio. "La antigua biblioteca de la Catedral de Salamanca," *HS*, 14 (1961), 281-289.

Omont, H[enri]. "Catalogue de la bibliothèque de Bernard II, archevêque de Saint-Jacques-de-Compostelle (1226)," *BEC*, 54 (1893), 327-333.

Pérez de Guzmán, Juan. "El libro y la biblioteca en España durante los siglos medios," *EM*, 202 (Oct. 1905), 111-152.

Pérez de Guzmán, Luis, Marqués de Morbecq. "Un inventario del siglo xiv de la Catedral de Toledo (La Biblia de San Luis)," *BRAH*, 89 (1926), 373-419.

Sánchez Albornoz, Claudio. "Notas sobre los libros leídos en el reino de León hace mil años," *CHE*, 1-2 (1944), 222-238.

Schiff, Mario. *La bibliothèque du Marquis de Santillana.* Bibliothèque de l'École des Hautes Études, Sciences Historiques et Philologiques, 153. Paris: Librairie Émile Bouillon, Éditeur, 1905.

Tailhan, Jules. "Appendix sur les bibliothèques espagnoles du haut moyen âge." In: *Nouveaux mélanges d'archéologie, d'histoire et de littérature sur le moyen âge.* Edited by Ch. Cahier. Vol. III: *Bibliothèques.* Paris: Firmin Didot Frères, Fils et Cie, 1877. Pp. 217-346.

3. Modern Libraries

Antolín, Guillermo. *Catálogo de los códices latinos de la Real Biblioteca del Escorial.* 5 vols. Madrid: Imprenta Helénica, 1910-1923.

Beer, Rudolf. *Handschriftenschätze Spaniens.* Bericht über eine im Auftrage der kaiserlichen Akademie der Wissenschaften in den Jahren 1886-1888 durchgeführte Forschungsreise. Vienna: In Commission bei F. Tempsky, Buchhändler der kais. Akademie der Wissenschaften, 1894.

Catalogue générale des manuscrits des bibliothèques publiques de France. Vol. I. Paris: Librairie Plon, 1886.

Delisle, Leópold. "Manuscrits de l'abbaye de Silos acquis par la Bibliothèque Nationale." In his: *Mélanges de paléographie et de bibliographie.* Paris: Champion, Libraire, 1880. Pp. 53-116.

Douais, C[elestin]. "Les manuscrits du château de Merville," *AM,* 2 (1890), 36-64, 170-208, 305-364.

Faulhaber, Charles. "Retóricas clásicas y medievales en bibliotecas castellanas," *Ábaco.*

Fernández Pousa, R[amón]. *Los manuscritos gramaticales de la Biblioteca Nacional.* Madrid, 1947.

García Larragueta, Santos, ed. *Catálogo de los pergaminos de la Catedral de Oviedo.* Oviedo: Diputación de Asturias. Instituto de Estudios Asturianos, 1957.

Inventario general de manuscritos de la Biblioteca Nacional. Dirección General de Archivos y Bibliotecas. Catálogos de Archivos y Bibliotecas, 18. 9 vols. Madrid: Ministerio de Educación Nacional. Dirección General de Archivos y Bibliotecas. Servicio de Publicaciones, 1953-1970. In progress.

Kristeller, Paul Oskar. *Iter Italicum. A Finding List of Uncatalogued or Incompletely Catalogued Humanistic Manuscripts of the Renaissance in Italian and Other Libraries.* Vol. I: *Italy. Agrigento to Novara.* Vol. II: *Italy. Orvieto to Volterra; Vatican City.* London: The Warburg Institute, 1963-1967; Leiden: E. J. Brill, 1963-1967.

Lacombe, Georgius, et al. *Aristoteles Latinus.* Codices descripsit . . . Union Académique Internationale. Corpus Philosophorum Medii Aevi. 2 vols. *Pars Prior.* Rome: La Libreria dello Stato, 1939. *Pars Posterior.* Cambridge: Typis Academiae, 1955.

Loewe, Gustav, and Wilhelm von Hartel, eds. *Bibliotheca Patrum Latinorum Hispaniensis.* Vol. I. Vienna: Carl Gerold's Sohn, 1887.

López, Atanasio. "Descripción de los manuscritos franciscanos existentes en la Biblioteca Provincial de Toledo," *AIA* (1ª época), 25 (1926), 49-105, 173-244, 334-382.

Mansilla Reoyo, Demetrio. *Catálogo de los códices de la Catedral de Burgos.* Madrid: Consejo Superior de Investigaciones Científicas. Instituto Enrique Flórez, 1952.

Millares Carlo, Agustín. *Los códices visigóticos de la catedral toledana: Cuestiones cronológicas y de procedencia.* Madrid: Ignacio de Noreña, Editor, 1935.

Millás Vallicrosa, José María. *Las traducciones orientales en los manuscritos de la biblioteca catedral de Toledo.* Madrid: Consejo Superior de Investigaciones Científicas. Instituto Arias Montano, 1942.

Morel-Fatio, Alfred. *Catalogue des manuscrits espagnols et des manuscrits portugais de la Bibliothèque Nationale.* Paris: Imp. Nationale, 1892.

Rius Serra, J[osé]. "Inventario de los manuscritos de la Catedral de Sigüenza," *HS,* 3 (1950), 431-465.

Rojo Orcajo, Timoteo. "Catálogo descriptivo de los códices que se conservan en la Santa Iglesia Catedral de Burgo de Osma," *BRAH*, 94 (1929), 655-792; 95 (1929), 152-314.

Torre, Martín de la, y Pedro Longás. *Catálogo de códices latinos.* Vol. I: *Bíblicos.* Patronato de la Biblioteca Nacional. Madrid: Tipografía de Blass, 1935.

4. STUDIES OF INTELLECTUAL AND LITERARY HISTORY

   a. Latin Studies

Alonso, Manuel. "Traducciones del arcediano Domingo Gundisalvo," *Al-Andalus*, 12 (1947), 295-338.

d'Alverny, Marie-Thérèse, ed. Alain de Lille: *Textes inédits, avec une introduction sur sa vie et ses œuvres.* Études de Philosophie Médiévale, 52. Paris: Librairie Philosophique J. Vrin, 1965.

Auerbach, Erich. *Literary Language and Its Public in Late Latin Antiquity and in the Middle Ages.* Translated by Ralph Manheim. Bollingen Series, 74. New York: Pantheon Books, 1965.

Bolgar, R. R. *The Classical Heritage and Its Beneficiaries: From the Carolingian Age to the End of the Renaissance.* Harper Torchbooks. The Academy Library. New York: Harper and Row, 1964.

Boskoff, Priscilla S. "Quintilian in the Late Middle Ages," *Speculum*, 27 (1952), 71-78.

Castro y Castro, Manuel de. "Gil de Zamora y la provincia franciscana de Santiago." In his edition of: Juan Gil de Zamora. *De Preconiis Hispanie.* Madrid: Universidad de Madrid. Facultad de Filosofía y Letras, 1955. Pp. xxxv-cxxvi.

Díaz y Díaz, Manuel C. "Isidoro en la edad media hispana." In: *Isidoriana (Colección de estudios sobre Isidoro de Sevilla).* Edited by Manuel C. Díaz y Díaz. León: Centro de Estudios "San Isidoro," 1961. Pp. 345-387.

—. "El latín medieval español." In: *Actas del Primer Congreso Español de Estudios Clásicos.* Publicaciones de la Sociedad Española de Estudios Clásicos, 2. Madrid: Talleres gráficos Cándido Bermejo, 1958. Pp. 559-579.

Elorduy, Eleuterio. "San Isidoro. Unidad orgánica de su educación reflejada en sus escritos: La gramática ciencia totalitaria." In: *Miscellanea Isidoriana.* Rome: Typis Pontificiae Universitatis Gregorianae, 1936. Pp. 293-322.

Gregory, Tullio. *Anima Mundi: La filosofia di Guglielmo di Conches e la scuola di Chartres.* Florence: G. C. Sansoni, 1955.

Grosser, Dorothy Evelyn. "Studies in the Influence of the *Rhetorica ad Herennium* and Cicero's *De Inventione.*" Unpublished Ph.D. dissertation, Cornell University, 1953.

Handley, Brian Patrick. "Wisdom and Eloquence: A New Interpretation of the *Metalogicon* of John of Salisbury." Unpublished Ph.D. dissertation, Yale University, 1966.

Haring, Nicholas M. "Thierry of Chartres and Dominicus Gundissalinus," *MS*, 26 (1964), 271-286.

Haskins, Charles Homer. "Hermann of Carinthia." In his: *Studies in the History of Medieval Science.* 3d ed. New York: Frederick Ungar Publishing Co., 1960. Pp. 43-66.

—. *Studies in Medieval Culture.* Oxford: At the Clarendon Press, 1929.

Hunt, Richard William. "The Introductions to the 'Artes' in the Twelfth Century." In: *Studia Mediaevalia in Honorem Admodum Reverendi Patris Raymundi Josephi Martin.* Bruges: Apud Societatem Editricem "De Tempel" [1948].

Lehmann, Paul. "Cassiodorstudien. IV. Die Abhängigkeit Isidors von Cassiodor," *Philologus,* 72 (1913), 504-517.

Lutz, Cora E. "Remigius' Ideas on the Classification of the Seven Liberal Arts," *Traditio,* 12 (1956), 65-86.

—. "Remigius' Ideas on the Origin of the Seven Liberal Arts," *MH,* 10 (1956), 32-49.

Marston, Thomas E. "Quintillian's *Institutiones Orationae,*" *YULG,* 32 (1957), 6-7.

Méril, Edélstand du. *Poésies populaires latines du moyen âge.* Paris: Firmin Didot Frères, 1847; Leipzig: A. Franck, Libraire-Éditeur, 1847.

Rico, Francisco. "Las letras latinas del siglo XII en Galicia, León y Castilla," *Ábaco,* 2 (1969), 9-91.

Sarton, George. *Introduction to the History of Science.* Vol. II: *From Rabbi Ben Ezra to Roger Bacon.* In two parts. Baltimore: Published for the Carnegie Institution of Washington by the Williams and Wilkins Company, 1931.

Vázquez de Parga, Luis. "Literatura latina medieval," *RUO,* 10 (1948), 5-23.

Vilchez, María Rosa. "El *Liber Mariae* de Gil de Zamora," *Eidos: Cuadernos de la Institución Teresiana,* 1 (1954), 9-43.

b. Spanish Studies

Amador de los Ríos, José. *Historia crítica de la literatura española.* 7 vols. I-III, Madrid: Imp. José Rodríguez, 1861-1863; IV-VI, Madrid: Imp. José Fernández Cancela, 1863-1865; VII, Madrid: Imp. Joaquín Muñoz, 1865; repr. Madrid: Editorial Gredos, 1969.

Artiles, Joaquín. *Los recursos literarios de Berceo.* Biblioteca Románica Hispánica. II. Estudios y Ensayos. Madrid: Editorial Gredos, 1964.

Ballesteros-Beretta, Antonio. *Alfonso X el Sabio.* Consejo Superior de Investigaciones Científicas. Academia "Alfonso el Sabio" (Murcia). Barcelona-Madrid: Salvat Editores, S. A., 1963.

Bidagor, Raimundo. "El derecho de las *Decretales* y las *Partidas* de Alfonso el Sabio de España." In: *Acta Congressus Iuridici Internationalis.* Pontificium Institutum Utriusque Iuris. Rome: Apud Custodiam Librariam Pont. Instituti Utriusque Iuris, 1936. III, 297-313.

Curtius, Ernst Robert. "Zur Literarästhetik des Mittelalters," *ZRPh,* 58 (1938), 1-50, 129-232, 433-479.

Dutton, Brian. "The Profession of Gonzalo de Berceo and the Paris Manuscript of the *Libro de Alexandre,*" *BHS,* 37 (1960), 137-145.

Foulché-Delbosc, R[aymond]. "Les *Castigos e documentos* de Sanche IV," *RHi*, 15 (1906), 340-371.

Gariano, Carmelo. *Análisis estilístico de los "Milagros de Nuestra Señora" de Berceo.* Biblioteca Románica Hispánica. II. Estudios y Ensayos. Madrid: Editorial Gredos, 1965.

Giménez Resano, Gaudioso. Rev. art. of Joaquín Artiles, *Los recursos literarios de Berceo.* In: *AEM*, 2 (1965), 683-684.

Giménez y Martínez de Carvajal, José. "San Raimundo de Peñafort y las *Partidas* de Alfonso X el Sabio," *AA*, 3 (1955), 201-338.

Gómez Pérez, José. "Manuscritos del Toledano," *RABM*, 63 (1957), 157-174.

Kahane, Henry and Renée, and Angelina Pietrangeli. "*Picatrix* and the Talismans," *RPh*, 19 (1966), 574-593.

Lapesa, Rafael. "Sobre el *Auto de los reyes magos*: Sus rimas anómalas y el posible origen de su autor." In his: *De la edad media a nuestros días: Estudios de historia literaria.* Biblioteca Románica Hispánica. II. Estudios y Ensayos. Madrid: Editorial Gredos, 1967. Pp. 37-47.

Lecoy, Félix. *Recherches sur le "Libro de buen amor."* Paris: Librairie E. Droz, 1938.

Letsch-Lavanchy, Antoinette. "Éléments didactiques dans la *Crónica General*," *VR*, 15 (1956), ii, 231-240.

Lida de Malkiel, María Rosa. "Fray Antonio de Guevara: Edad Media y Siglo de Oro español," *RFH*, 7 (1945), 34 i-388.

—. "La *General Estoria*, notas literarias y filológicas," *RPh*, 12 (1958), 111-142; 13 (1959), 1-30.

—. "Josefo en la *General estoria*." In: *Hispanic Studies in Honour of I. González Llubera.* Edited by Frank Pierce. Oxford: The Dolphin Book Co., Ltd., 1959. Pp. 163-181.

—. "Notas para la interpretación, influencia, fuentes y texto del *Libro de buen amor*," *RFH*, 2 (1940), 105-150.

—. "Perduración de la literatura antigua en Occidente (A propósito by [sic] Ernst Robert Curtius, *Europäische Literatur und lateinisches Mittelalter*)," *RPh*, 5 (1951-1952), 99-131.

—. Rev. of E. R. Curtius, "Zur Literarästhetik des Mittelalters," *ZRPh*, 58 (1938), 1-50, 129-232, 433-479, in *RFH*, 1 (1939), 184-186.

—. Rev. of Leonid Arbusow, *Colores Rhetorici*, Gottingen: Vandenhoeck und Ruprecht, 1948, in *RPh*, 7 (1953-1954), 223-225.

—. "Las sectas judías y los 'procuradores' romanos: En torno a Josefo y su influjo sobre la literatura española," *HR*, 39 (1971), 183-213.

López Estrada, Francisco. *Introducción a la literatura medieval española.* 3d ed. Biblioteca Románica Hispánica. III. Manuales. Madrid: Editorial Gredos, 1966.

—. "La retórica en las *Generaciones y semblanzas* de Fernán Pérez de Guzmán," *RFE*, 30 (1946), 310-352.

—. "Sobre la difusión del *Tesoro* de Brunetto Latini en España (El manuscrito de la Real Academia Sevillana de Buenas Letras)," *Gesammelte Aufsätze zur*

Kulturgeschichte Spaniens. Spanische Forschungen der Görresgesellschaft. 1. Reihe, 16 (1960), 137-152.

López Santos, Luis. "Isidoro en la literatura medieval castellana." In: *Isidoriana* (*Colección de estudios sobre Isidoro de Sevilla*). Edited by Manuel C. Díaz y Díaz. León: Centro de Estudios "San Isidoro," 1961. Pp. 401-443.

Maravall, José Antonio. "La estimación de Sócrates y del saber clásico en la Edad Media española," *RABM*, 63 (1957), 5-68.

Menéndez Pidal, Ramón. "La épica española y la *Literarästhetik des Mittelalters* de E. R. Curtius," *ZRPh*, 59 (1939), 1-9.

Michalski, André Stanislaw. "Description in Mediaeval Spanish Poetry." Unpublished Ph.D. dissertation, Princeton University, 1964.

Morreale, Margherita. "La lengua poética de Berceo: Reparos y adiciones al libro de Carmelo Gariano," *HR*, 36 (1963), 142-151.

Samonà, Carmelo. *Aspetti del retoricismo nella "Celestina."* Studi di Letteratura Spagnola, Quaderno II. Facoltà di Magistero dell'Università di Roma. Rome, 1953.

Sears, Helen L. "The *Rimado de Palacio* and the *De Regimine Principum* Tradition of the Middle Ages," *HR*, 20 (1952), 1-27.

Solalinde, Antonio G. "Fuentes de la *General estoria* de Alfonso el Sabio," *RFE*, 21 (1934), 1-28.

Valbuena Prat, Angel. *Historia de la literatura española.* 7th ed. 3 vols. Barcelona: Editorial Gustavo Gili, 1964.

Ware, Niall J. "The Date of Composition of the *Libro de Alexandre*: A Re-examination of Stanza 1799," *BHS*, 42 (1965), 252-255.

Waxman, Samuel M. "Chapters on Magic in Spanish Literature," *RHi*, 38 (1916), 325-463.

Willis, Raymond S. *The Relationship of the Spanish "Libro de Alexandre" to the "Alexandreis" of Gautier de Châtillon.* Elliott Monographs in the Romance Languages and Literatures, 31. Princeton: Princeton University Press, 1934; Paris: Les Presses Universitaires de France, 1934.

—. Rev. art. of Emilio Alarcos Llorach, *Investigaciones sobre el "Libro de Alexandre,"* in *HR*, 19 (1951), 168-170.

Zahareas, Anthony N. *The Art of Juan Ruiz, Archpriest of Hita.* Madrid: Estudios de Literatura Española, 1965.

c. Rhetorical Studies

Baldwin, Charles Sears. *Medieval Rhetoric and Poetic (to 1400), Interpreted from Representative Works.* New York: The Macmillan Company, 1928; repr. Gloucester (Mass.): Peter Smith, 1959.

Boggess, William F. "Aristotle's *Poetics* in the Fourteenth Century," *SPh*, 67 (1970), 278-294.

Buck, August. "Gli studi sulla poetica e sulla retorica di Dante e del suo tempo," *Cultura e Scuola*, 4 (1965), 143-166.

Caplan, Harry. "Classical Rhetoric and the Medieval Theory of Preaching," *CPh*, 28 (1933), 73-96; repr. in his: *Of Eloquence: Studies in Ancient and Mediaeval Rhetoric*. Edited by Anne King and Helen North. Ithaca: Cornell University Press [1970]. Pp. 105-134.

—. *Mediaeval "Artes Praedicandi." A Hand-List*. Cornell Studies in Classical Philology, 24. Ithaca: Cornell University Press, 1934.

—. "A Mediaeval Commentary on the *Rhetorica ad Herennium*." In his: *Of Eloquence: Studies in Ancient and Mediaeval Rhetoric*. Edited by Anne King and Helen North. Ithaca: Cornell University Press [1970]. Pp. 247-270.

Charland, Thomas M. *Artes Praedicandi: Contribution à l'histoire de la rhétorique au moyen âge*. Publications de L'Institut d'Études Médiévales d'Ottawa, 7. Ottawa: Institut d'Études Médiévales, 1936.

Chenu, M.-D. "Introduction" to Thomas M. Charland. *Artes Praedicandi. Contribution à l'histoire de la rhétorique au moyen âge*. Publications de l'Institut d'Études Médiévales d'Ottawa, 7. Ottawa: Institut d'Études Médiévales, 1936. Pp. 8-13.

Denholm-Young, N[oël]. "The Cursus in England." In: *Oxford Essays in Medieval History Presented to Herbert Edward Salter*. Oxford: At the Clarendon Press, 1934. Pp. 68-103.

Gaudenzi, Augusto. "Sulla cronologia delle opere dei dettatori Bolognesi da Boncompagno a Bene di Lucca," *BISI*, 14 (1895), 85-161.

Hamilton, Marie P. "Notes on Chaucer and the Rhetoricians," *PMLA*, 47 (1932), 403-409.

Kalbfuss, Hermann. "Eine Bologneser *Ars dictandi* des xii. Jahrhunderts," *QF*, 16 (1914), ii, 1-35.

Kantorowicz, E[rnst] H. "Anonymi *Gemma Aurea*," *MH*, 1 (1943), 41-57.

Langlois, Ch[arles]-V. "Formulaires de lettres du xiie, du xiiie et du xive siècle," *Notices et Extraits des Manuscrits de la Bibliothèque Nationale et Autres Bibliothèques*, 34, i (1891), 1-32, 305-322, ii (1895), 1-18, 19-29; 35, ii (1897), 409-434, 793-830.

—. "Questions d'histoire littéraire: Maître Bernard," *BEC*, 54 (1893), 225-250.

Lanham, Richard A. *A Handlist of Rhetorical Terms: A Guide for Students of English Literature*. Berkeley and Los Angeles: University of California Press, 1968.

McKeon, Richard. "Rhetoric in the Middle Ages," *Speculum*, 17 (1942), 1-32.

Manly, John M. "Chaucer and the Rhetoricians," *Proceedings of the British Academy*, 12 (1926), 95-113.

Murphy, James Jerome. "Aristotle's *Rhetoric* in the Middle Ages," *QJS*, 52 (1966), 109-115.

—. "Chaucer, Gower, and the English Rhetorical Tradition." Unpublished Ph.D. dissertation, Stanford University, 1957.

—. "Rhetoric in Fourteenth-Century Oxford," *Medium Aevum*, 34 (1965), 1-20.

—. "The Scholastic Condemnation of Rhetoric in the Commentary of Giles of Rome on the Rhetoric of Aristotle." In: *Arts libéraux et philosophie au moyen âge: Actes du Quatrième Congrès International de Philosophie Médiévale*. Mont-

164 Bibliography

real-Paris: Institut d'Études Médiévales-Librairie Philosophique J. Vrin, 1969. Pp. 833-841.

Naunin, Traugott. *Der Einfluss der mittelalterlichen Rhetorik auf Chaucers Dichtung.* Bonn, 1929.

Payne, Robert O. *The Key of Remembrance: A Study of Chaucer's Poetics.* New Haven: Yale University Press for the University of Cincinnati, 1963.

Pizzorusso, Valeria Bertolucci. "Un trattato di *Ars dictandi* dedicato ad Alfonso X," *SMV*, 15 (1967), 3-82.

Shields, Ellis Gale. "The Gawain-Poet and the Latin Rhetorical Tradition." Unpublished Ph.D. dissertation, University of Southern California, 1956.

Valois, Noël. "Étude sur le rythme des bulles pontificales," *BEC*, 42 (1881), 161-198.

Zumthor, Paul. *Langue et techniques poétiques à l'époque romane (XIᵉ-XIIIᵉ siècles).* Bibliothèque Française et Romane. Paris: Klincksieck, 1963.

C. REFERENCE WORKS AND MISCELLANEOUS

Aguirre, José Saenz de. *Collectio Maxima Conciliorum Omnium Hispaniae et Novi Orbis.* Edited by José Catalani. 6 vols. Rome: Antonius Fulgonius, 1753-1755.

Antonio, Nicolás. *Biblioteca Hispana Vetus, sive, Hispani Scriptores qui ab Octaviani Augusti Aevo ad Annum Christi MD. Floruerent.* 2d ed. Edited by Francisco Pérez Bayer. 2 vols. Madrid: Apud viduam et heredes D. J. Ibarrae, 1788.

Bresslau, Harry. *Handbuch der Urkundenlehre für Deutschland und Italien.* 4th ed. Vol. II. Part i edited by Harry Bresslau. Part ii edited by Hans-Walter Klewitz. Berlin: Verlag Walter de Gruyter & Co., 1968.

Carreras Artau, Tomás y Joaquín. *Historia de la filosofía española: Filosofía cristiana de los siglos XIII al XV.* Asociación Española para el Progreso de las Ciencias. 2 vols. Madrid: Real Academia de Ciencias Exactas, Físicas y Naturales, 1939-1943.

Castro, Américo. *Glosarios latino-españoles de la edad media.* *RFE*, Añejo 22. Madrid: Revista de Filología Española, 1936.

Corominas, Joan. *Diccionario crítico etimológico de la lengua castellana.* Biblioteca Románica Hispánica. V. Diccionarios Etimológicos. 4 vols. Madrid: Editorial Gredos, 1954-1957.

Cosenza, Mario Emilio. *Biographical and Bibliographical Dictionary of the Italian Humanists and of the World of Classical Scholarship in Italy, 1300-1800.* 2d ed. rev. 6 vols. Boston: G. K. Hall, 1962-1967.

Díaz Jiménez, Juan Eloy. "Inmigración mozárabe en el reino de León: El monasterio de Abellar o de los santos mártires Cosme y Damián," *BRAH*, 20 (1892), 123-151.

Díaz y Díaz, Manuel C. *Index Scriptorum Latinorum Medii Aevi Hispanorum.* Acta Salmanticensia. Filosofía y Letras, XIII. Salamanca: Universidad de Salamanca, 1958-1959.

Escalona, Romualdo. *Historia del real monasterio de Sahagún* .... Edited by Joseph Pérez. Madrid: J. Ibarra, 1782.

Eubel, Conradus. *Hierarchia Catholica Medii Aevi*. Ed. altera. Vol. I. Monasterii: Sumptibus et typis librariae Regensbergianae, 1913; repr. Padua: Typis et sumptibus domus editorialis ' Il Messaggero di S. Antonio,' 1960.

Fabricius, Johannes Albertus. *Bibliotheca Latina Mediae et Infimae Aetatis*. 6 vols. I-V, Hamburg: Sumtu viduae Felgineriae, ex officina piscatoria, 1734-1736; VI, Hamburg: Sumtu Joannis Caroli Bohn, 1746.

Fallue, Leon. *Histoire politique et religieuse de l'église métropolitaine et du diocèse de Rouen*. 4 vols. Rouen: A. Le Brument, Libraire-Éditeur, 1850-1851.

Fernández Duro, Cesáreo. *Colección bibliográfico-biográfica de noticias referentes a la provincia de Zamora o materiales para su historia*. Madrid: Imprenta y Fundición de Manuel Tello, 1891.

—. *Memorias históricas de la ciudad de Zamora, su provincia y obispado*. 4 vols. Madrid: Establecimiento Tipográfico de los Sucesores de Rivadeneyra, 1882-1883.

Floriano Cumbreño, Antonio C. *Curso general de paleografía y paleografía y diplomática españolas*. Oviedo: Imprenta La Cruz, 1946.

Fuente, Vicente de la. *Historia eclesiástica de España*. 2a ed. corr. y aum. 6 vols. Madrid: Impresores y Libreros del Reino, 1873.

González Dávila, Gil. *Teatro eclesiástico de las iglesias metropolitanas, y catedrales de los reynos de las dos Castillas. Vidas de svs arzobispos, y obispos, y cosas memorables de svs sedes*. 3 vols. I, Madrid: Francisco Martínez, 1645; II, Madrid: Pedro de Horna y Villanveva, 1647; III, Madrid: Diego Díaz de la Carrera, 1650.

Hopper, Vincent Foster. *Medieval Number Symbolism: Its Sources, Meaning, and Influence on Thought and Expression*. Columbia University Studies in English and Comparative Literature, 132. New York: Columbia University Press, 1938.

Kristeller, Paul Oskar. "Humanism and Scholasticism in the Italian Renaissance," *Byzantion*, 17 (1944-1945), 346-374.

Martínez Marina, Fernando. *Ensayo histórico-crítico sobre la legislación y los principales cuerpos legales de los reinos de León y Castilla*. Madrid: Hija de don Joaquín Ibarra, 1808.

Martyr Riço, Juan Pablo. *Historia de la mvy noble y leal civdad de Cvenca*. Madrid: Herederos de la Viuda de Pº. de Madrigal, 1629.

Menéndez y Pelayo, Marcelino. *Historia de las ideas estéticas en España*. 3d ed. Edited by Enrique Sánchez Reyes. In his: *Obras completas*. Edición nacional. Vols. I-V. Madrid: Consejo Superior de Investigaciones Científicas, 1962.

Millares Carlo, Agustín. *Nuevos estudios de paleografía española*. México: La Casa de España en México, 1941.

—. *Tratado de paleografía española*. 2a ed. corr. y aum. Madrid: Librería y Casa Editorial Hernando, 1932.

Morales, Ambrosio de. *Viage de . . . por orden del rey D. Phelipe II. a los reynos de León, y Galicia, y principado de Asturias. Para reconocer las reliquias de santos, sepulcros reales, y libros manuscritos de las cathedrales, y monasterios.* Edited by Henrique Flórez. Madrid: Por A. Marín, 1765.

Morgado, Alonso. *Historia de Sevilla, en la qval se contienen svs antigvedades, grandezas, y cosas memorables en ella acontecidas, desde su fundación hasta nuestros tiempos.* Seville: Andrea Pescioni y Iuan de León, 1587.

Pérez de Urbel, Justo. *Semblanzas benedictinas.* 2 vols. Madrid: Editorial Voluntad, 1926.

Procter, E[velyn] S. "The Castilian Chancery during the Reign of Alfonso X, 1252-84." In: *Oxford Essays in Medieval History Presented to Herbert Edward Salter.* Oxford: At the Clarendon Press, 1934. Pp. 104-121.

Ramírez y de las Cazas-Deza, Luis María. *Descripción de la Iglesia Catedral de Córdoba.* 4a ed. corr. y aum. Cordova: Imp. R. Rojas, 1866.

Sandoval, Prudencio de. *Antigvedad dela civdad, y iglesia cathedral de Tvy, y delos obispos qve se save aya auido en ella.* Braga: Fructuoso Lourenço de Basto, 1610.

—. *Primera parte de las fvndaciones de los monasterios del glorioso padre San Benito . . . .* Madrid: Luis Sánchez, 1601. Foliated 1-50, 1-96, 1-84.

Tilley, Arthur A. "The Early Renaissance." In: *Decline of Empire and Papacy.* Vol. VII of the *Cambridge Medieval History.* Ed. by J. B. Bury et al. New York: The Macmillan Company, 1932; Cambridge: At the University Press, 1932. Pp. 751-776.

Villanueva, Jaime. *Viaje literario a las iglesias de España.* 22 vols. Madrid: Imprenta Real et al., 1803-1852.